EXPLORING THE ISLES
OF THE WEST

Journeys to the Western Islands of Scotland

Skye and Tiree to the Outer Isles

Marc Calhoun

The Islands Book Trust

Published in 2012 by The Islands Book Trust

www.theislandsbooktrust.com

ISBN: 978-1-907443-31-2

All photographs © Marc Calhoun unless indicated otherwise
Text © Marc Calhoun

We are grateful to the Society of Antiquaries of Scotland
for permission to reproduce the pictures on pages 86 and 196.

The Islands Book Trust, Ravenspoint Centre, Kershader, South Lochs, Isle of Lewis, HS2 9QA. Tel: 01851 880737

Typeset by Erica Schwarz
Cover design by James Hutcheson
Printed and bound by Martins the Printers, Berwick upon Tweed

HIE
Innse Gall
Outer Hebrides

To my wife Shawna, the love of my life — yes, even the islands come second. Without her support, and endless patience, none of these adventures would have happened.

A note of caution

Some of the hikes described in these pages cover difficult terrain. If you choose to follow them I am obliged to say you do so at your own risk. Always carry a map, water, first-aid kit, compass, mobile phone (although chances are it won't work), and enough food and warm clothing so you could spend the night out in the open. And just as important, if you are walking alone always let someone know your plans.

A note on the illustrations

The maps that accompany each chapter are provided to illustrate the journeys, and should not be used for navigation. For that purpose the appropriate OS map(s) are listed. Unless otherwise indicated, all photos were taken by the author. Like the maps, they are provided to illustrate the journeys and, I hope, along with the stories they accompany, inspire you to see these magic isles for yourself.

This book continues the journeys described in the companion volume *Exploring the Isles of the West: Firth of Clyde to the Small Isles.*

Contents

CONTENTS

ACKNOWLEDGEMENTS

Dia Calhoun: Without my sister's mentoring, and editorial help, none of these adventures would have been readable.

My parents, Jim & Eva Calhoun: Without their interests in history and genealogy, I would never have known of my Scottish heritage or traveled to these wonderful isles.

Linda Grieve, John Humphries and the late Jeremy Smith; editors of *Scottish Islands Explorer*: Without the encouragement of seeing many of these stories appear in SIE I would not have continued writing them.

Roy Rogers, his son Nicol, and Susan Gill of Inchtavannach: One of the best rewards of my island-going has been to become friends with these wonderful people. Their home on St Kessog's isle has become my Scottish island home-away-from-home.

And last, but certainly not least, without the skilled piloting of the following skippers many of these adventures would not have been successful (or nearly as much fun):

Rob Barlow, skipper of *Elizabeth G* and *Poplar Diver*
Mark Henrys, skipper of *Hjalmar Bjørge*
Chris Jackson, skipper of *Chalice*
Andrew Johnson, skipper of *Petrel*
Donald Macleod, skipper of *Boy James*
Mike Murray, skipper of *Gemini*
Tim Wear, skipper of *Zuza*
Donald Wilke, skipper of *Annag*

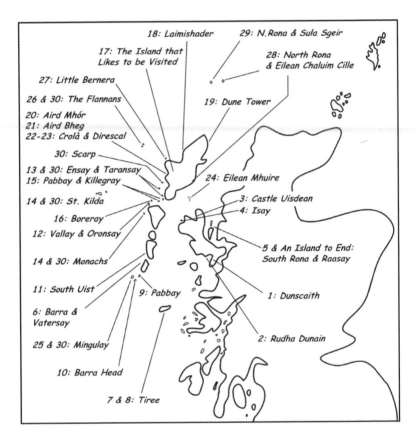

18: Laimishader

29: N.Rona & Sula Sgeir

17: The Island that Likes to be Visited

28: North Rona & Eilean Chaluim Cille

27: Little Bernera

26 & 30: The Flannans

19: Dune Tower

20: Aird Mhór
21: Aird Bheg
22-23: Crolà & Direscal

30: Scarp

13 & 30: Ensay & Taransay
15: Pabbay & Killegray

24: Eilean Mhuire

14 & 30: St. Kilda

3: Castle Uisdean
4: Isay

16: Boreray

12: Vallay & Oronsay

5 & An Island to End: South Rona & Raasay

14 & 30: Monachs

11: South Uist

9: Pabbay

1: Dunscaith

6: Barra & Vatersay

25 & 30: Mingulay

2: Rudha Dunain

10: Barra Head

7 & 8: Tiree

Skye and Tiree to the Outer Isles

Part I:

Round Skye

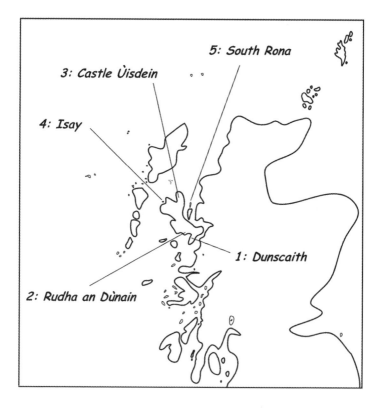

3: Castle Ùisdein

5: South Rona

4: Isay

1: Dunscaith

2: Rudha an Dùnain

1: The Fort of the Spiked Heads: Skye

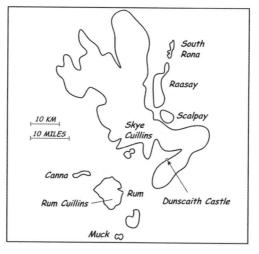

Map Reference: Ordnance Survey Landranger 32

ON THE western shore of the Sleat Peninsula of Skye stands the rock of Dunscaith. Clinging to the top of the rock is the ruin of a sixteenth century MacDonald castle. A drawbridge once spanned the gap between the rock and the mainland. The bridge is gone, but its arched support walls still stand. I was on the shore below, wondering how best to get up onto the rock. One way would be a direct scramble up the side, about a forty-foot climb. But I wanted to approach the fortress as the warrior Cuchulainn did some two thousand years ago. I wanted to cross the Bridge of the Cliff.

The MacDonalds were late comers to the site, as there has been a fortress of one sort or other here for thousands of years. Dunscaith was the Dùn Sgàthaich of the Red Branch sagas, where Cuchulainn came to learn the art of arms from the warrior Queen of Skye. To get here from Ulster he had to cross the dreaded Plain of Ill Luck. I could sympathize with Cuchulainn, as I'd had to traverse Heathrow airport to get to Scotland.

An iron palisade topped with spiked heads greeted Cuchulainn and his men as they approached Dùn Sgàthaich, the home of Queen Sgàthach. But before he could meet the queen Cuchulainn had to gain entrance to her fort. This meant crossing the Bridge of the Cliff; a devilish, supernatural bridge, said to grow narrower, shorter, steeper, and slipperier with every step. After three failed attempts to cross, Cuchulainn performed the salmon-leap, jumping high in the air and sliding down the far side of the bridge.

I left the shore and climbed to the top of the landward side of the gap between the mainland and the castle. There, a narrow built-up neck of land, with remnants of a stone roadway, extended towards the rock. At its end two parallel bridge supports, six feet apart, spanned a twelve-foot gap. That tricky bridge had shrunk to nothing since the days of Cuchulainn, for there was only open air between the support walls.

Not having practiced my salmon-leap in a while I chose a different way to cross. There were narrow ledges on the inside of each wall where the drawbridge would have rested. I carefully placed my toes on a ledge and side-stepped across. Now don't think I avoided all risk by not doing the salmon-leap. There were several hungry sheep on the rocks below. One mis-step and I'd fall into their waiting jaws.

It was at Dùn Sgàthaich that Cuchulainn learned the various feats of combat: the spear-feat, the rope-feat, the apple-feat, the thunder-feat,

The 'modern' replacement of the Bridge of the Cliff

and the cat-feat. Some of these feats involved the throwing of special spears grasped between the toes. There was a price for all this training. In return Cuchulainn agreed to fight the queen's rival, Princess Aoife. Cuchulainn did manage to capture Aoife during battle. And guess what? Several months after Cuchulainn returned to Ireland Aoife gave birth to a son, whom she named Conlaoch. Years later, on a battlefield in Ulster, Cuchulainn and his son faced off. Conlaoch, knowing he fought his father, mis-threw his spear on purpose. But Cuchulainn, not knowing he fought his son, mortally wounded Conlaoch with a deadly toe-throw of the gae bulga, a large barbed spear made from the skeleton of a sea-beast, given to him by Aoife.

There is nothing left of Sgàthach's fort. But bits and pieces of the old MacDonald castle still sprout from the rock. One corner stood to a height of six feet, and much of the defensive walling facing the mainland was intact. For a place renowned for deeds of violence a

Dunscaith Castle

more peaceful spot could not be found. Here, on an island packed with tourists and hill walkers, this bit of coastline is well off the beaten path. The only sounds to be heard were the waters of Loch Eishort lapping against the base of the rock. As for its history of violence, the only threatening things here now are clusters of stinging nettles growing amongst the ruins.

I left the rock where Cuchulainn learned to toss spears with his toes and tip-toed sideways back across the bridge to the mainland. The hungry sheep were still below me as I crossed, and I breathed a sigh of relief as I stepped onto solid ground. Not many people can claim to have performed the sheep-feat twice in one day (and live to tell the tale).

I had to catch the Mallaig ferry in half an hour, so the time had come to say goodbye to Skye. From where I stood the Cuillin Hills of Skye filled the horizon to the north-west. And fifteen miles to the south lay the equally impressive Cuillins of Rum. Those mountain names may mean 'The Handsome Hills', but I like to think they are memorials to the presence of the legendary Cuchulainn in the Hebrides.

2: A Nine Year Walk to Rudha an Dùnain: Skye

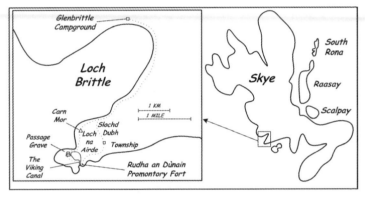

Map Reference: Ordnance Survey Landranger 32

Some pictures compel you to visit a place captured by the photographer. For me, one of those was Arthur Gardner's image of the fort of Rudha an Dùnain on Skye (*The Peaks, Lochs and Coasts of the Western Highlands*, 1930, plate 110.). This photo shows a small headland of rock jutting into the sea, a defensive wall separating a small bit of ground at its tip. It also shows an odd pinnacle, perhaps an intact bit of wall higher than the rest that looks like the crow's nest of a ship, which gives the fort the appearance of a pirate stronghold. *Rudha an Dùnain* means the headland of the little fort, and it is a small-scale version of the great promontory forts of Ireland.

It was at Rudha an Dùnain that MacLeod of Skye based his coastal watchmen; ready to light a warning beacon should Clanranald, sailing from the isles to the south and west, be on the warpath. It took three attempts before I finally stood atop the fortress walls of Rudha an Dùnain.

Neophytes at Scottish hill walking, my wife and I were in street shoes. The bog of the black-hollow seemed to be getting deeper with each step, and we could go no farther without sinking into the dark, mushy ground. It was frustrating, for we were so close to Rudha an Dùnain. We'd walked south along the shore of Loch Brittle for three miles from the campground at Glenbrittle, and had then turned into the ravine of *Slochd Dubh*, the black-hollow. The fort lay a mile away at the end of the peninsula. But we were not prepared to cross the bog and had to turn around.

Seven years passed. I was aboard the sailing boat *Annag* when the threat of gale force winds forced us to leave St Kilda early (see chapter 14). A few days later I was on my way home via the ferry that plies the waters between Lochmaddy and Skye. The gale, now in full force, blasted freezing rain against the large windows of the passenger lounge. But two hours later, as I drove south through Skye, the storm started to lessen.

So when I reached the road junction at Sligachan it was decision time. If I stayed on the main road I'd cross the Skye Bridge and be on the mainland in an hour, but a right turn would take me to Glenbrittle. I had a plane to catch in the morning, so if I was going to hike out to Rudha an Dùnain it had to be then. Desperately hoping the weather would continue to improve I turned right. A fifty-minute drive, the last ten miles along a single track road, led to the head of Loch Brittle. I drove into the parking area and shut off the engine. The car kept moving, the howling wind shaking it violently. Within seconds of turning off the wipers the outside world became smudged and blurred. I tried to open the car door. The wind pushed it shut.

I had a long talk with myself. I didn't want to admit it was a hopeless cause, but it was evident it would be an awful walk in that weather. I had anticipated doing it for years and wanted to enjoy it. So in a deeply depressed mood I switched the engine back on. The wipers swept away the smear and I could see the headland that had eluded me once again.

Another two years passed. I went to Skye to spend a week, hoping for at least one day of decent weather. One of those days dawned without a cloud in the sky, and I drove down to that sandy car park at Loch Brittle. I turned off the engine. This time I was able to open the door. Instead of a gale lashed headland barely visible in the pouring rain, Rudha an Dùnain lay spread out before me, its rock dappled heather slopes sparkling in the morning sun. I covered the three miles to the entrance of Slochd Dubh in an hour. But this time I didn't go into the hollow. That had been a mistake nine years before. Although it is the most direct route, it is the boggiest. Instead I kept to the coast and climbed the hill of Carn Mòr.

From the high ground the view opened out to the end of the peninsula, its moorland corrugated with fields of abandoned lazy-beds. It is tiring terrain to walk across, as you have to go against the grain, climbing over seemingly endless ripples of soft, grassy earth. Grazing sheep dotted the landscape, and they fled as I made my way across the fields. Just beyond the once-tilled land I came to Loch na Airde, a circular loch a thousand feet in diameter. Rudha an Dùnain lay within striking distance. But there were two other things to see first: a five thousand-year-old chambered tomb, and the Viking Canal.

At the north end of the loch I came to the large mound of the chambered tomb (NG 393 164). It was sixty-five feet in diameter, and

The Viking Canal

ten high. The round central chamber, open to the sky, consisted of a small slab-sided silo five feet in diameter. From the inside I could look out through the partially intact entrance passage, its giant lintel stones supported by equally large uprights. I didn't stay long, for a million midges were swarming in the damp interior of the tomb.

I rose from the grave and circled around to the south side of the loch. There I came to a canal, a quarter of a mile long, between the loch and the sea. The tide was low, and as the loch is barely above sea level, the black stones of the fifteen-foot-wide canal lay exposed. Some references call this The Viking Canal. It is not known who originally built it, but the MacAskills, MacLeod's coastal watchmen, are said to have made use of it to bring their sea-going ships to safe harbour in the loch. The terrain rose to form small promontories on both sides of the canal, and at the tip of one of them sat the fortress of Rudha an Dùnain.

The fort's defensive wall, eighty feet long and twelve feet thick, had once completely sealed off the tip of the headland. It was built of massive squared stones, the upper ones cloaked in moss. After climbing atop it I could see that the wall had small interior cells, and one of them, near the cliff top, lay open to the sky. The area of land the wall defended was small, and the cliff edge lay just forty feet beyond. If the defenders ever failed to keep out invaders there was nowhere to run.

The Uists and Barra lay forty miles to the west, and the isles of Eigg, Canna, and Rum were a dozen miles to the south. Those islands had been Clanranald land, and the MacLeods and MacDonalds were constantly killing each other. One only has to think of that infamous cave on Eigg, where several hundred MacDonalds were smoke-smothered by the MacLeods; or a half century later, when the MacLeods unfurled their Fairy Flag and proceeded to wipe out an army of MacDonalds at the battle of the spoiling of the dyke (see chapter 4).

Rudha an Dùnain

At the first sign of an approaching enemy the MacAskills of Rudha an Dùnain would light a warning beacon, and from here a series of lookouts along the coast could quickly relay information that trouble was afoot. But there's no need for watchman anymore, for the MacLeods and MacDonalds no longer feud, and only sheep stand watch at Rudha an Dùnain.

From the headland I walked north to the ruins of a small township where one large building stood out: Rudha Dùnain House. It was an odd structure. One end had a normal gable, but the other end was rounded, and solidly built. It looked as if the house had been a later addition to an older fortified structure. The last MacAskill of Rudha Dùnain lived here in the 1860s, long after the fort had been abandoned.

I left the township and started back to the car through the bog of Sloch Dubh. One spot looked familiar. It was where my wife and I had turned around nine years before. Of all the Hebridean walks I'd taken this had been one of the most rewarding. It took nearly a decade to complete, and had taught me to respect difficult terrain and plan ahead for bad weather. Knowledge that would make future walks on the islands successful the first time.

Some things are worth waiting for.

> *Would that thou to Rudh' an Dunain*
> *Mightest go at ebbing light,*
> *To review the phantom galleys,*
> *As they steal upon the night;*
> *Listen there with muffled breathing*
> *For the sweep of oars below,*
> *Dear was vengeance to Clan Ranald*
> *In the nights of long ago…*

From 'Watchmen of the Sea' — Alasdair Alpin MacGregor

3: The Castle with no Windows or Doors: Skye

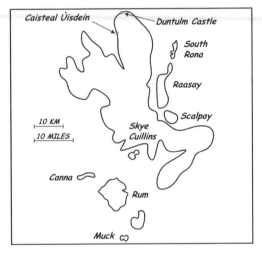

Caisteal Úisdein   *Duntulm Castle*

South Rona

Raasay

10 KM
10 MILES

Scalpay

Skye Cuillins

Canna

Rum

Muck

Map Reference: Ordnance Survey Landranger 23

Several times over the years, while driving the A856 to catch the ferry at Uig on the Isle of Skye, I'd driven by a nondescript side road that is the way to a ruined castle with an intriguing description: the castle with no windows or doors. The lane was always gated, and led to a farm that had no name on the map, and could not be seen from the road. Leery of trespassing I had never got up the nerve to open that gate and drive down this mysterious byway. I knew the castle could

14

also be approached by a walk from Cuidrach, a small village to the north. But whenever I was in the area I was always in such a rush to catch the ferry that I never seemed to have time to visit the castle with no windows or doors.

It was this odd description of a place built for refuge that made me curious to see it. Its entrance was said to be in the roof, accessed via a ladder that could be pulled up. And so I envisioned climbing a stony ruin, and looking down a dark opening into a castle impervious from attackers—although its owner did meet a horrible end.

Then one year, on one of those drives to the Uig ferry, I noticed a new sign next to the farm track. On it was the symbol of a walker, and the text *Path to Caisteal Ùisdein*. It was an invitation that could not be passed up. So my wife and I drove down the track to a parking area next to a large farm building, from where we set out on foot across grassy fields to the shore.

And there, on the cliff edge fifty feet above the sea, stood Caisteal Ùisdein; a tower house, fifty feet long by thirty wide, with walls nearly eight feet thick. It was a solid structure with only one opening, a narrow loophole placed five feet off the ground. The roof was gone, so any thoughts of climbing to a hidden entrance were for naught.

We approached the ruin and peered through the loophole. On its inside lay a deep embrasure, and beyond that the interior was a jumble of fallen stones, ferns, and nettles. I wanted to get a closer look at the inside. The loophole looked just wide enough to squeeze through, and I did.

Once inside I could see the remnants of a stairway and fireplace. The castle was small, 800 square feet at most, and I had to move carefully, for a trip on any of the hidden stones meant falling into lurking clumps of stinging nettles.

It was around the year 1600 that this little hidey-hole castle was built on the shore of Loch Snizort. Constructed from basalt quarried on

Caisteal Ùisdein

the Ascrib Islands six miles to the north-west, it was built for Ùisdean MacGhilleasbuig Chleirich, and was known as *Caisteal Ùisdein* (Hugh's Castle). At that time the stronghold of Duntulm Castle, ten miles to the north, was the seat of Donald Gorm Mòr, the chief of the MacDonalds of Sleat and North Uist. Hugh was the chief's cousin and could well afford to have his own castle, as he had been given the factorship of North Uist in the 1580s.

The MacDonald chief had no heir. So the idea came to Hugh that he might inherit his lands if he could eliminate the chief. (Hugh seems to have come from the same stock as the venomous Roderick MacLeod, who plotted, and carried out, mass murder for similar reasons on nearby Isay Island around the same time—see chapter 4.) And so Hugh wrote a letter inviting the chief to dine with him. He also sent a letter to a cohort who would do the dirty work, instructing him on exactly how to murder Macdonald when he arrived at Caisteal Ùisdein. The postal service was not very good back then, the letters got mixed up, and MacDonald received the letter intended for the henchman.

Hugh realised this occurred in time to escape MacDonald's wrath. But his little castle was too close for comfort to Duntulm. So he skulked away to Dùn an Sticir, the fort of the skulker, a safe haven on North Uist. But Hugh could not hold out forever, and was eventually captured.

MacDonald threw Hugh into the dungeon of Duntulm, where he was subjected to a gruesome torture. After being starved for a while he was given his fill of salted meat and fish. After gorging himself he became thirsty and asked for water. His captors obligingly lowered a jug into the dungeon. Hugh gratefully lifted it to his lips, only to find it empty. In another version of this story Hugh was chained to the centre of the dungeon, and a water jug left just out of reach. Either way our protagonist perished of thirst. And as Otta Swire put it in *Skye: The*

Caisteal Ùisdein from the south

17

Island and its Legends, 'His screams and curses are said to echo through the castle today.'

After crawling back out the loophole we returned to the car, leaving behind a bit of history, and an area that, until 1715, had been the centre of MacDonald power. Once mighty Duntulm Castle, where Hugh met his end, is also a ruined shell, its walls blown apart for stone, its towers fallen into the sea. After 1715 this was a quiet area until the summer of 1746, when a fleeing prince, escorted by Flora MacDonald, landed at what would come to be called Prince Charlie's Point, five miles north of Caisteal Ùisdein. Disguised as the Irish maid Betty Burke the prince marched past the castle on his way to shelter at Kingsburgh House. Three months later he escaped to France, and forty-four years after that, in 1790, Flora MacDonald died in a house just south of Caisteal Ùisdein.

Back in the car we shared a salty bag of crisps, and then quenched our thirst with a bottle of cold water, a taste we relished while pondering the fate of Ùisdean MacGhilleasbuig Chleirich.

4: An Isle of Song and Mayhem: Isay

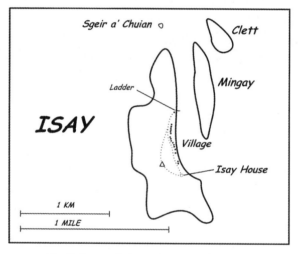

Sgeir a' Chuian

Clett

Mingay

Ladder

ISAY

Village

Isay House

1 KM

1 MILE

Map Reference: Ordnance Survey Landranger 23

I was afloat amongst the Hebrides, intent on reaching far off Sùlaisgeir, and making a long awaited return to North Rona. But it was not to be. The sea churned, and the forecast called for more. Even if the sea de-churned we would still need a few days of good weather for it to calm enough to land on those rocky isles. So three days out from Oban, as we lay at anchor off the Summer Isles, seventy miles south of Rona, we made the decision to turn back.

To ease the disappointment of missing Sùla and Rona, Mark Henrys, skipper of *Hjalmar Bjørge*, had a few alternative destinations up his sleeve. So after an early morning shore trip to Tanera Mòr, including a climb to the highpoint on the island's west side with its expansive view over the Summer Isles, we headed west to spend a few hours on the Shiants. The next day we set foot on Scalpay to walk to Eilean Glas lighthouse. Then, after a calm night at anchor off Scalpay, we headed south to the island of Isay. You may have heard of Isay as it is famous for its connections to Samuel Johnson, the singer Donovan, and mass murder.

Isay (Ìosaigh) appeared as soon as we rounded the Vaternish Peninsula of Skye. I also noticed something that made me realise it was not only the murders on Isay that made this area famous for dark deeds. What I saw was Trumpan Church, the site of another mass murder. Just below it was Ardmore Point where, after the church massacre, a battle occurred between the MacLeods and MacDonalds. We were motoring into an area with a grisly history.

The battle was called Blàr Milleadh Garaidh, the battle of the spoiling of the dyke, and was one of the few times that MacLeod's *Bratach Shìdhe* (Fairy Flag) had been unfurled to save the day. And a terrible day it was, for the MacDonalds had just burned Trumpan church while it was full of people.

The burning was done, as one version goes, in revenge for the Eigg cave massacre, when the MacLeods killed several hundred MacDonalds. But the MacLeods were to win the day at Ardmore with the help of their Fairy Flag, for, in the words of Seton Gordon, waving it caused the defending MacLeods to be multiplied in the eyes of the enemy. The flag worked its magic that day in 1578 and the MacDonalds were defeated. The bodies of the slain were laid out and the MacLeods tumbled a dyke over the corpses.

I tried to set aside thoughts of all those deaths as we neared Isay. But the sky was not helping the mood. A grey wall of cloud threatened from the south, while to the north a blue sky tried to stand its ground. In the forefront of this battling weather a large, ominous looking building could be seen on the island: the gaunt ruin of Isay House, last inhabited in 1860, and where the murders had been committed.

But all that grisly stuff was not the reason I wanted to visit Isay, it was because of the following passage from Boswell's journal of his trip to the Hebrides in 1773:

> *There is a beautiful little island in the Loch of Dunvegan, called Isay. MacLeod said he would give it to Mr. Johnson, on condition of his residing on it three months in the year, nay, one month. Mr. Johnson was highly pleased with the fancy... He talked a great deal of this island—how he would build a house, how he would fortify it, how he would have cannon, how he would plant, how he would sally out and take the isle of Muck.*

It was to see this island offered to Samuel Johnson, an offer he declined, that drew me to Isay. It is an island all readers of Johnson and Boswell's trip want to see; one made historical by a short and very bizarre mention, in one of the most well known accounts of a journey through the Hebrides.

By the time we stepped ashore the clouds from the south appeared to be winning the weather battle, and a light drizzle fell from a grey sky. We hiked through the abandoned village, passing, one by one, a dozen ruined houses. Upwards of ninety people called Isay home in the nineteenth century when it had been a fishing station with a general store. The community came in 1830, made up of people evicted from Bracadale, fifteen miles away on Skye. But life on the island came to an end in 1860 when it was cleared for sheep.

There were no sheep on the island, but it could be seen that some of the structures, their silent stones daubed with white lichen, had been altered for use as pens. The drizzle continued, dampening the

Isay Village

old houses, the tops of their walls tufted with soft fringes of newly wet grass. Here and there nettles and blue iris, but no people, greeted us as we explored the village. We then came to the ruins of several long houses, and below them stone fish traps could be seen on the foreshore.

At the south end of the village we came to Isay House. It is an eerie looking structure. The roof is missing, and the jagged and split gable ends looked like pincers pointing to the sky, lying in wait to clutch one of the gulls that soared overhead. Access to the first floor is via a stone-balustered staircase. The staircase is ten feet across at the ground, gradually tapering to three feet as it rises to the threshold of what had been the reception room. No door blocks the entrance these days, and if you step through you will fall ten feet down into the rocky ground floor, as the house is now just a shell.

I climbed to the top of the staircase to look out over the hollow interior. If he had taken MacLeod up on his offer this could have been Samuel Johnson's holiday home, from where he could have sallied forth to take Muck. But there was someone who stood here about forty years ago that did decide to make Isay a holiday home of sorts, and that was the singer Donovan.

Donovan bought Isay, the two neighbouring isles of Mingay and Clett, and some nearby land on Skye in the late 1960s. A lot of what you read says he established a commune on Isay, which is not true. He did establish a commune in the area, but he pretty much glosses over it in his autobiography, *The Hurdy Gurdy Man*. In a chapter entitled *Lord of the Isles*, Donovan describes how he met MacDonald of the Isles to discuss buying land, including the island of Isay. The chapter opens with the following:

My thoughts were drifting to the wild and windy land of my birth. I had some crazy notion of starting a commune with my artist friends, to pick up the threads of an early dream, to be a poet and painter. I felt that musical fame had led me astray.

He goes on to describe landing on Isay and sitting on tussocks of sea grass inside the ruin of Isay House. But other than a subsequent description about making arrangements to buy the land, no details are given as to where the commune would be.

In a later chapter he tells about establishing the commune on the land he owned on Skye in the winter of 1968 by buying 'a few old gypsy caravans'. Gardens were planted, and 'my friends and I had probably experienced the last wilderness of Europe before the coming tide of development'. He then writes briefly about the end of the commune. It was turning out to be expensive, and so he 'sold the Isles to a Dutchman'.

I descended the once grand staircase and stepped through a ground floor opening to wander around the nettle-grown interior. The tussocks of grass that greeted Donovan still sprouted on the ground, and I sat there wondering in which room the murders had been committed.

The killings happened in 1592 when Ruairaidh MacAilein MacLeod, known as *Nimheach* (the venomous) lived here. MacLeod wanted his son to inherit Raasay and the lands of Gairloch, but his family was third in line for the inheritance. So Ruairaidh decided to host a banquet, and the families that stood in the way were invited. During dinner he invited each attendee to have a private word with him and, one by one, they were quickly dispatched.

What grisly stuff, and what an area of grisly history. Three miles away lay Trumpan church, burned full of people to even the score for the Eigg massacre. And even closer lay Ardmore Point, where the MacDonalds had been put to the sword with the help of the Fairy Flag. I carefully picked my way across the stony ground to the crumbling entrance, left the house, and in the ongoing drizzle started the climb to the 100-foot summit of the island.

Hermetically encased in waterproofs it was a sweaty trudge to the top of the hill. After taking a seat on a spot overlooking Isay House I gazed skyward to see how the battle between the clouds and sun was

Isay House

progressing. The clouds still had the upper hand. As I sat there to catch my breath, I watched as the rest of the shore party headed back to the landing. The time had come to desert this deserted island with its sometimes dark history. It is an island that has had a few moments of fame in its time, but is now left alone, like a movie star in a retirement home; ignored most of the time, but brought to life every now and then by the occasional visits of adoring fans.

5: Two Voyages to South Rona

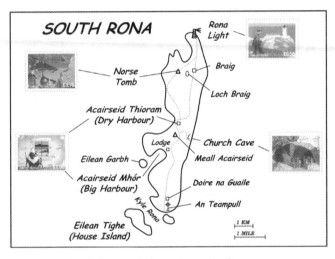

SOUTH RONA

Rona Light

Norse Tomb

Braig

Loch Braig

Acairseid Thioram
(Dry Harbour)

Lodge

Church Cave

Eilean Garbh

Meall Acairseid

Acairseid Mhór
(Big Harbour)

Doire na Guaile

Kyle Rona

An Teampull

Eilean Tighe
(House Island)

1 KM
1 MILE

Map Reference: Ordnance Survey Landranger 24
(South Rona stamp images used with permission – www.isleofrona.com)

My wife and I were the only ones staying at the Isle of Raasay Hotel when we heard an unexpected knock on the door. It was Sunday morning on an island where the Sabbath is seriously observed—so seriously that there are signs on the children's playground asking that it not be used on Sundays. We had gone to Raasay because I wanted to climb Dùn Caan, the island's flat-topped peak where James Boswell danced a reel centuries ago. But those plans changed drastically when the most incredible bit of island luck came knocking on a quiet Raasay Sunday.

I opened the door. It was Jane, who along with her husband Angus, ran the hotel.

"We were wondering if you'd be interested in going to Rona."

My eyes lit up. I may even have started salivating. I spend my vacations finding ways to get to remote islands. This was the first I'd been offered one on a platter, let alone one I'd wanted to visit for a long time.

She started to explain, "It's a little island to the…"

"Yes, I know it," I interrupted—a bit rudely. What I knew about little Rona was that it is a microcosm of Hebridean history. At its southern tip early Christianity found a base at An Teampull, where a medieval chapel still stands. Then there is Church Cave, another place of worship hidden in the cliffs on the island's eastern coast. And most interesting of all are its three abandoned villages, relics of the multiple clearances and subsequent land raids that marked the turbulent years of the nineteenth and early twentieth centuries.

That was Rona.

All these thoughts flashed through my mind as I looked at my wife Shawna. She saw that gleam in my eye, like an addict who's found a fix. She is not wild about riding in small boats, but nodded her head.

"Yes, we'll go!" I exclaimed.

It seemed a family reunion was taking place on South Rona, which lies to the north of Raasay. Several relatives of Fiona and Donald Macalman, who lived in Rona Lodge, the only inhabited house on Rona, were on Raasay. They had arranged for a fisherman to take them to Rona and the staff at the hotel wanted to go. But there was bit of a problem. They couldn't abandon my wife and me in an empty hotel. The knock on the door had been a bit hesitant. For why would two tourists want to spend the day travelling in a fishing boat to an obscure rocky island? An island, moreover, described by one writer as 'quite repulsive; presenting no picturesque features and but little verdure to chequer its grey and sterile surface'. However they had no idea whom they were dealing with. They hadn't the faintest inkling the offer they were making would be like dangling candy in front of a baby.

So that's how we found ourselves part of a convoy driving the single track road to Loch Arnish at the north end of Raasay. The last two miles of this track is the famous Calum's Road, built over a ten year period by Calum MacLeod. (His epic feat in building this road is told in Roger Hutchinson's *Calum's Road*.)

From the end of Calum's Road it took some time for all eight of us to trek down the wet grassy slopes to the rocky shore of the loch. Once at the shore we slid into a small inflatable to be ferried over to a worn, red-painted fishing-boat named *Ocean Unity*. Her engine fired up, and we were soon rumbling north at eight knots. After six miles of motoring we approached Acairseid Mhòr, the Big Harbour of Rona. Its narrow entrance was hard to spot. But a white arrow with a big 'H' painted on the rocks of Eilean Garbh, a small island that almost blocks the entrance, pointed the way to the inner harbour.

The harbour once had a more colourful name, Port Robaireann, Robber's Bay: a name that matches a description of it in the sixteenth century as a haven for thieves, robbers, and reivers. At its head lay Rona Lodge. Built in 1866 as a hunting lodge for the Raasay estate, the natural colour of its stone blended into the hillside beyond. An aluminium dingy, appropriately named *Tin Can*, was tied to a buoy in the bay. We transferred to it and, after a couple hard yanks on the starter cord its outboard sprang to life. A minute later we stepped ashore on Rona, increasing the population by 400 percent in one fell swoop.

Once the reunion got underway my wife and I went for a walk, following a steep muddy track behind the lodge to the hill pass at the centre of the island. From the top of the pass the summit of Rona was soon conquered: *Meall Acairseid*, the hill of the anchorage. We realised that there would not be time to visit the medieval chapel two miles to the south. Nor would there be time to pay proper attention to the abandoned village at *Acairseid Thioram* (Dry Harbour). To truly appreciate Rona would require many days of exploration. We would have to come back someday to give the island her due. So we savoured what time we had atop the island.

The view was one to remember. To the south on Raasay we could see the flat topped peak of Dùn Caan. Farther south the jagged Cuillin hills of Skye formed a black outline against a grey sky. And to the west, on Skye's cloud-shrouded Trotternish ridge, we could see where the rocky pinnacles of the Needle and Prison guard the narrow entrance to the Quirang.

When we returned to the lodge we were invited in for tea, and asked to sign the substantial guest book. Although the Macalmans lived on a remote island they were far from lonely. The sheltered bay is a haven for 'yotters' who anchor for the night and make use of the onshore showers and washing facilities. One indication of Rona's popularity is this excerpt from the *Yachtsman's Pilot*. In discussing Big Harbour it says: 'Holding is poor in places, consisting of soft black mud, well ploughed by yachts' anchors.'

Once the reunion came to a close we boarded *Ocean Unity* and motored south to Loch Arnish—the sea smooth as glass all the way. Back at the hotel drinks were offered to all who'd visited Rona. But not before the window blinds in the bar were drawn, reminding us it was still a Raasay Sunday.

That visit took place in 1995. Eight years later, while perusing the magazine rack at a large bookstore in Seattle, I picked up a glossy Scottish tourist magazine and started skimming through its pages. In between stories on golf, whisky, and Nessie, a small ad flashed by. I almost continued flipping pages, but the word 'Rona' caught my eye and an old memory became new. The ad described how the derelict mission hall on Rona had been converted into holiday cottages as an effort to revitalize the island. On that visit eight years before we'd had only a few hours ashore. Here was an opportunity to spend a week. There are no stores (or pubs) on Rona, so we'd need to bring a week's worth of food (and beer). We'd have to get all these provisions to Portree on the Isle of Skye, load them on a boat, and then set off for the unknown.

On a Saturday afternoon in May we met Peter Urquhart at the quay in Portree. Peter operated *MV Brigadoon*, and made regular runs to Rona. With our gear and supplies stowed away we set course for the hour long crossing to Rona. As *Brigadoon* cut north across the calm Sound of Raasay we saw puffins out foraging from the Shiant Isles. Then several porpoises spotted the boat. They darted over, like excited children finding someone new to play with, and for several minutes joyfully surfed our bow-wave. We motored past Loch Arnish and, as we neared Rona, saw the white arrow on Eilean Garbh. With a fresh coat of paint its big H still pointed the way to Big Harbour. Since our previous visit the lodge had also been whitewashed, and was now a bright landmark crowning the head of the bay. As we neared the lodge we saw *Tin Can* lying high and dry on the rocks. A pontoon dock had been built since our last visit, so we wouldn't need her to get ashore.

Peter throttled the engine back as we approached the pontoon. We were still a hundred yards out when a figure astride a red quad-bike zipped down the track from the lodge, a small empty trailer bouncing behind. The Macalmans were long gone from Rona Lodge, having left in 2000. The driver of the motor-bike was Bill Cowie, who became island manager in 2002.

Bill loaded our gear on the trailer and took it over the pass to Dry Harbour. We followed behind on foot, climbing a road we'd end up traversing several times during our stay. It is a steep, mile long twisting track, that after a few days we'd start to call the Burma Road. A layer of stone covered the track, so our climb was more pleasant than last time, when we'd had to pick our way across stretches of black mud.

Rona Lodge

After twenty minutes of walking we reached the summit of the pass; or, as Donald Macalman called it in Gaelic on our first visit, the *bealach*, and then started the descent to Dry Harbour. We could not see any of the settlement until we reached sea level. Then the road turned sharply to the north and the mission hall appeared, sitting above the shore of Dry Harbour. The reason for the name was readily apparent. With the tide out the floor of the shallow bay lay completely exposed, the sun shining on curly worm casts and beds of drying kelp.

Our quarters for the week would be the restored mission hall. Built in the 1870s as a Presbyterian Free Church, it is sixty feet long and fifteen wide, with several sky-lights embedded in its slate roof. The hall had lain derelict for decades. Then, in 2003, it was remodelled into two side-by-side cottages; one named Seascape, the other Skyescape. No one would be staying in Seascape during our stay, so we had the whole place to ourselves. We were soon settled in and, as we unpacked, three eggs were found to be the only casualties of our long trek over sea and hill—thankfully, all the beer had survived.

31

South Rona suffered from decades of neglect until Dorte Jensen acquired it in 1992. She hired Scottish Woodlands to manage the island habitat, deer and Highland cattle have been introduced, and the sheep cleared off—though three rogue escapees from that clearance still warily trot the hills. Once the lodge had been refurbished they remodelled the mission hall into two fully equipped cottages. With their battery powered inverters, electricity is available with only the intermittent running of a well muffled generator. (Windmills were installed a few years later). Radiant heat keeps you cosy, a washer-dryer cleans the bog-mud from your clothes, and a gas stove cooks your meals. It would be interesting to bring back some of the long dead residents of Dry Harbour and show them the cottages. Their jaws would drop in wonderment, a bit of heaven now found in their old church.

Rona provided me with several fascinating destinations for walks: three abandoned villages, their stones still in place; the Norse Tomb,

School ruin and Mission Hall at Dry Harbour

a legend that led me through rough country to climb the Eagle's Hill; the medieval chapel of An Teampull, built where a Celtic monk once found solitude, as did I; and Church Cave, another remote place of worship embedded in the cliffs above the sea.

We will explore all those places shortly. But as we lived next to it for a week, let me first describe the saddest sight on Rona. Standing next to the mission hall is the roofless ruin of the schoolhouse. At one time there were three schools on Rona. This had been the largest, with over thirty pupils, ranging in age from five to thirty years old. Its two large doorways faced the harbour, with an arched opening above for a bell, though it's not known if they ever installed one. The school's two chimneys still stand tall, their fireplaces once warming the teacher's quarters on the upper floor and the schoolroom below. The school closed in 1930. Its windows, doors, and floors are long gone, bushes sprout from the chimneys, and all about the ground lay shards of the slate roof.

During our week on Rona I hiked some forty miles. It was gloriously difficult walking country. Short bits followed old tracks used by the Rona people. But much of the walking entailed crossing trackless glens, and climbing through deep heather to the tops of the rocky knolls that dot much of the island.

But instead of describing the various walks one by one, let's put ourselves in the place of the postman, a position once held by Norman Cumming. Norman lived for a time on Eilean Tighe, a small tidal-island between Rona and Raasay, and then at Kyle Rona on the north end of Raasay. When the lighthouse was manned Norman rowed across to Rona, and then carried the mail to the lighthouse at the north end.

Our walk will start where Norman came ashore when the sea was rough, and he couldn't row all the way to Big Harbour. This is *Port an Teampull* (the Port of the Church), the nearest point to Eilean Tighe and Kyle Rona. We climb the hillside and, on a level bit of ground a hundred feet above the sea, come to An Teampull, a chapel and burial ground that date to the fourteenth century. The chapel, being in such a remote spot, may have been built on the site of a monk's cell. Perhaps St Maelrubha, who in the seventh century founded a monastery at nearby Applecross, had a retreat here.

The chapel is oriented east-west, with a walled burial ground abutting its western gable. We enter the site through a modern steel gate, its metalwork forming a chi-rho cross. This puts us into the burial ground, its walls refurbished by a visit from the Skye Dry-Stonewallers. Although generations must rest here there is only one recognizable tombstone. Now propped against the wall it once marked the grave of a family named Graham, some of the last residents of the nearby village of Doire na Guaile.

From the burial ground we have to stoop low to pass through the chapel door. Above it is a niche where a cross, or a statue of the saint this place had been dedicated to, may have once stood. High above the niche is a small window that when the chapel's roof was intact would have been the main source of light. The only other window is a narrow splayed opening, like an arrow slit, embedded in the eastern gable above where the altar would have been. No other internal features have survived, though on the north side bits of a circular stone frame possibly mark where a memorial had been built into the wall. There are also bits of nature built into the walls. For if we examine them closely we'll find sea-shells embedded in the mortar.

We leave the chapel and follow a meagre track to the north for a third of a mile to *Doire na Guaile* (the grove on the shoulder). Here there are some twenty structures that had been Rona's second largest settlement. The village is a mix of black houses and a few 'modern' ones; modern in the sense that they are made of squared, dressed stonework. And in several of the houses remnants of stone fireplaces, and rusting bedsteads, lay open to the sky. In 1883 eight families lived here, and at one time there were over twenty pupils in the school. If we were delivering mail in the early 1920s we might have a letter or two to drop off. But in 1926 Doire na Guaile died when its last family moved to Raasay.

From Doire it's a mile and a half walk along the boggy track to Big Harbour and the lodge. On a spring day it is slow going in places, in the winter it must be a terrible slog. The residents of Doire lobbied for years to have a decent road built—pleas that fell on deaf ears.

After a while we come to a junction. Here we turn left and descend to Rona lodge, where as postman we would have delivered mail to the Macraes; who for many years, other than the lighthouse keepers at the far north of the island, were Rona's only residents. The Macraes left in 1943, and since then the population has never exceeded three. The only written glimpses I've found of the Macraes are in *I Remember: Memories of Raasay*, by John Nicolson, and *Leaves from Rowan's Logs*, by RB Carslaw. The latter describes a series of sailing adventures along the Scottish coast in the 1930s, Big Harbour being one of the author's favourite ports of call. The last mention of the Macraes in this book is telling. When describing his final visit, in 1939, the author says: '…here everything is as it was except that the Macraes are like us, getting older.' Four years later they would be gone.

From the lodge we follow the track back to the top of the pass. Here we'll set down our mailbag and make a detour the postman would not have made. From a stone cairn we follow a series of posts to the south-east. We gradually lose altitude as we near the coast, and soon come to a ravine where a thick rope has been strung down as a handrail. With one hand on the rope we gingerly descend a step at a time. Where the rope-rail ends, a worn path leads over to *Uamh an Fhuamhair*: the cave of the giant, better known Church Cave (NG 6265 5700).

It is a large cavern in the cliff, sixty feet wide and a hundred feet deep. Inside it six rows of stones are set up as pews, and in front of

Candles burning in Church Cave

them a small font has been worn into the bedrock by water falling from a natural seepage in the roof. An enclosure of stones has been built around the font and, drip by drip, it is continually refreshed, never running dry. At the mouth of the cave sits a large square rock. Some three feet high, this is the altar stone of Rona.

The cave had been used as a Free Church meeting place until they built the mission hall, and after that baptisms were still performed here. In 2002 an Easter service was held, the first in several decades, the worshippers coming from Portree by boat. Several have been held since then, and today you'll find candles and a bible in case you're tempted to have an impromptu service.

From the cave we return to the pass and walk down to Dry Harbour. In the 1870s over a hundred people called Dry Harbour home. Here are the remains of over forty structures; a dozen black houses, a similar number of 'modern' stone houses, and an assortment of byres and gardens. Roughly half the village sits on the northern side of the glen, the rest on the south; between runs a track, Rona's old main street, which winds its way up through the village.

Most of the people who once walked along this now abandoned street came from Raasay, whose population swelled in the 1800s, when MacLeod of Raasay sold out and moved to Tasmania. Starting in 1846, George Rainey, the owner of Raasay, wanted to reduce the population and make room for sheep. So he sent many of the people to Australia, and forced others on to the poor ground of Rona.

Raasay and Rona have traded hands many times since. Rainey sold to George Mackay in 1872, the man responsible for creating the forlorn village of Braig we'll be visiting next. Mackay owned the islands for just two years, as did the next owner, William Armitage. In 1876 the estate was bought by Edward Wood. During his reign fifteen families

Dry Harbour village ruins

lived in Dry Harbour, eight in Doire na Guaile, and three in Braig. The estate changed hands again thirty-five years later, when William Baird & Company acquired it in 1911, with an eye on mining Raasay's iron-ore deposits.

Rona started losing its people in 1921, when the seven families of the Raasay Raiders left to settle Fearns and Eyre on the southern end of Raasay. Long denied decent land on Raasay, land their ancestors once called home, they took that land back. They were briefly sent to prison, and their actions spurred the sale of the estate to the Government in 1923.

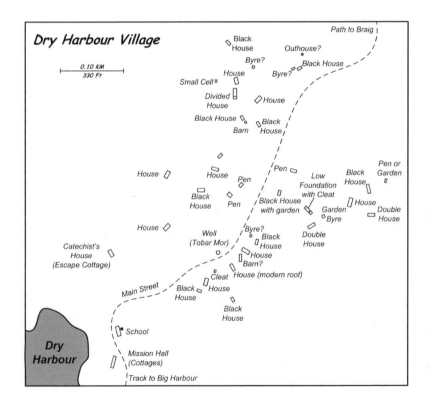

38

As we ascend the glen the first building we come to is a black house, twenty by twelve feet in size, and just beyond it a 'modern' stone house, thirty-two feet by sixteen, both overgrown and empty. Continuing up what's left of the narrow main street we come to Tobar Mòr, the village well. And as we continue east we soon reach an enclave of a half dozen dwellings that mark the end of the southern part of the settlement. From here the harbour below is obscured by a dense grove of birch trees, a billowing canopy of green floating over the lower part of the glen. After peering into a few of the homes— many are not easily accessed, being blocked by thick growths of thorny brambles—we cross the grassy track of main street and climb to the north-west.

If it were the 1920s we might have a letter or two to deliver here, for we've come to a couple of the most modern houses in the village; each two storeys high and solidly built. (One of these houses would be refurbished two years after our visit into a self catering cottage.) The view from them is quite different than from the south side of the glen. Off to the west Rona's small knobby middle peninsula, *Gob a Mhill* (the lumpy beak), which shelters the south side of Dry Harbour, juts into the Sound of Raasay. And beyond, on the distant Skye coast, we can see the pinnacle of the Old Man of Storr.

One of Rona's cottages in the early nineteenth century was known as the Widow's Cot. Because of the view over the harbour, it may have been one of the houses up here on the north side of the village. In this cottage lived Janet Mackenzie, and there are several versions of her story, her name, and where she lived. It is usually accepted she lived in a house at Big Harbour. But in T Ratcliffe Barnett's *The Land of Lochiel and the Magic West*, there is a version of the story that says she lived here in Dry Harbour. It tells how she kept a light burning in her window to guide fishermen through the rock–strewn waters of the bay. One night she did not notice the light had gone out. Later that evening she became a widow, when her husband's boat came to grief on the rocks. From that day on she religiously maintained her beacon.

Walking north-east to the far end of the village we come to another neighbourhood of houses. Some are tiny, some are built into the hillside, and some make use of large boulders to anchor their walls. The last dwelling is a black house. Like most of the others it's twenty by twelve feet in size and has a single entrance. The empty threshold faces south-east. But where the morning sun once warmed a family, it now warms bracken and brambles.

From the north end of the village a track passes through a narrow gully with the remnants of a gated wall that once closed it off. Once through the gully we find ourselves on the floor of a valley hemmed in on both sides by low hills. We're now following the path to Braig (the village at the top), and after a mile we reach the reed fringed shores of Loch Braig.

From the loch a right turn to the north-east takes us up a ravine. A few outlying buildings appear, and then the half dozen stone houses of Braig come into view. George Mackay, the owner of the estate from 1872 to 1874, created Braig in an effort to increase the rent return. It was a failure and had been abandoned in the 1890s. In 1881 there were five families living here. But by 1891 only two were left, and the heads of both households were widows. The postman in the early twentieth century would not have stopped here, having no mail to deliver to this ghost town clinging to the barren hillside.

From here we can follow our nose, for next to a crumbling house a cluster of mint marks the beginning of the way to the lighthouse. We leave Braig behind and follow a slight trail up and over a ridge cloaked with heather. And as we reach the next rise the yellow and black lantern house atop Rona lighthouse appears.

But as with all walks on Rona, just when you think you've arrived at your destination you discover yet another glen to cross, and yet another hill to climb; for we've come to a hilltop south of the lighthouse, only to realize that the light sits atop the next hill. Our way today is made a bit easier thanks to the Ministry of Defence, for at the bottom of the hill we reach the only paved road on Rona. The road starts at the pier in the bay below and climbs to the lighthouse. But its main traffic has nothing to do with the lighthouse, it's used to ferry workers at Rona's small military base to a helipad next to the lighthouse, from where they come and go on a regular basis. The base is a range control centre for submarine testing, the channel between Rona and the mainland having some of the deepest water in the Hebrides.

We follow the road to a gate in the whitewashed wall surrounding the lighthouse. Once inside the enclosure we pass two side-by-side slate-roofed houses. These were the keeper's homes from 1857 until the light was automated in 1975. These were the most modern homes on Rona for decades. And it must have been quite a stark contrast in the 1890s between the keeper's lives here, and those of the widows' families in the primitive stone houses of nearby Braig.

From our viewpoint at Rona's land's end several interesting places can be seen. On the tip of the Applecross peninsula, five miles to the west, lies An Uamh Shianta, the sacred cave. And twenty-five miles north-west, but hard to spot in the salty sea-haze, lie the Shiant Isles. These are the sacred isles, with their small ruined chapel and one of the largest puffin colonies in the islands. With all of these sacred places about it's not hard to imagine the early Christian monks using them as rest stops during their visits to the various settlements along the coast and among the isles. Perhaps St Maelrubha traveled from Applecross to Rona's An Teampull, and then worked his way north to Lewis via these havens.

Courtesy of a web-cam we're probably being watched by a security officer somewhere as we explore the lighthouse grounds and walk around the tower. It is locked up tight, so we won't be climbing it today.

Norman Cumming would have delivered the last of his mail here, and with his load lightened it would be time to head home. Walking down from the lighthouse we're tempted to continue to the pier. But because of the base below, when exploring Rona it's advisable to go no further than the lighthouse without asking. So we tip-toe to the helipad, sneak a peek at the cluster of buildings below, then start our way back.

As we walk south we have a choice. Shall we return the way we came, or go a different way? The postman would return as he'd come. But because we don't have to walk this route on a regular basis let's do something different. So we head to the south-west and, after a bit of hard work, reach the shore of lighthouse bay. The glen to the south ripples with overgrown lazy-beds, and out on the water we spot otters swimming between two rocky islets in search of lunch.

From the shore it's a fight uphill through dense vegetation. Weird honey-scented dust clouds erupt from the five-foot-tall heather as we plough through; a choking brew of pollen and midges. As we approach the top of a hill we see a dozen noisy gulls swarming around a cairn at the summit. Reaching the cairn we find it sits atop a cluster of rock slabs four feet deep. We've come to *Leac Nighean Righ Lochlainn*, the Tombstone of the Danish Princess; a cairn also known as the Norse Tomb (NG 6268 6006).

Our appearance at the top of the hill scares the gulls away, and we see what they found so interesting. The stones seem to be alive, as they're covered with a mass of squirming caterpillars. Here we can stop for a rest and lunch. (We'll leave the caterpillars for the birds. A sandwich washed down with a can of lager sounds better, and should keep us going for a few more hours.)

It may be a Norse seamark, but to the Rona people the traditional story of this airy cairn tells that it's the grave of two dead lovers. A Prince of Greece went to woo a Princess of Denmark. When he arrived he found several other suitors vying for her attention. The two fell in

Looking towards Skye from the Norse Tomb

love, and he convinced her to run off with him. Furious, one of his rivals, a Swedish Prince, pursued them across the sea, catching up to them here on Rona. A duel was fought, and the Greek slain. They prepared a grave for the Prince atop *Beinn na Iolaire*, the Eagle's Hill. The distraught Princess asked to be buried alive with her lover. They granted her wish, and the tomb was covered with slabs of rock.

From the Norse Tomb an easy stroll down the west side of the island looks possible—oh, the foolishness of youth! So we descend the hill to the south-west where we come to a hidden loch nestled against the hillside. We continue our descent to the coast, and then turn south to cross a short stretch of white shell sand. But, such as Rona is, our easy hike does not last long. The shoreline becomes a series of sheer rock walls plummeting to the sea. So back inland we head, climbing high over more rocky ridges, one after the other, until a familiar sight comes into view, the cottage at Dry Harbour.

The postman had to continue to the south and then row his way home, having covered a dozen hard miles on foot. But unlike the postman, our walk is finished, and we can take a well deserved rest in the cottage. (Note: There is a wonderful book called *Whirligig Beetles and Tackety Boots*, written by Julia Mackenzie, a daughter of the postman Norman Cumming, about growing up in Kyle Rona and Eilean Tighe.)

On the last evening of our stay I climbed Meal Acairseid, Rona's highest point. On the way up a rain squall blew through from the Skye Cuillins and a vertical rainbow rose to the heavens above St Maelrubha's monastery at Applecross. I then recited that poem-song that I intend on saying atop all the isles of the west. Its second verse begins *It's by Shiel water that the track is to the west...* After saying the poem I popped open my last can of beer—now we had to go home! White foam spewed out of the can, and I blew it, my own sort of blessing, onto the heather.

An Teampull

To the south dark clouds brewed over Raasay and the flat top of Dùn Caan. It is strange how accidents steer your course. How a desire to climb that peak, and dance in the footsteps of Boswell, had taken us to Raasay. How that endeavour had been waylaid by an unexpected knock on the door. How years later, killing time in a bookstore half a world away, an ad had caught my eye while flipping through the pages of a magazine. The word 'Rona' flowing directly into my brain, an unexpected knock on the door of memory. That had led to a week of memorable hikes and silent island nights. It was a silence we'll remember forever, for it's something hard to find these days. We had been fortunate to call Rona home for a week.

Postscript

I was struck by the many similarities between the abandoned village of Dry Harbour and the more famous one on far off St Kilda. Both confront you with a period of time frozen in stone. But unlike St Kilda, Rona had no mass evacuation that made headlines. Kilda's village died on August 29, 1930. There is no precise date for Rona. It had a slow death. A death by neglect, but hastened by courage; the courage of the Raasay Raiders taking back land their ancestors once called home. St Kilda had some famous last residents, such as Finlay MacQueen, immortalized in black and white images snaring puffins. But no one will ever know the name of the last resident of Dry Harbour.

I like exploring in solitude. Although its windswept main street is far out in the sea, St Kilda is anything but remote. It is a busy place, a place where sometimes you will find almost as many people as at a mainland attraction. Rona, on the other hand, had been a quiet place that welcomed us. Long may she remain that way.

PART II:

FLYING TO THE ISLES

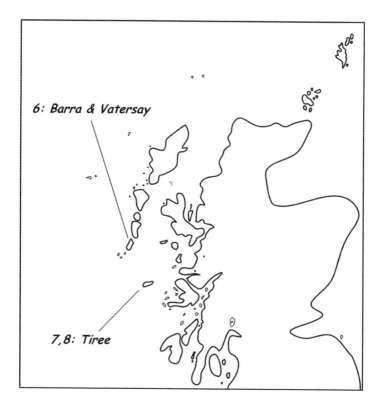

6: Barra & Vatersay

7,8: Tiree

6: A Winter Visit to Barra

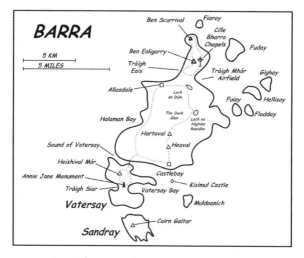

Map Reference: Ordnance Survey Landranger 31

AFTER several springtime trips to the islands I had a growing desire to see them outside the usual tourist season. Then one February my work took me to Manchester. I couldn't be so close and not visit an island. But after I'd finished work I needed to be home in relatively quick order, so whatever island was chosen had to have an air service. So I had five wonderful choices: Lewis, Benbecula, Islay, Tiree, or Barra.

Looking at those islands on the map one thing stood out. Next to Barra the map showed an airport symbol in the sea. This was the famous beach landing, and there had recently been talk of its demise. Two issues threatened its continuation: removal of the government subsidy, and use of the beach as a landing field, as salt water and sand are not an aircraft's best friends. That settled it. I would fly to Barra.

At first everything went as planned. I flew from Manchester to Glasgow, where I made my way to gate twenty-three at 9am on a frigid Saturday in February. Then things started to go wrong. The in-bound flight from Barra was late.

Glasgow had just been pummelled by a snowstorm. I had wanted to see Scotland in the winter, and this was the real thing. When the plane finally arrived it brought more bad news. The snowstorm had hit Barra. We were told the pilots needed to see some markings on the beach. If these were obscured by snow they could not land. In other words, we might take off, only to have to turn around and return to Glasgow. So we were told to wait for the next weather report.

The next report came at noon. Good news. Barra was basking in sunshine. We marched one by one into a DeHavilland Twin Otter, where I took a window seat hoping to see some of the Hebrides as we flew west. The first break in the clouds came over Tiree where, far below, I could see the large strand of Gott Bay covered with a light dusting of snow. Fifteen minutes later we started to descend.

Looking out the small window, a thousand feet in the air, I saw Barra appear through the clouds: a snow-white mountain in a grey sea. We made one pass over the beach and the pilots looked happy, the markers they had to see were visible. We splashed down at eighty knots as seawater churned up by the wheels spattered the windows. Turning around, we taxied up the beach to the small terminal building on Tràigh Mhòr, the Great Beach. The engines spun down to a stop and, stepping from the aeroplane, we waded through an inch of sandy seawater to make landfall.

The flight had arrived several hours late. The small post-bus I had counted on to take me to Castlebay, eight miles distant, was nowhere

Twin Otter on Tràigh Mhòr

to be seen. What I had not noticed was that while I had been collecting my luggage the little post-bus had driven to the far side of the aeroplane to collect the mail. So while I was wandering around the front of the terminal it had set off for Castlebay, leaving this ignorant tourist stuck in the back of beyond.

The terminal emptied out fast and I found myself alone. Fortunately I came across a list of taxi providers pinned to a wall. The first three numbers got me nowhere. Using my last coin I dialled the last number. Thirty minutes later I was in Castlebay.

From the window of my room at the Castlebay Hotel I could see Kisimul Castle on its rock in the bay, its tower crowned by the iron basket of the balefire beacon. Kisimul is the most interesting of all the Scottish castles. To be taken to Kisimul on a small boat, to wander its halls, see its chapel, and climb the narrow stairway to the top of the tower, is one of the best castle experiences a tourist can have in Scotland. Various portions of the castle date from the eleventh to the fifteenth century, and in season it's open to the public.

51

There were a few hours of daylight left so I set out on foot to visit Vatersay, an island linked to Barra by a causeway built in the 1980s. Once over the causeway I climbed the frozen slopes of Heishival Mòr to the survey pillar 625 feet above the sea. Three miles to the south lay the deserted island of Sandray, its summit, Cairn Galtar, white with snow. And below me white-capped breakers were rolling in from the Atlantic to pound the western shore of Vatersay.

There was tragedy under all that beauty. For on the shore below lay a mass grave for over 300 people. I hiked down to Tràigh Shiar, the West Sands of Vatersay, where a monument stands among the dunes. Its inscription reads:

ON 28th SEPR 1853 THE SHIP ANNIE JANE WITH EMIGRANTS FROM LIVERPOOL TO QUEBEC WAS TOTALLY WRECKED IN THIS BAY AND THREEFOURTHS OF THE CREW AND PASSENGERS NUMBERING ABOUT 350 MEN WOMEN AND CHILDREN WERE DROWNED AND THEIR BODIES INTERRED HERE AND THE SEA GAVE UP THE DEAD WHICH WERE IN IT   REV: XX 13

The ship *Annie Jane* sailed from Liverpool on August 23, 1853. Two days later she suffered severe storm damage and returned to Liverpool for repair. She sailed again on September 9, carrying a full load of emigrants. A few days later she encountered another storm, but this time they did not return to port. Instead, she floated about for a week while the crew made what repairs they could. Then, on September 28, she fought her last storm and ran aground in Vatersay's west bay. Only a hundred survived the disaster, and the bodies of the rest covered the beach. The dead were gathered together and buried in this mass grave, which has since been used to inter victims of other shipwrecks. The biblical quote on the memorial is from a verse that describes Judgement Day, when all the dead, including those drowned at sea, stand before God. It must have been a horrific scene that September day, when the sea gave up so many dead.

Vatersay west beach seen from Heisival Mhór

It snowed that night, and after a solitary breakfast in the hotel I set out to cross the hills. I followed the road east from Castlebay then, leaving it at its highest point, started up the steep snowy slopes of Heaval.

Nine hundred feet above the sea I came to the lichen stained white marble statue of Our Lady, Star of the Sea. Star of the Sea is the name of the Catholic Church on Barra, and was a title given to Mary in the twelfth century, a name that may come from this prayer attributed to St Bernard: 'If the winds of temptation arise, look to the star. If you are tossed upon the waves, look to the star; call on Mary.' Intercession for help while being tossed upon the waves was very important for island communities, whose livelihood depended on the sea, and where drowning deaths were common. The statue, carved by Hew Lorimer, is lovely; the child Jesus sits on Mary's shoulder, his left hand holding aloft the Star of the Sea. The two of them have held this beacon of hope over the Barra Isles for fifty years.

To the south, snow squalls moved across Vatersay, heading in my direction. It was an impressive sight, the storm clouds funnelling their fury in concentrated blasts onto the sandy bay I'd visited the day before. Just after reaching the 1256-foot summit of Heaval the storm hit, and for several minutes freezing rain pelted the hillside. I pictured myself in a Scottish Tourist Board brochure. Picture it for yourself. In a thick fog, battered by wind and icy sleet, a soggy figure huddles for shelter on a snow-covered hillside. The caption proclaims: *Scotland's for me!*

After the storm blew through I slid down the back of the hill and climbed the next peak, Hartaval. Just as I reached the top a second ice storm blew through. From Hartaval I descended into *Gleann Dorch*, the dark glen, and walked over to the wind blown waters of *Loch na Nighinn Ruaidhe*, the Loch of the Red Haired Girl. Out on the loch sat a crannog, a small man-made island linked to the shore by a stone causeway. On the island stood the remnants of a dùn—unfortunately

The Star of the Sea shines from Heaval

there was no sign of the red-haired girl. I could not cross to the crannog, as a high water level submerged its causeway. I was disappointed about this, as I wanted to see if the causeway's *Cloch Ghlagain*, the rattle stone, still rattled. If someone steps on this stone it knocks against another rock, alerting the dùn-dwellers that someone was approaching—an ancient alarm system of sorts; a clever idea, and no monthly fees.

I followed a track north through the Dark Glen. Its name comes from the black, peaty soil, and square depressions of old peat cuttings covered the valley. The sun came out as I reached the main road at Loch an Dùin, and along with it a stiff wind. Sustained blasts of twenty to thirty knots, with gusts of forty were blowing in off the Atlantic. I started trudging west, directly into the wind. Every step felt like walking in glue, as if the force of gravity had doubled, pulling me down and backwards. Several times I had to shelter behind stone walls to catch my breath before going on.

At Allasdale the road turned south. Walking became easier, as the wind hit from the side, instead of head on. I continued past the Isle of Barra Hotel at Hallaman Bay. Except for the bar, it appeared to be closed for the season, and I resisted the temptation to stop in for a pint. A half-hour later I stumbled into the Castlebay Hotel, where my resistance to the same temptation failed.

On the Monday morning I hauled my luggage down to the pier and caught the bus to the airport. The beach-side terminal was open so I was able to check in early. With four hours to kill before the flight left I decided to make a wander around the north tip of the island.

From the terminal I walked the single-track road to the old chapels at Cille Bharra. Barra may be named after the sixth century St Finbarr, and this could have been the site of his cell. Inside one of the chapels stood several medieval tombstones, and in the centre of the floor, mounted on a pedestal, is a replica of a 1000-year-old rune inscribed cross-stone that had been found here. The front of the stone has a design like those you find in an illustrated Celtic manuscript, patterns of thick interlaced tracery, and each side of the stone is decorated with double-spirals and square fretwork. The runes on its back have been translated to read something like *this cross was raised to Thorgerth, Steinar's daughter.* Sadly, in the nineteenth century, the original stone was taken away to a museum in Edinburgh.

Reaching the northern tip of Barra I climbed to the summit of Ben Scurrival, and then started the final ascent of the trip, 335 feet to the top of Ben Eoligarry. On the way up I heard a buzzing sound, and looked up to see the aeroplane arriving from Glasgow. Fighting its way into the wind it appeared to be flying in slow motion as it gradually set down on the beach. A few minutes later, as I descended the slippery southern slopes of Ben Eoligarry, I heard the little plane take off and head north to Benbecula—it would be coming back for me shortly. I walked onto the west beach just as another storm blew in, and was sand blasted clean while crossing the dunes to the airfield.

Inside the terminal I joined ten others waiting for the flight. The aeroplane arrived on time, and we heard the loud drone of the props as it rolled to a stop on the beach. We tip-toed our way through puddles of seawater to board the plane, and once everyone was aboard the co-pilot latched the door, and took his seat on the right side of the cockpit.

We taxied to one end of the beach and turned around. There was no waiting for takeoff clearance. We were number one on the runway. The pilot raised his hand to the throttles and pulled them back. Fifteen seconds later we were aloft.

Postscript

I'd been fortunate to see a side of the islands only the people who live there see. I'd been pelted with sand, wind, and freezing rain, but I'd also seen the sun break through to illuminate endless rows of white breakers, sweeping in off the Atlantic over the beaches, and the graves, of Vatersay. I thought to myself that I had to find a way to do something like this again. Looking out the tiny window of the aeroplane I watched the snowy top of Heaval slowly merge into the clouds and disappear.

7: Four Days to Tiree

The distance from Manchester to Tiree is only 300 miles. But the following journey between those two points took four days, and involved flying 2000 miles in a series of loops high over the British Isles.

A Saturday in November: Four Days to Tiree

Although the British Aerospace Regional Jet (RJ) could seat eighty-five, there were no passengers aboard. Two test pilots, a few BAe engineers, and I, made up the entire crew. With all four engines at full throttle the RJ pitched up steeply as it roared into the sky above Woodford Aerodrome, ten miles south of Manchester.

We jetted west for eighty miles to Anglesey Island near the northern tip of Wales. Twenty-five hundred feet over tiny Puffin Island, off the north shore of Anglesey, we turned around. With the aircraft aimed back at the mainland we set a course directly towards the mountain ridge behind the coastal town of Penmaenmawr. Unfortunately I could not enjoy the scenery, as I had to work. Work that involved monitoring a computer and listening to the pilot's comments and questions. It was hard to concentrate, for the scenery below offered up non-stop temptations to daydream. Oh, to be afoot down there on Puffin Island. But, if everything went well over the next few days, I would be heading north to another island: distant Tiree, in the Inner Hebrides.

Our flight test plan called for flying towards a mountain over safe, low ground (in this case the sea), and checking that the aircraft's warning system would alert us to the fact that some hard rock would soon be in the way. The Penmaenmawr ridge rises to 2000 feet, and if the aircraft's altitude was correct we'd clear it by a few hundred feet. That is not a safe margin for a commercial aircraft, so a warning should sound.

We approached the mainland at 300 knots. A minute before the ridge was upon us a computerized voice shouted "Pull Up!" The system had passed the test. We then started a gradual climb, and I glanced out the cockpit window in time to see the top of the ridge pass below.

We turned around and flew out over Conwy Bay: our next destination the Isle of Man, sixty miles to the north-west. The pilot called the tower at Ronaldsway Airport and requested permission for a touch-and-go. We would make a normal approach, then once the wheels touched ground we'd throttle up and head back to the sky. This would be another test of an aeroplane flying at the ground. But this time the system had better hold its tongue. A landing is in reality a controlled crash, and a useful warning system had better know when *not* to give a warning.

I was still fighting to concentrate on the work at hand. Just out the window rose the heather topped hills of the Isle of Man. No false warnings sounded as we dropped to touch the runway, rolled along for a few hundred feet, and then lifted off. My total amount of time on the island was (and shamefully, still is) eight seconds.

Sunday: Three Days to Tiree

Sunday was our dress rehearsal. We would fly several more tests, and if all went well, demonstrate the system to a representative from the Civil Aviation Authority on Monday. It was that Sunday flight I had looked forward to most of all, for it could have been entitled *Once Round Scotland*.

After lifting off from the aerodrome we jetted north. As we neared Glasgow the window filled with island distractions galore, and I managed an occasional glance to see Arran, Holy Island, and Bute, floating below in the Firth of Clyde. We started our descent to Glasgow, and every now and then I looked to the north, searching for a glimpse of the islands in Loch Lomond. At one point, Inchtavannach, and its Hill of the Bell, broke through the cloud cover that obscured much of the loch. After a touch-and-go at Glasgow we continued north over the snow flecked Grampian Mountains and then started an approach to Inverness. Our wheels lightly kissed the runway, and a few seconds later we were back aloft. Oh how I wished we'd kept going north; to soar over Orkney, Fair Isle, and Shetland. But from Inverness we turned south, and after one more touch-and-go at Edinburgh we returned to Woodford.

Monday: Two Days to Tiree

I hoped this would be my last day of work. I had a ticket for a flight to Tiree in two days, and if things did not go well I'd miss it. With the CAA representative aboard the RJ blasted into the skies and we flew back to Penmaenmawr. After several successful runs at the ridge we headed south to London City Airport for a touch-and-go. Anyone who has landed there is familiar with the steep approach angle, twice that of most airports. The unusually fast descent would be another test to see that the system kept quiet when it should. We flew in over the city and dropped down to the runway, a strip of concrete near the Thames. No false warnings sounded and we were soon flying back north.

It was dark when we landed back at Woodford. There was one more hurdle to overcome: the post-flight debrief. It seemed to go on forever. Even though we were now on solid ground, questions on how the system behaved were flying right and left. I managed to stumble my way through them, hoping each would be the last. I was dead tired and sleep deprived. For in addition to recovering from jet lag, firecrackers had been going off outside my hotel every evening, as it was the week of Bonfire Night.

Around 9pm everyone seemed satisfied. We would get the system certified, and the customer could take delivery of a new aeroplane. In the dark, wet, November night, I made my way back to the hotel.

Tuesday: One Day to Tiree

In the morning I drove 200 miles to Glasgow. It was raining as I continued up the west shore of Loch Lomond, where I took the Luss bypass off the A82 to get another, and much closer, glimpse of the Hill of the Bell. I checked into the Lodge Hotel at Luss, getting my first full night of sleep in a week. In the morning, after a short drive to Glasgow airport (hadn't I just been there?) I boarded yet another aeroplane. But there'd be no touch-and-goes with this one. It would stop. I would step out. I would touch Tiree.

8: An Autumn Visit to Tiree

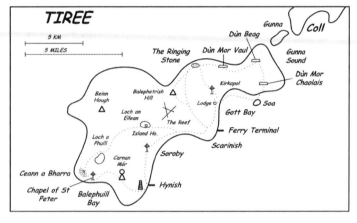

Map Reference: Ordnance Survey Landranger 46

At Glasgow airport I boarded a DeHavilland Twin Otter for the forty-five minute flight to Tiree; free to visit it after three long days of work. This particular Otter, tail number G-BVVK, was an old friend, as she had taken me to Barra on my last flight to the Hebrides. There was heavy cloud cover, so the little plane had to fly low over Argyll and the isles.

Once airborne we passed Dunglass Castle on the shore of the Clyde. To the north I briefly glimpsed Loch Lomond and its constellation of wooded isles. We then flew by the rock of Dunadd, the ancient capital of Dalriada, where I could see the River Add winding through the bogs of the Mòine Mhòr to the sea. Then all too fast we passed over Luing and the Isles of the Sea. Reaching the southern coast of Mull we soared over the dark tower of Moy Castle, its water-filled pit-prison hidden behind thick stone walls. David Balfour's adventures in *Kidnapped* came to mind as we neared tiny Erraid. Then ten minutes after passing the once blood soaked sands of Iona's Martyrs' Bay we made landfall above the eastern shore of Tiree. After one circle around Balephetrish Hill we descended to a soft landing on the Reef.

A few weeks earlier I'd called the Tiree Lodge to book a room. When I asked if there was a post bus to take me from the airport to the hotel, a woman's voice from far, far away, had said "No worries, we'll put you down for a Reef pickup." The Reef, as I learned, is the low-lying central area of Tiree where the airport, originally built for the RAF in the 1940s, is located. Suitcase in hand I walked out of the terminal and met Glen, my Reef pickup. At the hotel, as on the aeroplane, I was the only tourist. After getting settled in I put on hiking gear and headed outside. With the short November days there was only two hours of daylight left. Two hours to search for some Tiree gold.

In front of the lodge lay the vast expanse of Gott Bay, and its firm sand made for easy walking. At its east end I went overland to the ruin of *Dùn Mòr Chaolais*, the big fort of the narrows. The area was fenced off and a large sign said *Strathclyde Water Supply.* The old fort site is now a wellhead. I sat on the adjacent trig-pillar and had a taste of the water I carried, which was probably from the well, as I had filled my bottle earlier from a tap at the lodge.

I hiked on across the north tip of Tiree. Near a roofless croft house I came upon a large earthen mound where yet another fort, Dùn Beag, once stood. Dùn Beag and Dùn Mòr Chaolais once worked together to guard Gunna Sound, the narrow seaway between the islands of Coll and Tiree. Someday these two forts may stand watch over a causeway that could connect Coll to Tiree via the small island of Gunna.

I was truly in a land of forts. Dùn Mhòr Vaul, Tiree's most intact broch, lay just two miles away, and I set out to find it. After crossing several boggy fields I came to the adjacent bays of Salum and Vaul, and a few minutes later found the broch. Its circular foundation, thirty-five feet in diameter, stood six feet tall, and when originally built it had been some thirty feet high.

On the inside wall sat the base of the stairs that once wound all the way to the top of the tower. The ruin is twenty centuries old, and during excavations Roman and Norse objects were found. These show that the site had been occupied in various ways from the first to the tenth century. Other items dated to 800 BC, so people lived here long before the broch had been built. Many features of the defensive nature of the building were evident: holes for the bar that held the door closed, and a guard chamber next to the entrance.

From the broch I walked west to Clach a Choire, a large boulder lying above the shore. There are several names for it in English: the Kettle Stone, the Cauldron Stone, the Singing Stone, or more commonly, the Ringing Stone. Over thirty cup-marks cover its surface, and I have seen cup-markings like these elsewhere, some set within circles and looking like drawings of constellations. But I could not make out any pattern to these. There are some who believe that carvings like this were methods of directing energy fields that flow across the earth. That large stones like this served as a neural nexus of sorts for this energy, and the act of chiselling out a cavity established a specific projection of that energy. Thus each cup-carving had been placed to send energy out to encircle a dwelling, one that may even have been quite far away, where the energy field had a beneficial effect on the residents. If you're interested in reading more on this unusual subject, refer to the books *Ley Lines and Earth Energies*, by David Cowan and Chris Arnold, and *Lines on the Landscape*, by Nigel Pennick and Paul Devereux.

Clach a Choire – The Cup-Marked Ringing Stone

It was here that my search for Tiree gold ended. For although the Ringing Stone is said to be filled with gold, I'd have to split it open to get at it. And it's also said that if the stone is ever broken Tiree will sink into the sea. So even if I did get manage to get my hands on the gold, I'd not have long to enjoy it. So instead of a gold one I settled for a ring of a different sort. I tapped on the stone with a pebble and listened as it sang out its high pitched metallic chime.

The sun had set an hour earlier, and a hard mile of streams, bogs, and fenced fields separated me from the lodge. In increasing darkness I carried on across the moorland. There was no moon, stars, or street lights to illuminate the way, but off in the distance I could see the glow of the lodge. Then a storm hit and I had to walk headlong into forty knot winds. A half-hour later I stumbled into the warm lobby with one thing on my mind. But it was not to be. The bar was closed.

Over dinner I perused a copy of *An Tirisdeach*, the island newsletter. It had a story about a recent mass mailing from American Express to the residents of Tiree. The ad proclaimed: 'The card is welcomed in over 200,000 establishments in the UK. In the Scarinish area alone, you can use the card in 133 restaurants, 917 supermarkets and 436 other outlets.'

In the morning I bundled up and walked the beach to Scarinish. At the co-op (there was no sign of the 916 other supermarkets) I picked up snacks for lunch and a can of beer I planned to drink atop Carnan Mòr, the highest point on Tiree. A few minutes later, as I walked along the old harbour of Scarinish, a rainstorm blew in from the sea. So I ducked into a phone box to put on waterproofs.

After walking for a few minutes in the driving rain a passing car stopped, and I was offered a lift. One of several I would get that day. I sat in the back seat next to Faith, a little one new to this world, and as we drove along the driver asked why in this world I had come to Tiree, when sunny Spain was a cheap flight away. No quick reply came to my lips. How do you explain an obsession to strangers? In the back of my mind I knew why. But to express it I'd have to describe a desire inspired by a glimpse of a snow-dusted Gott Bay, a brief vision seen from the window of an aeroplane on its way to Barra two years before.

The question had caught me off guard. I was tired and not up to the challenge. So the first words that came to mind were lame ones, the equivalent of the island-bagger's creed "Because it's there." Instead I said something to the effect that I enjoyed out-of-the-way places. The driver and her companion both laughed, agreeing that in Tiree I had indeed found someplace out-of-the-way. They dropped me off in Crossapol, and a few minutes later I reached the cemetery at Soroby, which lies on the site of a monastery founded in the year 565.

In the rain at Soroby an elderly man was putting flowers on a grave. No ruins of the monastery remain, but set amongst the tombstones, slightly tilted and partially sunk in the earth, stood Maclean's Cross. One side had a bold cross carving, at its centre a large boss. The other side showed a worn, flat Celtic cross. The cross's dedication is due to this being the burial place of the Maclean chiefs during their ownership of the island from the fifteenth to the seventeenth century.

From Soroby I followed the road south to Hynish. Here you will find the pier and signal tower used in the construction of Skerryvore lighthouse. First lit in 1844, Skerryvore sits on a rock in the sea eleven miles to the south-west. The signal tower is now a museum, which I'd hoped to see. But I found the door locked, and other than a friendly tabby cat there was no one around to let me in. Hynish has a unique feature, one that would be interesting to see in action. The harbour is subject to silting and they needed a way to periodically clean it out. So a reservoir that can hold a million gallons of water had been constructed on the hillside above. When needed, all that water could be released to scour out the harbour. I looked around for the flush lever, but it was nowhere to be found.

The two faces of Maclean's cross

From Hynish I climbed Tiree's highest hill, Carnan Mòr, and hopped atop the trig-pillar, 462 feet above the sea. That may not sound like much. But it is when you consider Tiree is such a low lying island that its Gaelic name is *An Rioghachd Bàrr fo Thuinn*, the Kingdom whose Summits lie beneath the Waves. Usually, a trig-pillar, like the one I was sitting on, marks the highest point of an island. But not on Tiree, for looming above me, blocking out half the sky, and sitting on its own fat pillar, was an immense white sphere. Locally called the golf ball, it's an air-traffic control radar, and I could hear the humming sounds of electrical equipment coming from inside the dome. Like a captive lab rat I was probably being zapped with all kinds of radiation. But you only live once, so I sat on the pillar to eat lunch and drink the beer. I had hoped the radiation would warm my cold feet. It didn't.

From the top of Carnan Mòr I could see out over a wide horseshoe of white sand embracing Balephuil Bay. Descending to sea level I rounded the bay through wet grassland and, on its north side, searched unsuccessfully for the remains of *Kil Phedrig*, St Patrick's chapel. I did find a small rectangular stone foundation in the short grass above the shore. But it was too small to have been a chapel. (I learned later I'd missed the chapel ruin by a few hundred feet.)

One story says a chapel had been built here to honour the spot where, in the year 563, St Columba first set foot on Tiree. As the story goes, on his journey from Ireland a storm blew Columba's coracle to this lonely place, twenty miles north-west of his intended destination of Iona. In 1898 two boys knocked down the chapel. Both supposedly died shortly afterwards.

I gave up trying to find the chapel and climbed *Ceann a Bharra*, the Headland of the Sea. At its top, overlooking the sea in all directions stood the meagre remains of *Dùn nan Gall*, the Fort of the Strangers, where watchmen would have given the first warning of raiders from the south. I was ten miles from the lodge, and wanted to continue north, to

Looking to Ben Hough from Ceann a Bharra

climb Ben Hough, and explore the west of the island. But the daylight would not last much longer, and I had to fly home the following day, so I'd have to save Ben Hough for my next visit. It was time to start back, and so from the headland I crossed over a stretch of gentle sand dunes to reach the road near the grey waters of Loch a' Phuill.

Then I heard gunfire. The sounds grew louder as I walked on, and five minutes later I saw the shadowy figures of four men with shotguns blasting away at something, something I could not see. Not feeling safe, I hurried by. Then the Gods smiled on me. A passing shepherd stopped his car and asked if I wanted a lift. I gladly accepted, and as he drove the shepherd told me the men were snipe hunters. He didn't seem to care for the sport, telling me he thought they wounded more birds than they killed.

I left the shepherd to tend to his flock and continued on. The lift had saved me a good deal of walking, but there were still six dark miles to go. A few minutes later I reached Loch an Eilean. A castle once stood on a little island in the loch, and in its place now stands a mansion known as Island House. A drawbridge would have reached the castle, but a filled in land bridge now connects the island to the mainland. As I passed by a Land Rover towing a small trailer turned into the property. I was told later that this would have been the head gamekeeper, the trailer filled with the evening's snipe harvest.

I walked on into the dark night, the silent blackness broken only by the rare passing motorists. Then kindness illuminated the darkness. When I reached Crossapol a car stopped and I was offered a lift, my third of the day. Where in the world would someone stop and offer a ride in the pitch blackness of a winter night to a sweaty, soggy stranger? Fortunately for me, Tiree is one of those places. I was dropped off in Scarinish, and after wiping up the puddle of rainwater I'd left on the passenger seat I carried on. Forty minutes later I reached the warmth of the lodge. I was in luck this time. The bar was open.

Back in my room I used every available spot to lay things out to dry, and then crawled under the thick duvet to sleep. The wind howled through the night. It also howled through the open gap between the wall and the bathroom window, which I'd tried unsuccessfully to plug with towels.

Friday morning dawned with promise. The sun rose orange in the east over the mainland, and there was no sign of rain. My flight to Glasgow left in the afternoon, so I had a few hours to explore.

I set out to visit Kirkapol, which has a medieval church and a chapel dedicated to St Columba. Amongst the ruins at Kirkapol stood a sign warning that the old buildings were dangerous, so I did not enter them. The smaller of the two churches, Columba's Chapel, is set atop a large rock said to have cup-markings like those on the Ringing Stone, but I could not see any. A cross once stood at Kirkapol, a tall, exquisite monument that may have originally come from Iona.

Kirkapol Church Ruin

The Campbells took it away many years ago and it now stands in the garden of Inveraray Castle.

I decided to pay a last visit to the Ringing Stone. I climbed up on it and, lying down on the hard stone, closed my eyes for a short nap. Then out of nowhere hail stung my face. For three minutes I huddled next to the stone under the thin shield of a raincoat, the sound of the surf drowned by the clatter of hail. As suddenly as it started, the hail stopped, and a double rainbow arched across the sky. I walked a few feet away from the stone to take a photo, and from where I stood the two arcs of the rainbow pierced the Ringing Stone, which fit in well with the legend that the stone is filled with gold.

It was time to say goodbye to Tiree, so I climbed nearby Balephetrish hill. From up top I could see all the places I'd visited: the Ringing Stone; the broch of Dùn Mòr Vaul; the Hynish signal tower; and the golf ball

71

Rainbows pierce the Ringing Stone

atop Carnan Mòr. I also thought of all the people who'd offered me, a total stranger in their midst, rides wherever I went. So often on the mainland you meet people inured and dismissive to tourists. There was none of that here. I'd found Tiree to be a very welcoming place. Everyone I had met invariably asked me the same question: Why had I come to Tiree? As I said before, I had no simple answer. Before my visit I would have said I'd come to see the beaches, the ruined forts, and the early Christian sites. All which had repaid my efforts many times over. But after my visit I realised that, for a brief time, I had been part of an isolated community that has inherited, and still holds special, thousands of years of history. Not something you find very often.

PART III:

BACK TO THE BARRA ISLES

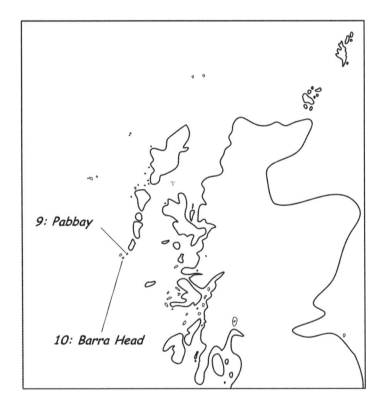

9: Pabbay

10: Barra Head

9: The Blood of the Merry Dancers: Pabbay

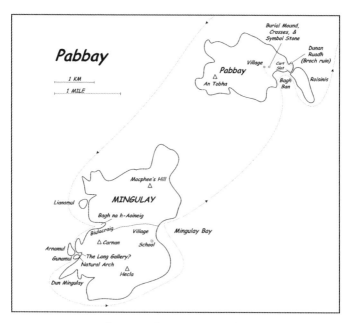

Pabbay

1 KM

1 MILE

Burial Mound,
Crosses, &
Symbol Stone

Dunan
Ruadh
(Broch ruin)

Village

Pabbay

An Tobha

Cart
Slot

Bagh
Ban

Roisinis

MINGULAY

Macphee's Hill

Lianamul

Bagh na h-Aoineig

Biulacraig

Village

Mingulay Bay

Carnan

School

Arnamul

Gunamul

The Long Gallery?

Natural Arch

Hecla

Dun Mingulay

Map Reference: Ordnance Survey Landranger 31

My fingernails were nubs. My stomach churned like Corryvreckan. I was in an incredible place, a place to savour, an island in the Outer Hebrides. But my thoughts were elsewhere. British Airways had lost my luggage.

I had been in Scotland for three days, and there was still no sign of my suitcase. So there I stood on Tràigh Mòr, the great beach on the Isle of Barra, watching, along with a busload of forty tourists, as a Twin Otter aeroplane approached from the east.

Unlike those tourists I wasn't there for the fun of it, to watch the little plane land on the beach. I was there as I had faint hopes my wayward luggage would be aboard. The Otter touched down and rolled to a stop on the hard grey sand. Several passengers, and a dozen bags, came out of the plane. None of the bags were mine.

Twenty-four hours later I stood on the beach again; watching along with a different busload of tourists as the same aeroplane, tail number G-BVVK, splashed down on Tràigh Mòr. I have fond memories of G-BVVK, as she had taken me to Barra beach and Tiree beneath the waves in times gone by. I would shortly have another fond memory of her. The hatch to the plane's hold opened up and various items were hauled out. A gold ribbon tied to a black bag brought joy to my heart. My fingernails could start to re-grow. My stomach could stop churning.

When I got back to the Castlebay Hotel I looked at the paperwork that had shepherded my wayward luggage from London to Barra. I was amazed the bag made it. The shipping directions said to send it to "The Isle of Arra in the Heberdese".

Still weary from jet lag I went to bed early. At 10pm the phone jolted me awake. The voice on the other end brought even more joy to my heart. It told me that in the morning I would be going to a small island I had long desired to see. An island that cruise ship itineraries rarely include, for the simple reason her next-door neighbour, glorious Mingulay, outshines her like a blinding supernova. And it was to see this other island, home to the most mysterious stone in the Hebrides, that I had dedicated a week's stay on Barra.

The voice on the phone was that of Donald MacLeod, skipper of *Boy James*. The forecast looked promising, unlike the last three stormy days I'd been on Barra, and he told me to be at the pier in the morning, where I would join a group going to Mingulay. After he set the rest of the passengers ashore there I would be taken to Pabbay, the isle of the symbol stone.

An ecstatic 'Mingulay Bound' sense of adventure emanated from the group I met at the pier the following morning. I have had that same feeling, and my days ashore on Mingulay are ones to remember. But that day I was 'Pabbay Bound'. As we set out from Castlebay there was no rain, and little wind. But the high top of Heaval, the summit of Barra, was cloud shrouded.

We passed the eastern tip of Vatersay, where a turn to starboard took us down the west coast of Sandray, the heavy Atlantic surf battering the rocky shore of the island. Then came Pabbay, and as we motored down her west side I saw something that battered my spirits. Most of the island lay hidden under a thick blanket of cloud. Hopefully conditions were better on the east side, where I hoped to be set ashore in an hour. Mingulay was then in sight, and we set course for the cliffs that rise high on her southern coast.

'It's in the long gallery in Mingulay, on the ledge below the blood of the Merry Dancers'. The quote is from Neil Munro's *The Children of Tempest*, and was a hint to the location of *MacNèill's Ulaidh*, MacNeil's Treasure, £20,000 left from the '45 that had been hidden on Mingulay. The climax of the novel is a climb up the cliffs of Mingulay, to a ledge where the treasure was said to lie. I had long wished to see those cliffs up close, and to journey through the narrow channel that separates the 400-foot-high sea stack of Arnamul from Mingulay, something only possible in calm seas. My wish was about to come true.

After rounding the west side of Mingulay we passed the stack of Lianamul, which had been connected to Mingulay by a precarious rope bridge in the 1880s. Just beyond it we came to the base of Biulacraig, a 700-foot-high sea cliff, its sheer rock walls cloaked with a spattering of green moss and white guano. Because of the low clouds we could not see the top of the cliff. But though our eyes could not see to the top, our ears could, for the echoing caws of seabirds bounced down through the mist from the thousands of nests on the precipices above.

We next came to the massive stack of Arnamul, and after traversing its north side we entered into the slender slot of sea that separates it from Mingulay. The slot narrowed as we continued on and, after reaching its narrowest point, we passed through to a pool of stippled sea, where the boat was surrounded by vertical walls of rock. It seemed as if we were floating in the nave of a giant cathedral of sea-cliffs, and the place that must have been the inspiration for Neil Munro's Long Gallery.

If this was the gallery then it was here that Col of Corodale, the antagonist of Munro's novel, drowned after a greedy climb to seek the treasure said to lie high on a ledge below the blood of the Merry Dancers. This blood was a patch of lichen, a red stain on the cliffs, and its name a reference to *Fuil nan Sluagh*, the blood that spills from the wounds of the Spirit Multitude that battle in the heavens above; the other visible sign of their clash being the Merry Dancers, also known as *Na Fir Chlis* (the Nimble Men), the Aurora Borealis.

No blood was to be seen on the cliffs that summer morning, for it takes a frost to turn the lichen red. But colours galore there were; splashes of green moss sparsely cloaked the rock, pearl grey tipped fulmars swooped through the air, and several black-green shags roosted on some of the low ledges above the sea.

After twenty minutes of staring at the cliffs; the boat rocking in the swell as countless seabirds soared overhead, we motored under a 60-foot-high arch that connects the stack of Gunamul to Mingulay; a passage that can only be made at low tide. After exiting this eerie stone portal we left the cliffs behind and set course for Mingulay Bay. Along the way we passed a flotilla of kayakers, battling the waves as they headed north. I did not know it at the time but, like me, they were Pabbay bound.

The clouds were only 100 feet above the sea as we approached Mingulay Bay, so most of the island was obscured. But what was visible, poking into the ceiling of mist, was the ruin of the Priest's House. It looked to be in even sadder shape than when I'd last seen it, as the southern gable had collapsed.

The boat came to a stop 200 feet off the rocks on the north side of Mingulay Bay. The other passengers boarded the tender to be taken ashore. And I watched as they made the difficult landing onto the rocks and climbed to the grassy slopes above.

A half hour later we approached Pabbay. Her high ground lay shrouded in cloud, but the rocks on her eastern shore were visible. It is an easier landing than Mingulay, and the tender nosed into a slot in

Approaching the Long Gallery, Mingulay

the rocks on the south side of Bàgh Bàn, the white bay, where I stepped ashore.

As I walked across the beach I passed a large rocky outcrop, one that would become an islet at very high tides. On its turf-clad top sat a deserted encampment of several tents, cooking gear lying atop assorted rocks. I realised this must be home to the kayakers I'd seen near Mingulay. I then selfishly hoped they'd not reach Pabbay for a while, so I'd have the island to myself. At the head of the beach I went inland, following a narrow stream that cut through the sands. Then, after crossing an old, turf-grown bridge, I found myself standing amongst the ruins of the village.

It had been a small settlement, for there were only ten acres of arable land on the island, and the population never exceeded more than two-

Taigh nam Bòchdan – the House of Spectres

dozen. Many of the men drowned on a fishing expedition in 1897. And by 1912, a year after Mingulay had been abandoned, Pabbay became a deserted island. The ruins of a half dozen black houses are grouped closely together here, and standing above them is the only 'modern' house. The black houses are barely recognizable, having been altered for use as sheep pens. But the shell of the big house, constructed in 1891, is still in relatively good shape. Its roof is gone, but its dressed stone walls, including both gable ends, still stand tall.

The house is known as *Taigh nam Bòchdan* (House of the Spectres), and was built for Ranald Morrison. Slate roofed, and with wood-lined rooms, it cost him ten pounds. When the Morrisons lived there they often heard strange noises, noises that sounded like a turbulent sea. These same noises had been heard in an older house on the site, that of John MacCormick, Ranald's uncle. That home, for some unknown reason, had been abandoned, and stones from it had been re-used in the making of the new house.

On the night before the drownings of 1897 the sea-sound was heard louder than ever by Ann, Ranald's wife. She learned she was a widow the next day. Afterwards she felt uneasy in the house, and eventually moved her family to Vatersay. After that a widowed cousin of the drowned Ranald, Mary Ann MacCormick, moved into the house with her three children. It is said that Mary Ann and her children sailed Pabbay's last boat to Barra when the island was abandoned in 1911.

After that the house was occasionally used by fishermen, and when the roof collapsed in 1937 the fallen timbers and slates were taken to Vatersay to make byres. But they did not use the material in their homes, concerned that the Bòchdan, the ghosts of Pabbay, would return.

Just below the House of the Spectres is the most interesting piece of ground in the Hebrides, the large burial mound with its carved stones, and to see it was the main reason I'd come to the island. The mound is twenty feet high, and proudly stands out from the smaller grass

*Fog-shrouded burial mound with the Pictish Stone lying prone at its base;
the stone has since been mounted upright*

grown dunes and the nearby rolling terrain. I climbed to its summit to
find the stump of an old cross. It had an odd finger of stone pointing
skyward from its broken top, and on its face were the remnants of a
now indecipherable design. Two other cross-marked stones stood below
the summit. The larger, three feet high, had a double cross carved on
its upper face, and had the look of a Christianized standing stone. The
smaller stone appeared to be a simple tombstone, with an incised cross
that completely spanned its face.

The time had finally come to take a look at a mystery. So I dropped
down to the base of the mound and took a seat next to Pabbay's
crowning glory, her Pictish symbol stone. These islands were Pictish
into, and beyond, the time of St Columba, and the stone dates to

sometime between the sixth and the early ninth century. It had been found in the sand here by Father Allan Macdonald in 1889, and it was both a joy and a sorrow to see.

The symbol stone is sadly worn. So worn, that at first glance I saw no sign of its carvings. Where was the lily symbol? Where was the crescent and-V-rod? I crouched down and ran my hands over the stone's surface. As I did I could feel the shallow outline of the lily's stem, and the curved top of the flower. Looking closely above the flower some of the incised V-rod could be seen, but the arcs of the crescent were virtually non-existent. One thing that I could see was the cross carved into the top of the stone, its rounded grooves, a half inch deep, thickly crusted with white lichen.

There are about 250 symbol stones in Scotland, and no one knows for certain what they are, or what their symbols mean. There are several theories. One is that the symbols are ancient heraldry, emblems of the person honoured with what may be an elaborate tombstone. In W A Cummins' *The Picts and their Symbols*, the author deduces that the crescent and V-rod is the symbol for the name Brude, but he has no theory for what name might be represented by the lily. So a partial translation of the Pabbay stone could be: Here lies Brude, descendant of 'Flower'.

The stone is a rare thing to find in the Hebrides. Of all the known symbol stones, Pabbay's is the most remote, and one of only six in the Western Isles. Three of the island stones have since been moved to museums, but the others still stand in the open air of their island homes. The two other freestanding island stones are much easier to visit than Pabbay's. One is on Skye at NG 418 492, the other is on Raasay at NG 547 368.

I wanted to see more of Pabbay, so after snapping too many photos of the stone—none of which turned out well, for photographing them is an art—I left the mound and walked to Dùnan Ruadh, the Red

Fort. It sits on a rocky promontory at the east end of the island, and is a galleried dun, whose outer walls have fallen into the sea. It was an easy walk out onto the promontory, and I could see that a substantial bit of the fort still stood, an arc of wall facing inland, the fort's first line of defence. It had also been Pabbay's last line of defence, for if the dun was overrun there'd be nowhere for its defenders to escape. Like many island duns this one has a sister fort perched high on the slopes of Cairn Galtar, two miles away on the isle of Sandray (NL 637 912).

As the persistent cloud cover made climbing to the top of the island pointless, I then set my sights on reaching the summit of Roisinis (the headland of the horse). It is a detached peninsula said to be reachable at low tide, and its low summit (141 feet) could be seen beneath the clouds.

As I walked towards Roisinis I came across an odd looking cart embedded in the turf. It appeared quite old, and had obviously not been used for decades. Its wooden frame was six feet long by two wide, and it had two small iron wheels rusted solidly to its single axle. I would shortly stumble upon something fascinating that would tell me how the cart had been used.

Ten minutes later I found myself in a precarious situation. The pack was wobbling on my back, and the sloping rocks, a foot below my dangling feet, looked slippery, so I called it quits. I was trying to get over to Roisinis. But although the tide was low, a two-foot-wide channel of sea had to be crossed. At first I thought it would be easy. I would only have to lower myself down a short ledge of stone above the channel, and then step across. I started to do just that, and as I dangled midway down the ledge I could almost touch the far side with my foot. Then it occurred to me I'd have to return the same way. I would have to jump back across the channel and climb the ledge. Being alone has it advantages, and disadvantages. In that situation it was a definite disadvantage, and discretion was called for. So I pulled myself back to the top of the ledge.

I looked around, but could not find an easier way to cross. While I was searching I came upon an odd looking slot in the rocks above the shore. It was unnaturally square sided, a blackened channel carved out of bedrock that formed a chute down to the sea. The inner sides of the chute had flat ledges, halfway down, that were obviously for wheels, and the sloping floor of the slot consisted of a series of small steps chipped out of the rock. I realised that this had been a ramp for the rusting cart I'd stumbled upon earlier, part of a trolley system designed to bring supplies up onto the island.

After giving up on my attempt to reach Roisinis I decided to spend what time I had left back in the village. So I made my way there and took a seat atop the burial mound, where I stayed for an hour, surrounded by its silent stones. One was trying to tell me something. But, sadly, I didn't know its language.

Burial Mound and Taigh nam Bòchdan seen through the fog

So what story was the stone trying to tell? And what legends did the Pabbay people have of its mysterious images? Did they have stories of the *Sluagh* and *Na Fir Chlis*, the Spirit Multitude and the Merry Dancers, or of the *each-uisge*, the water-horse? One of the most common figures carved on the symbol stones—it shows up on over fifty—is something called The Beast. It has a mane, a tail, and appears to be swimming. It is a figure some think represents a water-horse, a beast well known to the Picts, as the first recorded encounter with one (Nessie) came from St Columba's visit to the king of the Picts in the fifth century. Mingulay's water-horse legend has survived to this day, and from its home in the haunted hollow on MacPhee's Hill it would be an easy swim to Pabbay for this wily creature. So perhaps tales of it were once murmured on dark winter evenings around peat fires in the Pabbay homes.

Drawing of the Pabbay stone by John Romilly Allen (1887 – 1907)
Proceedings of the Society of Scottish Antiquaries, Vol. XXXI (1897)

The sound of an approaching boat brought my thoughts back to the present. It was time to go. So I left the mound and started walking across the white sands of Bàgh Bàn. When I approached the kayaker's camp I saw it remained deserted. They were still out battling the sea. As I passed their camp I decided to leave a message. It would be one that would either mean nothing to them, or if they knew anything about the lore of these islands, one they would appreciate. And, if they did, it would be something for them to talk about around their campfire that night; though the fire would be one of driftwood, not peat. Finding a patch of smooth sand above the rolling surf, I scrawled, in giant letters:

Beware, the Pabbay water-horse rides tonight!

Erskine Beveridge's photo of the Pabbay Stone from 1895
© Royal Commission on the Ancient and Historical Monuments of Scotland; C/65811. Licensor www.scran.ac.uk

10: Berneray of the Children's Graves:
Barra Head

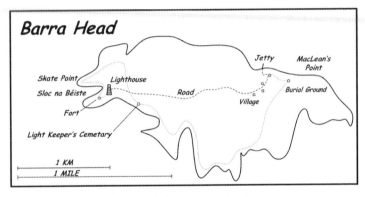

Barra Head

Skate Point

Lighthouse

Sloc na Béiste

Fort

Light Keeper's Cemetary

Jetty

MacLean's Point

Road

Village

Burial Ground

1 KM

1 MILE

Map Reference: Ordnance Survey Landranger 31

The deserted *Beàrnaraidh nan Easbaig*, Berneray of the Bishop, was an island I'd tried to get to for many years. The reasons were many. The island has centuries of human history, having been occupied from prehistoric times up until 1980. Its population peaked at 57 in 1881, but declined to just the lighthouse-keeper's families after 1910. Berneray also has a religious history, as there was once a chapel, and its old burial ground still remains.

Another reason to go was its unique location. It is Land's End of the Outer Hebrides, the next stop south is Ireland, 100 miles away. I also wanted to see its spectacularly placed lighthouse, the highest in the

UK, 700 feet above the sea on the cliff-edge site of an Iron Age fort. Berneray is also a Land's End of Hebridean literature, as it is the island TS Muir chose to finish the Hebridean portion of his writings on the ecclesiological ruins of the Scottish Islands—more on this, later.

Berneray, also known as Barra Head, lies twelve miles south of Barra, and the 'of the Bishop' designation comes from it having once been controlled by the Catholic Bishop of the Isles. On the several occasions when I was near Berneray, and the sea calm, which it needs to be to land, her sister island of Mingulay was always there, a half mile away to play her trump card, demanding a visit: Mingulay of the immense cliffs, Mingulay of the Long Gallery, Mingulay of the marooned McPhee. And so Berneray went unseen for many years.

The nearby island of Pabbay is also eclipsed by Mingulay, and getting there had been a challenge. In 2007 I had made a long stay on Barra in order to set foot on Pabbay. So three years later I decided to return to Barra for another extended visit; hoping that obliging weather, and an obliging boatman, would allow a visit to Berneray.

And so a week's stay in late spring was booked at the Craigaird Hotel on Barra. I also sent an email to Donald MacLeod, who operates the boat *Boy James* out of Castlebay. Donald had taken me to Pabbay on one of his regular Mingulay runs, and in his reply he said it would be no problem to drop me on Berneray if, that is, the sea-state was good.

Three months later, at noon on a sunny Thursday, the boat *Boy James* left Castlebay with a full load of passengers—all but one destined for Mingulay. It was the boat's second trip of the day, and when I asked how the sea-swell had been on his earlier run the skipper ominously replied "Not good, not good a'tall."

Although I had made the journey around Mingulay before, it was as amazing as the first time. Motoring over a rough sea we rounded the cliffs on the south side of the island, where we saw dozens of rock-climbers clinging to the high cliffs, some descending, others ascending, with nothing below them but rock and sea. We would later see their tents, about forty of them, dotting the ground near Mingulay's deserted village.

In the choppy sea Donald expertly motored *Boy James* into the narrow sea-slot between Arnamul and Mingulay, then slowly manoeuvred between the sheer rock walls that rose just feet away on each side of the bouncing boat. After threading this needle's eye of stone we came to a stop below the dramatic cliffs of the Long Gallery, where all of us stared up to the high cliffs above to see hundreds of sea-birds wheeling overhead. (See chapter 9 for the story of the Long Gallery.)

Once out of the gallery we motored past the headland of Dùn Mingulay and then traversed the narrow channel between Mingulay and the stacks of Geirum Mòr and Geirum Beag. The other passengers were preparing to set foot on Mingulay, but they would have to wait a little longer. The sea-state was good and, when the skipper set a course to the west, I knew I'd be landing on Berneray.

Berneray faces the western winds off the Atlantic, so the only habitable area was at its low, north-east end. This was where Donald intended to set me ashore at the island's only port, a small storm beach where a cement jetty had been built in preparation for war in 1930.

I had been warned that the jetty could be a skating rink, as it is usually covered with slimy seaweed. But the hot weather had dried the seaware to a crisp, making it an easy landing. A minute after stepping ashore I reached a storehouse that had been built for supplying the lighthouse. A tractor and trailer stood inside. The tractor, an old rusted relic, looked to have made its last run many years ago.

From there it was an easy walk in the tall dry grass to the burial ground. It had the look of a typical Hebridean mound-cemetery, and the outlines of several structures could be seen. One, a circular foundation eight feet in diameter, probably marked the site of a beehive cell or chapel. Unfortunately there is no record of a name for the site, or to what saint it may have been dedicated.

Burial ground mound, Berneray

Thick green rushes covered the burial ground, and amongst them lay several sun-bleached boulders. None looked like grave-markers, but two were quite remarkable. One had a cup-mark carved into it, and incised in the other was a delicate cross; a foot high, with circular depressions at the ends of the shaft.

Above the burial ground a grassy track led west to the lighthouse road. Once on the road I passed a four-foot-tall standing stone, and then started the climb towards the top of the island. From the road it was easily seen how most of the island's arable ground sloped to the sea. This kept the land drained, which meant no peat could develop. So the residents of Berneray had to go to great effort to get peat from Mingulay, a half mile across a sometimes treacherous Sound of Berneray. There was a school here for a while, but due to the small number of children

Worn cross stone, Berneray

it closed in 1887. The population fell after that, and other than the light house keepers Berneray became a deserted island in 1910.

The track curved left as it climbed the grassy slope, and soon the entire lighthouse enclosure came into view. Its thick stone walls surrounded several large fields, the southern walls abutting the cliff edge. Behind the walls sat the lighthouse buildings; nine tall chimneys rising from three keepers' houses. I entered the paved courtyard to find all the buildings locked. A glance through the windows showed dereliction; empty rooms, peeling paint, and soiled floors. Also locked were several rectangular fibreglass pods, where maintenance workers stay when they service the lighthouse.

Built in 1833 from granite quarried on the island, the sixty-foot-high tower was the second lighthouse built in the Outer Isles—the first was Eilean Glas on Scalpay. Keepers manned Barra Head for nearly 150 years until automation came in 1980. The light is so elevated that, on a clear night, its flash every fifteen seconds can be seen thirty-five miles away. Being high is also a weakness, as on cloudy nights its visibility is drastically reduced.

TS Muir, author of *Ecclesiological Notes on some of the Islands of Scotland* (1885), chose Berneray to end the Hebridean portion of the book. Here is how he opens the chapter entitled *Barra Head*, writing as he sat here in the keeper's house:

July 15, 1866: Here, after innumerable jumblings by land and by sea, I am – thanks for it! – at the end of my journey, and taking a few days' rest in the lighthouse. My worthy hostess, the head-keeper's wife, has assigned to my use the spare chamber, and, the more to conduce

Barra Head Light

me to its salubrity, maintains, notwithstanding the sultry weather, a perennial blaze in the chimney, feeling, perhaps, I might take hurt from the fog which ever and anon gathers thickly around our aerial habitation… From the crofter's little township a continuously ascending path of more than a mile leads you to the pharos, grandly seated within a few yards of the edge of a precipice rising sheer 600 feet above the sea.

One can be truly jealous of Mr Muir, enjoying a stay with the keepers high atop Berneray. *Ecclesiological Notes*, the result of all his jumblings by land and by sea, remains one of the most remarkable works on the antiquities of the Scottish isles.

Just beyond the lighthouse a thirty-foot-thick stone wall cut off the end of a narrow promontory. The wall had a small section cut out of its

Remnants of the fort, Barra Head

middle, so that the beam from the lighthouse would not be obstructed. This wall is all that's left of an Iron Age galleried dun that had been the first in a string of forts that guarded against threats from the south. A beacon fire lit here could be seen from forts on the islands of Pabbay and Sandray, from where a warning could be relayed on to Barra.

A portal through the stone wall is still in place, and after passing through it I came to a sunken grassy area, surrounded by natural stone slabs and boulders; the heart of the fort, the last resort for the residents of Berneray in times of trouble. To the south, north, and west there were sheer drops to the sea, and I could hear the raucous calls of seabirds nesting on the cliffs below. The north side of the fort faced *Sloc na Bèiste*, the ravine of the beast, that splits the end of the island into two great claws of cliff; cliffs that the Berneray people once descended to harvest birds.

I circled around the head of the beast's ravine to the tip of Skate Point, the westernmost point of the island. (Dried skate was once called the currency of Berneray). From there all of Mingulay could be seen, a mile across the sound. Also to be seen were the two rock stacks of Geirum Mòr and Geirum Beag. Sheep were once grazed on the grassy plateau atop 160-foot-high Geirum Mòr; sheep who managed

Mingulay seen from Berneray

to survive on what meagre grass grew around the remains of an old structure, either a chapel or a fort that once stood atop the stack.

Nearer at hand, on the grassy slopes of Berneray, lay a cluster of four massive square pillars. In the years leading to WWII a radar station had been built here, along with the jetty at the landing place. The radars were eventually dismantled. But the pillars it stood upon remain to this day.

I climbed back through a break in the wall to re-enter the lighthouse enclosure. There, at its far north-west corner, lay an odd vaulted building, ten feet high. It had the look of a Celtic Christian oratory, but was of much more recent date. Its purpose is a mystery (to me, anyway). But one could conjecture it is the most sturdy donkey barn ever made, as that may have been how the keepers originally hauled supplies to the lighthouse.

From there I followed the cliff tops east to a circular structure, thirty feet in diameter. Its walls were eight feet high, and a solid block of granite carved in the shape of a flame stood atop them: an eternal flame if ever there was one. I stepped inside to find a truly sad place; a cemetery made for the lighthouse keepers. Inside of it there were several tombstones set into the walls; one for two-year-old Catherine Black, who died in 1818: 'This stone was erected by her mourning parents'; another for two-year-old Alexander McIntosh, who died in 1842: 'Son of the Principal Lightkeeper, the Lord gave and the Lord taketh away'; and one to Donald Reid, 'Born 22nd, died 29th July'. Little Donald was only a week old.

My time on Berneray was nearly up. From the children's graves I followed the cliff-tops to the east, peering over the edge every now and then to see puffin burrows, and old bits of wall built in precarious places to keep sheep from tumbling to the sea. From the southernmost high point of the island an easy stroll led down to the old burial ground, where generations of Berneray's people rest in unmarked graves. I sat

Lighthouse keeper's Cemetery, Barra Head

there for a while to enjoy what time was left; precious time, time alone on Berneray.

That time came to an end when I heard the boat motoring over from Mingulay. I had to say goodbye to *Beàrnaraidh nan Easbaig*, Berneray of the Bishop. But that name seemed too distant, too impersonal. The island needed a better name. So as I stepped onto the boat I said goodbye to *Beàrnaraidh Uaighean na Cloinne*, Berneray of the Children's Graves.

PART IV:

SOUTH UIST, THE SOUND OF HARRIS & ST KILDA

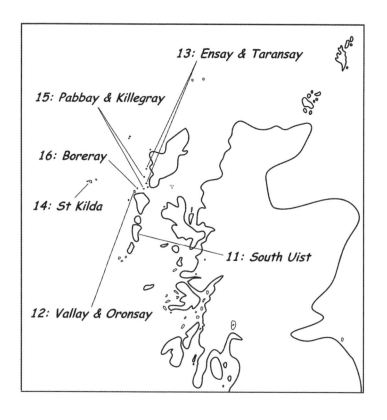

13: Ensay & Taransay

15: Pabbay & Killegray

16: Boreray

14: St Kilda

11: South Uist

12: Vallay & Oronsay

11: The Loch of Weapons: South Uist

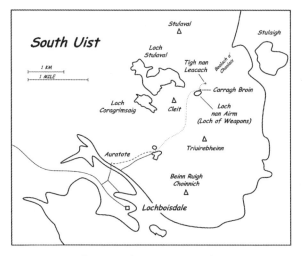

South Uist

Stulaval △

Stulaigh

Loch Stulaval

Tigh nan Leacach

Bealach ó Chadais

Carragh Broin

1 KM
1 MILE

Loch Coragrimsaig

△ Cleit

Loch nan Airm (Loch of Weapons)

Auratote

△ Triuirebheinn

Beinn Ruigh Choinnich △

□ Lochboisdale

Map Reference: Ordnance Survey Landranger 31

A SERIES of walks on the Outer Isles are described in Daphne Pochin Mould's *West Over Sea*. On one of them, entitled *The Ridge on the Edge of the World*, she wandered from Lochmaddy to *Loch nan Airm*, the loch of weapons, set high in the hills of South Uist between the mountains of Triuirebheinn and Stulaval. Then after paying a visit to the earth house of Tigh nan Leacach, she continued to the north-west to climb Stulaval. To end this eight-mile hike she followed the Hornary River to the sea at Mingary on the west coast.

Aside from the magnificent wander itself, the two historic sites seen on this walk sounded fascinating: the earth house and the Loch of Weapons. The earth house is one of five on South Uist; underground structures that were either hiding places, storage for valuables, or religious shrines of some sort. And the loch is the traditional site of the last Viking battle in the Hebrides. At its bottom are said to lay the weapons used during the fight.

With the sky above Lochmaddy grey with cloud, and a series of showers sprinkling the ground to the north, I followed in Daphne Pochin Mould's footsteps to the bridge to Auratote (NF 787 205). The bridge took me across the narrow channel that connects *Loch a' Bharp* (loch of the tomb) to the sea, from where a soggy footpath led up to the reservoir of *Loch nan Smalag* (loch of the coal-fish, or cuddy), the water supply for Lochmaddy.

From the loch I started across the trackless moorland to the north-east. It was oppressive terrain, sinister and soggy, surrounded on three sides by dark mountains. Due south lay *Ben Ruigh Choinnich* (the hill of Kenneth's shieling); to the north sat the low hump of the hill known as Clett; and to the west stood the triple heights of *Triuirebheinn* (the hill of three peaks). Adding to this gloominess the hill pass ahead of me lay shrouded in a heavy, dark fog.

After rounding the west shoulder of the hill of three peaks I climbed to *Bealach na Doillaid*, the pass of the saddle. At the top, 525 feet above the sea, the view opened to the east. Three-hundred feet below lay *Loch nan Airm* (NF 812 226), the loch of weapons; a dark, circular loch 600 feet in diameter, nestled in a bowl at the bottom of the surrounding slopes; the crater of an extinct volcano.

From the pass I could see my first destination on the hillside above the loch. It was a grey scattering of stones that stood out against the green heather and bracken. To get there I dropped down the hillside to cross the stream that flows from Loch nan Airm to

The entrance to Tigh nan Leacach

Loch Stulaval, and then climbed into *Bealach a' Chaolais*, the pass of the narrows.

Fifteen minutes later I stood atop *Tigh nan Leacach*, the house of flagstones (NF 813 225). Under the ground—and piles of stone that have fallen from the hillside above—lay a narrow, S-shaped chamber, twenty-five feet long. Wet nettles covered the ground and I carefully pushed them aside as I tried to crawl into the structure. I didn't get far, for fallen stones blocked the entrance. If I had been a bit skinnier I might have wiggled my way in. Another thing that discouraged me from trying harder was that an enterprising spider had spun a web across the opening. (He's probably bragging about the big one that got away.)

Too small to have been a permanent home, Tigh nan Leacach had probably a place of refuge when unfriendly visitors were in the

Loch nan Airm

neighborhood. The local residents may have found sanctuary here during the battle that gave the loch its name. And as for that loch, the time had come to see it up close, so I descended to the Loch of Weapons.

At the south-east corner of the loch I came to a boulder on the shore and sat on it to eat lunch. Current maps mark this as *Carragh Bròin* (the stone of sorrow). Older maps indicate that the stone lies higher up the hillside, but my search up there had failed to find any large stone. The story of the stone's name, and that of the loch, is in Otta Swire's *The Outer Hebrides and their Legends*, where she recounts the tradition that the last battle between the Vikings and the people of South Uist occurred here. The battle was indecisive and both sides stopped fighting. The wounded were brought to the stone of sorrow, and the combatants threw their weapons into the water as a sign of peace.

As much as I wanted to complete Daphne Pochin Mould's route to Mingary, doing so would require a six-mile road walk back to Lochmaddy, so I returned to the pass of the saddle. From there the loch, far below, could still be seen; a round spot of black water surrounded by deserted, shadowy hills. Like that dark portal into Tigh nan Leacach, the loch resembled an entrance hatch to an unknown land, and I wondered if a cache of once bloodied weapons still lies mouldering in its depths. The hidden loch sees few visitors these days and, with the stone of sorrow at its side, it was once again left in peace.

12: Two Walks across the Waters:
Vallay & Oronsay

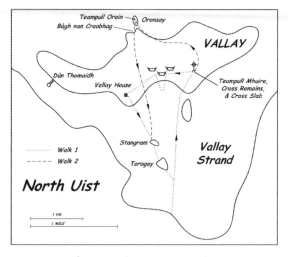

Map Reference: Ordnance Survey Landranger 18

I BEAT the bulls to the beach by fifty feet. Once safe on the rocks I turned to face them. They came to a halt, their eyes twinkling in the sunlight. They looked mad, and I heard a snort or two as they discussed their next move. They were young bullocks, castrated bulls, still in their early, formative years. (I'd be mad, too.) I hadn't seen them until I was halfway across *their* field. Fortunately I'd found sanctuary on Vallay Strand.

Earlier that day I'd tried to get to the island of Pabbay in the Sound of Harris. But I couldn't find anyone to take me there. So, I thought, since I couldn't take a boat to an island, why not walk to one? Why not visit the tidal island of Vallay? Someone suggested I speak with Lexie ——, who lived near the crossing. Lexie pointed out where to go and, an hour before low tide, I started out. I should have waited longer. A few hundred yards out a shallow tidal stream blocked the way. So off came the boots and I covered the remaining mile barefoot.

Once on Vallay I made my way to the site of its pre-reformation church, Teampull Mhuire. In 1703 Martin Martin wrote of Vallay that: 'It hath three chappels, one dedicated to St Ulton, and another to the Virgin Mary. There are two crosses of stone, each of them about seven-foot high'. Although the tall crosses have disappeared, I was curious to see the site of the chapel dedicated to Mary, and something referred to on the map as 'cross remains'.

Only a scattering of rocks marked the site of Teampull Mhuire, as its stones had been robbed to build a nearby burial enclosure. Cloaked in thick, yellow lichen, the enclosure is mentioned by Erskine Beveridge in his book *North Uist* (1911), which has a wealth of information on antiquities in the area. Whoever is buried in the enclosure would not be happy with its condition. To get into it I had to chase out a squatting cow. The ground inside was an aromatic stew of ashy soil and cow-pies—one still steaming. Inside the enclosure I looked in vain for a cross-marked stone shown in a photo in Beveridge's book. Only one slab protruded from the ground. But since cattle have used it as a scratching post, its inscriptions, if it ever had any, have been worn away.

I eventually found the stone I was looking for lying outside the enclosure. Its incised crosses are hard to see, but if you run your hands over the large slab you can feel their faint outlines. This unusual stone must have strong pagan roots, as someone thought it needed two crosses to Christianize it. Perhaps it is the Brownie's Stone, described

The burial enclosure

by Martin as a flat stone on which an offering of milk was made on Sundays.

Adjacent to the enclosure is a burial ground that was used until the 1930s. It has been sadly trampled by livestock, and here and there the stubs of old tombstones peek above the turf. The largest is what must be the 'cross remains' marked on the map; a tilted, moss-grown cross, three feet high with only one arm intact.

I left the hoof-trodden holy ground and, walking to the west, came upon a colony of terns. The screeching birds started to whizz past my head. The attack was such a distraction that it was only the sound of pounding hooves that alerted me to the approaching bullocks. An adrenalin powered trot took me to the safety of a rocky section of beach. Then, once they wandered off to find someone else to play with, I continued to the centre of the island.

Several historic houses sit close together here. One is the tacksman's house, which dates to 1727, and served as a school and laundry in its later years. Adjacent to it is the Farmhouse (1797). It was once the home of Finlay MacRae, the minister of Bayhead, ten miles away on North Uist, who had to time his services based on the tides. A later resident was Richard Perry, who recounts living here in *I went a' Shepherding*. Perry's account of the house is depressing: 'An indescribably filthy farmhouse. Smelling vilely of unclean dogs and rats, who left their disgusting traces in every room, while the kitchen stank like an open drain'.

The most imposing ruin here is Vallay House. This two storey grey-stone mansion with its circular entrance tower, crow stepped gables, and slate roof, presents an impressive front from a distance. But as I neared it I could see that the windows and doors had been removed or broken, letting the wind and rain in to do their worst.

The house had been built in 1902 for Erskine Beveridge. In 1833 his father started a linen factory in Dunfermline. In the 1850s steam-operated

Vallay House

power looms replaced hand looms, and the business rapidly expanded. Erskine took sole charge of the business in 1887, and all this wealth allowed him to pursue an interest in Scottish archaeology, publishing such works as *North Uist* and *Coll and Tiree*; books filled with details and photographs of hundreds of sites on the islands. Until his death in 1920, Beveridge spent his summers in Valley House. His son George, who inherited the estate, drowned while crossing to the island in 1944.

I couldn't resist stepping inside the house, testing out the floor strength with each step. At every turn I came across remnants of brightly painted walls, shattered tile-covered fireplaces, and built-in bookcases— indications of lost grandeur. The fireplaces, now mantle-less and covered with graffiti, still retained some of their dignity, but not much.

Back outside I took a look at the map. There were interesting possibilities for further exploration. The ruined chapel of Teampull Orain stood on the adjoining tidal island of Oronsay. And there was *Bàgh nan Craobhag*, the bay of little trees, where ancient stumps are said to be visible at low tide, remnants of the forest that once covered the Hebrides. However the tide was calling. I had to start back, but only after making a promise to return.

Once back on North Uist I sat on a sandbank and rubbed my frozen wet feet. From that spot Valley House looked quite grand, the sad decay well hidden behind its walls, and I wondered if someone would rescue it before it completely crumbled away. I doubt it. But, if I ever win the lottery, you'll know where to find me in my retirement years.

It took five years to make good on that promise to return. A heavy rain poured from a grey sky as I again crossed the strand. Once on the island I walked to its northern shore, where a sand bar connects Valley to the island of Oronsay.

Oronsay is narrow; so narrow that a storm could easily wash the sea over its entire surface. Apparently that is not an uncommon occurrence,

Oronsay

as a scattering of stones lay spread out over the north end of the island. Sadly this is all that's left of Teampull Orain. Only slight bits of walls remained, and a small circular stone formation that looked like the remnant of a beehive cell. Several nests dotted the ground around the ruin, a pair of large green eggs nestled in each. And at my approach several roosting ducks took flight.

Was the chapel of Teampull Orain dedicated to St Oran? Or is its name a reference to it being on a tidal island? I don't know. But St Oran's missionary activities could have brought him here, as it's only 100 miles from Iona. And if I had to pick my own Hinba, my own hermitage in the sea, this little island-off-an-island would be a good choice. Perhaps it had been a true island fifteen centuries ago, and the tombolo linking it to Vallay a recent development of the shifting sands.

The last item on the day's agenda was not to be. Gentle Atlantic combers were rolling across Bàgh nan Craobhag. Although it was low

Vallay House (centre) and the farmhouse (right)

tide, sea still covered much of the bay, and there were no signs of the tree-stump relics of the ancient forest. It must require an extremely low tide to see them if, in fact, they are still there to be seen.

But what I could see as I made my way back across Vallay was the gaunt ruin of Vallay House. Its roof had collapsed a little more since I last visited. I thought about having another look inside, but decided against it as the weather was deteriorating. When I made landfall on North Uist a downpour was in full force. Looking back towards Vallay House I could barely see it through rain smeared glasses.

I had not won the lottery in the preceding five years. And I'm not likely to win one in the future. So Vallay House is probably doomed to end up like Teampull Orain: a scattered ruin, open to the sky and inhabited by birds.

13: The Sea-Gate and St Taran's Cross: Ensay and Taransay

Six hours before my wife and I were supposed to be on a flight to Scotland the phone rang. A voice from 4000 miles away said my boat trip to St Kilda had been cancelled. Several years' worth of anticipation, of planning what I would do and see was for naught. The voice on the phone told me there were mechanical difficulties with the boat, and that my fare would be returned (it never was). We had already paid for airfare, car rental, ferry tickets and hotels. It being too late to cancel our trip, we decided to go to Scotland anyway. When we got to Tarbert (Harris) we were told that the boat, *Eilean na Hearadh*, was still not running. I would definitely not be going to St Kilda.

The only way raise my spirits would be to try and set foot on some of the other remote islands I'd always wanted to see. I spread out my most cherished map, OS Landranger 18, which includes the Sound of Harris. It was worn, torn, and covered with dozens of scrawled notes. Isles galore lay sprinkled out before me. There were many intriguing temptations. But which of the 'ays' should I pick: Taransay, Ensay, Killegray, Pabbay, Shillay, or Boreray? Forty miles out in the Atlantic, and depicted in a small inset on the map, lay St Kilda—I tried not to think about it.

I was immediately drawn to Ensay. Alasdair Alpin MacGregor wrote lovingly about it in his 1933 book *Searching the Hebrides with a Camera*, one of the best books about the islands in the Sound of Harris. Ensay also had something that sounded intriguing: a 700-year-old chapel buried in sand. Another island also called out, and that was Taransay. Ever since reading Seton Gordon's *Afoot in Wild Places* I had wanted to visit Taransay to see the carved standing stone known as St Taran's cross. So the decision was made; I'd try to set foot on Ensay and Taransay. Now all I had to do was to find someone with a boat, and hopefully one that worked.

Ensay

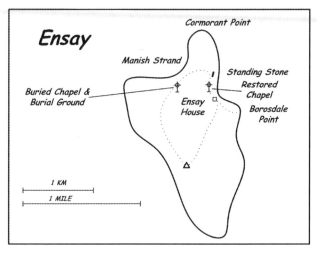

Map Reference: Ordnance Survey Landranger 18

I met Alison and Andrew Johnson on Leverburgh pier. Alison Johnson's book *Islands in the Sound* is a favourite of mine, and as a sideline to their publishing work the Johnsons took people out in their boat *Petrel* for wildlife viewing. I had asked if they could drop me on Ensay for a few hours, and they had agreed. Ensay House was currently occupied, and they asked me to introduce myself when I got there, and explain that I'd been brought over by the Johnsons. I'd be asking permission, after the fact so to speak, to wander about. In other words, I should show some common courtesy. The *Petrel* motored west through the shallow Sound of Harris to Ensay where I jumped ashore on the black rocks of Borosdale Point.

Ensay (*Easaigh*, Ewe Island) is one and a half miles long, and less than a mile wide. The only dwelling on the island, Ensay House, is a large grey two-storied mansion that sits above a sheltered bay on the island's eastern shore. I walked across the sandy grassland and stood at the sea-gate next to the house, where cement steps, pitted by a century of blowing sand, descend to the beach. Three hundred feet to the north I could see Teampull Easaigh, also known as Christ Church, a beautifully restored sixteenth century chapel. And there was something even more ancient there, for on a nearby knoll a solitary standing stone looked down on the house and chapel.

Until 1779 Ensay belonged to the MacLeods of Harris. It was sold several times between 1779 and 1841, and during those years most of the island's residents were evicted. In 1856, Archibald Stewart, who had Ensay house re-built, bought the island. The Stewarts sold out in 1937, after owning the island for seventy-nine years.

A ladder was set up against the house, and some members of the David family, who had acquired Ensay in 1957, were busy making repairs to the slate roof. I told them I'd been brought over by the Johnsons, and asked if it would be possible to borrow the key to the chapel. They kindly invited me in while they searched for the key. I was soon handed a key chain attached to a large wooden disk. The rusty chain held several keys, and the wood disk was smooth from years of handling. Still visible on the disk was the faded crest of Stewart of Ensay.

Keys in hand I walked to the chapel. It is thought that this chapel, which dates to the sixteenth century, is constructed on the ruins of an even older church, as portions of its west wall may date to the eleventh

*Ensay House and Christ Church Chapel – standing stone
on the horizon to the right*

Christ Church Chapel – Inset: piscina and the Ensay keys

century. Due to its nearness to a spring this site may have originally been the cell of an early monk. Embedded in the wall above the chapel door was a granite plaque, which read in Gaelic: 'This chapel was rebuilt in 1910 in remembrance of St Columba and the monks who brought the Gospel to these islands and founded this church'. In 1931 the chapel was bequeathed by the Stewarts to the Bishop of Argyll and the Islands, on the condition that at least two services are held every year, and in June there is an annual pilgrimage to this lonely chapel.

I struggled to get the heavy oak door to open, as its bottom was embedded in the earth. After a bit of hard tugging it opened enough to slip inside. The interior walls were bare rock, and the ceiling beautifully paneled in redwood. At the front of the chapel stood a mahogany lectern, but the most intriguing thing was something set into the cement floor next to the altar; a white stone piscina. After communion, water used to cleanse the chalice is drained to the earth through a hole in the stone.

After leaving the chapel I returned the keys, paid my respects to the standing-stone sentinel on its knoll, and then followed the coast north towards the white sands of Manish Strand. Amongst the dunes at Manish (gull headland) are an old cemetery, and a chapel that has been buried under sand for four centuries. The chapel was a strange sight, just the top of each gable end protruding from the sand. Strewn about the site were fallen sections of an iron fence that once surrounded the cemetery. The gate was the only part that still stood upright, and a sign on it said the chapel was of the fourteenth century, and had been buried by shifting sands in the sixteenth century. It also mentioned that bones are exposed every year, and pleads with the visitor to tread the site softly.

I did tread softly. And as I wandered about I was glad to find no exposed bones among all the tumbled stones. Dr AEW Miles examined this eroding cemetery at intervals from the late 1960s to the 1980s and hundreds of burials were studied. (British Archaeological Reports;

The gable ends of the buried Manish chapel rise from the sands

Series 212; 1989.) It was during this period that they discovered the chapel, and partially excavated it to floor level, which turned out to be twelve feet below the level of the sand. After examining the chapel it was back-filled for protection. I stood next to the inner wall of the east gable. About eight feet below lay the buried altar of Manish chapel. This site has yet to be fully excavated, so this incredible buried treasure of the Western Isles still awaits complete discovery. Partly preserved by protective sands for centuries, it is still there today, waiting for caring hands to uncover more of its mysteries.

I left the burial ground and hiked to the survey pillar that crowns the top of Ensay, 160 feet above the sea. I found it hard to believe this small island once supported over a hundred people. But as I walked south I went up and down over endless waves in the earth, fields of overgrown *feannagan*, lazy-beds—signs of the intense cultivation carried out on Ensay before its people left.

I crossed back to Ensay House and sat down at the sea-gate. Steps from the gate led down to a white sandy beach, a sheltered spot in the Sound of Harris. This spot had been a haven centuries ago when the chapel was built. And it had been a haven over a thousand years ago when a Columban cell may have stood here—the sandy bay providing a safe landing place for those braving the seas in hide-covered coracles. This bay had also been a haven several thousand years ago when the standing stone was planted. It had been a privilege to tread these sands.

Petrel motored into sight and I made my way back to Borosdale Point. Andrew threw me a line and I stepped aboard. Twenty minutes later we were back in Leverburgh. I asked if he could take me to Taransay the next day. My spirits sank when he told me it was too far for him to go. But those spirits soared when he gave me a name and a phone number. A few hours earlier I'd held the keys of Ensay. I now had the keys to Taransay.

Taransay

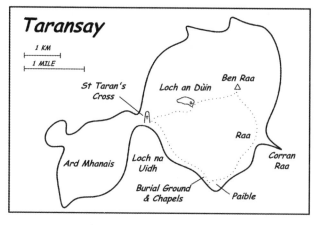

Map Reference: Ordnance Survey Landranger 18

On the following day I called Angus Mackay, and made arrangements with him to drop me on Taransay for a few hours. Angus, whose father bought Taransay in 1967, ran sheep on the island, and had agreed to take me there on one of his regular visits. Taransay is really two islands joined together by a narrow isthmus. The larger, eastern portion is three miles by two, the western part, Ard Mhanish, just a mile across. We took a small rowboat out from the sands of Tràigh Nisabost to a bright red RIB anchored in the Sound of Taransay. The dual outboards were fired up, and we were soon skimming the surf west towards Taransay. Flying along at thirty knots it took just a few minutes to cover the mile and a half to the island. We motored in near the rocks off the deserted village of Paible where I easily stepped ashore.

Paible, whose last residents left in 1974, means place of the priest. And it is here that Taransay's two recorded churches once stood; *Teampull Tharain* and *Teampull Che*, the chapels of St Taran and St Keith. Nothing is left of Teampull Tharain, but a few stones of Teampull Che are still standing, and next to it sheep were grazing contentedly amongst the stumps of tombstones sticking up through the sandy machair (grassland).

I have been unable to find out anything about these churches other than the often repeated tradition that woman were buried in St Taran's, and men in St Keith's. It was believed that if they did not follow this practice the corpse would be found above ground soon after its burial. Supposedly they tested the superstition to, in the words of Martin Martin, 'undeceive the credulous vulgar.' There are two different endings to this story. The first, and most common, relates that they found the body above ground the next day. The second ending, which Martin repeats, and not nearly as interesting, states that nothing happened—and thus the credulous vulgar were indeed undeceived.

I followed the shoreline to Ùidh, the isthmus that connects the two parts of Taransay. Planted solidly in the short turf above the sheltered lagoon of Ùidh is a five-foot-tall standing-stone (NB 013 007). Known as St Taran's cross, it is slightly tilted, and there are signs it had once been surrounded by a cairn or small stone circle. With one amazing exception it is a twin to the pillar-stone I'd seen on Ensay. The difference is that someone, perhaps St Taran, Christianized this stone by incising a cross on it. There is a wonderful picture of it in Seton Gordon's 1937 book *Afoot in Wild Places*. In the foreground of the picture the carved cross stands out boldly on the face of the stone, while in the background the ruin of a lifeless croft house, its roof gone, its hearths exposed to the sky, stands on a barren hillside. The old croft house is still there, but it now has a metal roof and is a comfortable bothy.

From St Taran's Cross I climbed inland towards the top of Ben Raa, the island's peak, which rises 876 feet above the sea. On the way up I came to *Loch an Dùin*, the loch of the fort. Out on the loch stood a stone fort on a circular island, possibly a crannog, linked to the shore by

Causewayed fort in Loch an Dùin

121

a slender causeway. Like the causeway to the fort in Loch na Nighinn Ruaidhe on Barra, this one has a *Clach Ghlagain*, a rattle stone. And as I stepped on a large boulder, a third of the way across the causeway, it rocked under my feet, sending out a loud clank to alert a hungry colony of midges I was about to invade their island sanctuary.

A small, ruinous guardhouse of sorts, stood where the causeway connected to the island. I clambered over it to stand atop the five-foot-high walls of the fort. It was not a pleasant place to linger. The interior was overgrown with nettles, and the midges were eating me alive. So I made my way back over the causeway and continued up the hillside.

A half hour later I reached the top of Ben Raa, the highest point on the island. A cold wind blew in off the Atlantic. A sturdy stone windbreak surrounded the trig-pillar, so I took advantage of the shelter and ate lunch high atop Taransay. Across the sea to the west the sharp outlines of Hirta and Boreray of St Kilda could be seen. I should have

The Summit of Taransay – St Kilda in the centre distance

been afoot on Hirta that very day, and was disappointed not to be there. I would have to try again someday to get to those far-off islands; but at that moment there wasn't a spot in the isles I'd rather have been than on the top of St Taran's isle.

On the way down the slopes of Ben Raa I came to the high ground above the old village of Raa. Striking out from the shoreline below was Corran Raa, a sickle of golden sand visible under the turquoise water. The arc of sand reached across the shallow sound to almost touch the Harris shore. The time to leave Taransay had come, so I started back to Paible. While taking a second look at the burial ground of St Che I heard the motors of the powerboat. Five minutes later we were speeding back to Harris.

Postscript

I live several thousand miles from Taransay, and it was not until a year later that I learned the *Castaway* television show had invaded the island a few months after my visit. I returned to Taransay in the spring of 2003. The castaway's pod houses were gone, and the island seemed to have survived its moment of modern fame. Several of us from the ship *Poplar Diver* hiked the two rough miles from Paible to see St Taran's cross set above the tranquil waters of its sheltered lagoon. Its dignity was still intact, and it appeared to have taken no notice of recent events.

Note: Taransay is much easier to get to these days. As for Ensay, you're on your own. The Johnsons no longer provide boat trips on *Petrel*. But, as I've come to learn, where there's a will, there's always a way.

14: A First Voyage to St Kilda

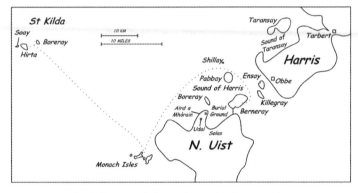

Map References: Ordnance Survey Landranger 18 & 22

Part 1: A St Kilda Sail

THOUGH I didn't know it at the time, I had my first sight of Scotland from 35,000 feet. It was May of 1988, seven months before Lockerbie, and a year before I knew anything about the Hebrides. The Pan Am 747 was heading east towards London's Heathrow airport, and we were an hour from landing when the cloud cover over the Atlantic parted. Far below I saw a snow flurry above a green mountain surrounded by sea. Next to this island several large stacks rose from the sea, their tops speckled white with snow. As it was late May, it surprised me to see snow. A larger island lay a short distance away but, strangely, it had no snow. I opened the airline magazine to the route map. It indicated we would make landfall over the Western Isles, but showed no islands farther to the west. As the plane flew on, clouds gradually obscured the snowy island.

Later I learned we had flown over Boreray, one of the islands of St Kilda, which lay forty miles west of the Western Isles. I also learned it had not been snow I'd seen. It had been one of the largest gannet colonies in the world. But more than a decade would pass before I would find myself underneath that gannet snowstorm; before I would be amongst the farthest of the Hebrides; before I would be floating on the sea next to Boreray and its immense guardian stacks, looking up instead of down, as thousands of seabirds wheeled overhead.

Ten years after that trip my first attempt to reach St Kilda went awry. I had made the mistake of booking on a three-day cruise to the islands. This period of time, as I've subsequently learned, almost guarantees you won't get there. On top of that, the boat operator was having difficulties, and cancelled the trip at the last minute. My wife and I went to the UK

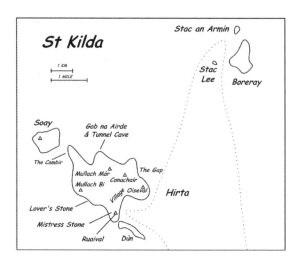

anyway, as I still hoped to get to Kilda. From London I made several calls to Scotland trying to make other arrangements. But it was not to be, though I did come close. I contacted Iain Murray, whose yacht *Annag* made five-day trips to Kilda from the island of Berneray. Iain had a spare berth on a trip that was about to depart. But I couldn't get to Berneray in time to make the sailing.

So I made arrangements to go on *Annag* the following spring. On a clear June afternoon twelve months later, I arrived on Berneray, where I lodged with Gloria and Donald Alick 'Splash' MacKillop. The MacKillops ran Burnside Croft, made famous as the location of Prince Charles' crofting holidays. As I'd arrived a day before *Annag* was to sail, I went for a long walk on North Uist to shake off the jet lag. My destination: the ruins of Udal and the Well of the Cross.

I parked in Solas, above the beach where flights to the Western Isles landed in the 1930s. The Well of the Cross was near the tip of the Àird a Mhòrain peninsula ('arsht-a-voran' as Splash told me it was pronounced). Penciled in on my treasured and torn OS map 18 was a hint to its location; a quote from Daphne Pochin Mould's *West Over Sea*: 'Two-hundred yards west of the burial ground, on a flat face of dark gneiss facing the sea.' She was speaking of a stone with an incised cross that stands above the holy well. After three miles of sandy hiking I reached the end of the peninsula and Caibeal Bhororaigh, a cemetery once used by the people of the nearby island of Boreray.

On the shore below the cemetery I paced west across the pebbly beach. After 200 steps I stopped to look around. The cross and well were nowhere to be found. I looked all along the shore, working back and forth for an hour, to no avail. I thought at the time that the cross and well must be buried under beach rocks pushed in by the tide. Disappointed, I gave up the search.

I left the beach and climbed to the trig-pillar that capped the high ground of the peninsula, a vantage point that looked out over the isles

Caibeal Bhororaigh at Àird a Mhòrain

The sand cliffs of Àird a Mhòrain

in the Sound of Harris. To the south the curving sand cliffs of Àird a Mhòrain faced Vallay, where the abandoned hulk of Erskine Beveridge's mansion sat rotting away.

With not another soul in sight I walked south on Tràigh Udal, a small beach on the west side of the peninsula. Finding a break in the sand cliffs I climbed over the soft, grey dunes to the east, where the wind kicked up, giving me an eye-full of sand. After splashing water in my face I got all but one speck out—a speck that would torture me for the next few days.

In amongst the dunes at the centre of the peninsula I came across the remains of a dozen stone dwellings. This was Udal, once home to the Sìol Gorrie MacDonalds, the seed of Gorrie. In the fifteenth century the Gorries of Udal were massacred, and their homes destroyed, by their rivals, the Siol Murdoch MacDonalds. In the blowing sand I explored several of the exposed cells, and then returned to Solas along the vast flat curve of the east beach.

The day's hike; seven sandy miles, on top of an eight-hour time change, ten hours of flying, 200 miles of driving, and a thirty mile ferry ride—all within a period of thirty-six hours—had taken its toll. After one of Gloria MacKillop's wonderful dinners I slept the sleep of the dead.

The next morning Gloria made French toast, a tasty change from the usual B&B full-fry breakfast. After that wonderful start the day got even better, as an hour later I was sailing out of Berneray Harbour on the forty-foot yacht *Annag*. Aboard were five passengers: Mairi, a student from Aberdeen; Annemiek and Christian, who were doctors working in Stornoway; Gareth Robinson, who worked for a chemical company in Cheshire; and me. The crew consisted of the cook, Seija, and our skipper, Donald Wilke. It was an international expedition, with representatives from Scotland, England, Germany, Finland, and America.

A half hour later Ensay passed by as we sailed north through the Sound of Harris. I'd visited Ensay, and its sand-buried chapel, the year before—an unbeatable consolation prize when I'd been unable to get to Kilda. Once past the island of Pabbay we sailed twenty-five miles down the coast of North Uist to anchor in Croic Harbour, between Ceann Iar and Shivinish, two of the Monach Isles.

The *Monachs* (the Monks' Isles, from the Gaelic 'math neach', meaning the good ones) consist of five small islands: Stockay, Ceann Ear, Shivinish, Ceann Iar, and Shillay. We were soon ashore on Ceann Iar, and I had to dodge clusters of fulmar nests as I crossed the small sandy isle to sit atop the trig-pillar that marked its highest point. On Shillay, a mile and a half away, stood the 133-foot-tall tower of the Monach light. Built by the Stevensons in 1864, its white light flashed over the sea every ten seconds for seventy-eight years—my calculator tells me this was about 250 million flashes.

But this impressive red-brick monolith no longer shines at night. It went out of operation in 1942, leaving the seas in the dark for over a half-century. Then, in 1997, a utilitarian minor light was put in place near it. The old lighthouse is on the site of a Celtic monastery, whose monks had maintained a fire beacon. So lights of one form or other have guided wayfarers here for centuries. (The old lighthouse was reactivated in 2008, nine years after my visit.)

There was nothing much to see on Ceann Iar, as the main settlement had been on the larger Ceann Ear. There was, however, a small cluster of a half dozen stone dwellings, possibly once used as shielings by the people of the east island. There was also one modern structure, a two-storey building built of the same red brick as the Shillay light. It had been a storehouse for the lighthouse keepers, but it's now a roofless derelict, falling apart brick by brick with every passing year.

After exploring the island we sat on the dunes overlooking Croic Harbour to watch seals playing in the water. And later that evening, as

Storehouse ruin on Ceann Iar

the sun set over the western sea, we watched them surfing the tide as it poured like a river over the sand-bar between Ceann Iar and Shivinish.

The next morning we listened, with some trepidation, to the forecast from Stornoway Coast Guard. The triple repetition of their call sign would become familiar to us over the coming days: "Stornoway Coastguard, Stornoway Coastguard, Stornoway Coastguard." And what followed would be the basis for the plans we'd make each day.

The forecast did not bode well. Winds were from the south-west, and the conditions at Kilda were marginal. Donald told us things could get unpleasant if we attempted the voyage. But the vote to continue was unanimous—no surprise there. So we weighed anchor and set sail for the forty mile crossing.

We scudded north like a skilled surfer, riding with the wind atop six-foot swells, all the while keeping a watch out for drifting obstacles. Stray shipping containers and submarines could cause some grief if we came upon them. But the only obstacles we came across were gannets sleeping on the water, and the occasional stray float. At one point we could not see land in any direction. Then, out of the sea-haze, the peaks of Kilda gradually materialized, and Donald decided conditions were good enough to visit Boreray and the stacks before sailing into Village Bay.

That snowstorm I'd seen a decade before from 35,000 feet was still in progress. And as we approached Boreray, those flakes of snow slowly resolved into gannets endlessly circling the island and the adjacent stacks. These are some of the highest stacks in the world. *Stac Lee*, the stack of the blue fulmars, rises 564 feet out of the sea. And *Stac Armin*, the steward's stack, is an incredible 644-foot-high tooth of rock, which from some vantage points resembles the dorsal fin of a mammoth shark. Donald brought *Annag* to a stop, and we floated for an hour looking up to the stacks and the thousands of gannets soaring overhead.

It was amazing to watch them dive. Like guided missiles, certain of their targets, they dropped from altitudes of up to 200 feet straight into the sea. I don't know if they're true, but there are tales of gannets crashing through the wooden boat decks of early visitors to Kilda.

The stack tops were thick with nesting gannets, and every available nook and cranny on their vertical walls had a nest. The smell was a vibrant elixir that triggered memories of previous sea-bird encounters; the ozone of the sea topped off with a not so subtle aftertaste of guano wafting on the salty wind.

Necks aching from looking up, we then crossed four miles of sea to Hirta, where we arrived in the gathering dark to anchor in Village Bay. It took two trips in the inflatable to get us all ashore. Then, first things first, we went into the Puff Inn, a bar with roots dating back to when the military came in the late 1950s to establish a missile tracking station. We paid our membership dues of one pound and ordered a drink. (Reader beware, the pub is no longer open to non-residents. And while we're on the subject, I want my pound back!)

After an hour in the Puff Inn we took a brief walk in the dark along the village street. The row of old houses, abandoned since 1930, tempted further exploration. But it had been a long day and, totally exhausted, we made our way back to *Annag*.

Once aboard Gareth and I stretched out our sleeping bags on the settees in the ship's saloon, which we preferred over the narrow coffin-like berths above them. But as tired as I was, I did not sleep well. That speck of sand still chafed my eye, and the pots and pans in the galley clanked whenever a swell rocked the boat. But I would not have to listen to them the following night. I would be camping on the island.

Ashore the next day we met Andy, the National Trust warden. He gave us an overview of the island; and also advised against wearing waterproofs on the steep grassy slopes, as one slip could send you sliding hundreds of feet to the rocky shore. Anxious to be on the hills, Gareth and I set out to circle the island. We crossed the steep grassy slopes to the base of Ruaival, and then climbed a jumble of boulders to its summit. Three-hundred feet below us the sea flowed through the narrow channel that separates the long, narrow island of Dùn from Hirta. Dùn's undulating knife-edge ridge stretched for a mile into the sea, and swarming in the air above it were thousands of puffins.

On the north-west side of Ruaival we found the Mistress Stone; one of two lustily named stones on the island, the other being the Lover's Stone. There are tales of young Kildan men proving their cliff prowling prowess, impressing possible wives in the process, by performing various balancing acts atop these precarious perches. The Mistress Stone bridged a narrow gully of rock in the side of the hill, and I sat on the airy roost for a rest. No prospective mistresses were about, so, sadly, I wasn't able to impress one with my version of Cuchulainn's salmon-feat; where I spring into the air like a fish, and then throw a spear with my toes. Maybe next time…

Village seen from atop Conachair

Following the hills to the west we came to the second of the famous stones: the Lover's Stone. It was a tongue of rock, which, like the Hangman's Rock on Colonsay (minus the handy hole for the rope) protruded from the cliff. Like the Kildans of old, I started to test my nerve by crawling up the stone. While doing so I startled a fulmar roosting near its base. The bird's head heaved back and forth, its bill pointed directly at me, a sure indication it was about to vomit some stinky stomach fluid. Unlike the Kildans of old, I ran away as fast as possible.

We reached land's end at the Cambir, the headland that looks out over the western-most of the Kildan archipelago, the isle of Soay. From there we turned east to enter Glen Mòr, where we came to an ancient village of horned structures, stone cells that are some of the oldest dwellings on Kilda. The name comes from the shape of their open ended forecourts, where the low stone walls arc towards each other, but do not touch, which gives them a horn-ish look. The most impressive is marked on the map as the Amazon's House, a large complex of linked cells and mounds. Unfortunately there were no Amazons about.

North of Glen Mòr we came to the headland of Gob na Airde, where a sloping stone ledge along the cliff face led down to the sea. At first it was an easy descent. Then came a point where a trickle of water fell from the cliffs above, creating a slippery stretch along the steep ledge. It would have been a difficult passage, but fortunately someone had strung a thick rope along the base of the cliff. Using the rope for insurance, I slid down the slime to sea level. (Reader beware, the rope is no longer there.)

At the end of the rope was the entrance to a 400-foot-long tunnel that cuts through the headland; Boreray and the stacks, four miles away, framed in its far exit. I had been told seals were to be found

The headland of Gob na Airde, Boreray and stacks in the distance.
Note the walkway down to tunnel cave

here, swimming in the waters of the sheltered sea-cavern, but none were about. It was a lonely spot. The only sound the echoes of the surf bouncing off the rock walls; the only sign of life, the small creatures swimming in tide-pools that lay on the slabs of dark stone that rose from the sea.

Back up top Gareth and I traversed the grassy slopes of Mullach Mòr. We were now in bonxie country, and what at first I thought were tufts of Soay sheep fleece on the ground were actually great skua chicks. And as we walked through the lush grass we were repeatedly dive bombed by their anxious parents.

The higher we climbed on Mullach Mòr, the fiercer the wind got, and the skuas finally quit their attacks. Reaching the top, 1200 feet above the sea, we sought shelter in the doorway of one of the radar buildings. We took a break to eat lunch—sandwiches that had been

Tunnel Cave

smashed flat in our packs—and with the small brown bottles of beer we'd been carrying all day toasted the day's accomplishments.

After dinner on *Annag* we returned to the island. While everyone else made for the Puff Inn to get a drink, I went around back to pitch my tent. My only neighbour for the night was a large tent set far off in one corner of the field, its occupants currently warming themselves in the pub. After a dram (or three) in the Puff Inn, I returned to settle in for the night. Sleeping on solid ground was a nice change from the previous evening of rolling with the swell and the clanking of pots and pans. But as tired as I was, sleep came only after the noisy generator shut down. During the night tremendous gusts rolled down from the hills to rock the tent, and I awoke several times thinking I was back aboard the boat.

In the morning I enjoyed a hot shower in the small ablutions shed, the force of the water finally flushing away that persistent speck of sand from my eye. The shower was a real luxury, as its use is a privilege offered only to National Trust workers—and campers (like me) with paid permits.

An hour later I was ferried back to *Annag* for breakfast. As we ate we listened to the forecast. Gale force winds from the south were due early the following day, so we needed to leave by late afternoon. I still hadn't spent much time in the village. Neither had I climbed to the Ultima Thule of this western Ultima Thule, the 1400-foot summit of Conachair, which rises above the highest sea-cliffs in Britain. That was something that had to be done. So once ashore Gareth and I climbed up the valley of An Lag to the Gap, the precipice-saddle between the peaks of Conachair and Oiseval. Another half hour of steep climbing took us to a small pedestal of stone, the remnant of a sundial that once crowned the top of Conachair.

Reaching this spot was the culmination of years of anticipation. Looking out to Boreray and the stacks we had a celebratory drink—I'd

The campground: In Village Bay float four regular visitors to St Kilda (left to right): Hebridean Princess, Poplar Diver, Annag, *and* Cuma

brought along two whisky miniatures from home for the occasion. Before descending we took a last look towards Boreray. From this distance the flurry of gannets looked once again like that snowstorm I'd seen from six miles up, so long ago. It was hard, but we turned our backs on that wondrous view and headed down to Village Bay.

St Kilda had been a place of contradictions. When we were on the hills, with Boreray and the stacks gleaming through the sea-mist, we felt as if we were indeed in another world, a place apart, one of the farthest Hebrides. Yet there had been a busy pub and gift shop. And at times I felt as if I was in an episode of the Twilight Zone. For example, one morning the *Hebridean Princess* appeared. Until 1989 she had been the *Columba*, a MacBrayne's ferry, but has since been converted to an upscale cruise ship. We watched from *Annag* as stewards escorted the well dressed folks ashore in the ship's tender. Some of the women were in heels—and I'd just finished scraping sheep poo from my soggy boots.

Another odd thing, considering what I'd expected to find on this distant speck of land in the sea, were the radio telephones. I'd been able to call my wife back in the States, which was as much a surprise to me, as it was to her. She thought I'd be out of touch for a week among the most remote of the isles.

"Hi honey."

"Where are you?"

"St Kilda."

She could hear the music from the Puff Inn in the background. I was supposedly on an island far out in the Atlantic, but it sounded like a Manchester pub on a Saturday night.

"Where are you?" she asked again.

"I'm on St Kilda." And I went on to tell her of all the marvellous things I'd seen and done in just one week. After I hung up I thought about that day a decade before, when I'd flown over these islands in a far off sea; islands that had been lived on for thousands of years, until events forced the people away. But the gannets on Boreray and the stacks were certainly the better off. No regular deathly visits to

Boreray and the stacks

their nests, only occasional wide eyed folks, like myself, staring in wonderment, like children on their first visit to the zoo, at a mass of life not seen before—a snowstorm of life.

So if you ever have the privilege of flying over the sea to the Western Isles, make sure you look out the window. Perhaps, just perhaps, the clouds will part, and you'll be blessed with a glimpse of that snowstorm. It is a rare sight. I've looked for it many times since that first flight, and have never seen it again. Better yet, see it from the sea. Watch the gannets plunge from the air. Watch them bring food to their hungry young on their cliff-side perches. Best of all, watch them ignore you; for out there you really don't matter, and that puts the whole world in perspective.

Part 2: The Well of the Cross

A few years after returning from Kilda I purchased a large scale Ordnance Survey map for Àird a Mhòrain, as I wanted to try again to find the Well of the Cross. On the map the words *Incised Cross and Well* were printed in the centre of the peninsula. But, frustratingly, unlike pirate maps of old, there was no 'X marks the spot' showing where the treasure lay. I had read that the well lay on the shore west of the burial ground. And while scanning the map with a magnifying glass I noticed a tiny blue circle set between the high tide line and the street of the dead that led to the graveyard. From this symbol for a spring I drew lines to the map grid, and came up with the coordinates NF 8349 7869.

Then it was time to put my tax money to good use. On some future visit I'd enlist the aid of a constellation of GPS satellites I'd help to pay for. They could guide me to within a few feet of these coordinates, and hopefully the well and cross. Standing outside my home in Seattle I entered the coordinates into the waypoint page of my hiker's GPS and punched the 'GO TO' button. The display showed that the well lay 4290 miles to the north-east.

Seven years after the Kilda trip I punched 'GO TO' again. But this time I was standing on Sollas beach, and the distance readout showed just two miles to go. The tide was on the ebb, so I could walk a direct line across the hard sand towards the burial ground. Familiar territory, but even if I did find the exact location, I wondered if the well and cross would be buried under beach rock.

I started walking, following the guidance arrow on the GPS display, which pointed towards a spot west of the burial ground. The distance readout counted down: 1.0 mile, then 0.5 mile, then 0.1 mile. Then the read-out changed to feet: 500, then 400, 300, 200, 100, 50...

I reached a vertical face of rock with bits of gold lichen splotched here and there, and I wish I had a picture of the smile that filled my face. Right in front to me was the cross, six inches high, etched a quarter inch into the stone. Just as Daphne Pochin Mould's book said, it had been carved on a flat face of dark gneiss facing the sea. I ran my fingers over it, becoming part of the cross for a brief time.

But now that I'd found the cross, where was the well? From Erskine Beveridge's photo of it in *North Uist*, I knew the well lay at the end of a vertical crack in the rock, below, and to the right of the cross. No well was visible, only a bed of pebbles piled against the rock. I started scooping stones out by the handful and, after digging down a foot, the resulting cavity started to fill with water. I took a tentative taste; a good taste indeed, fresh, not salty. Several large flat rocks were amongst those I'd dug out, and I laid them out to frame the top of the well.

It was a fragile thing. The next high tide would push the stones in to bury it again. The cross will last a little longer. But not forever, for the constant battering by the sea will eventually scour it from the face of the rock. I had been fortunate to share its presence for an hour, a work of faith, patiently etched in stone by a monk long ago. Amongst all the

The Well of the Cross

pebbles dug out of the well I came across a nugget of white crystalline stone, which I took with me, thinking I needed a tangible souvenir of my visit. Whenever I touch it I'm taken back to the beach and the well; taken back to a place of peace and faith. It is a place I must return to someday. For the feel of the cross left an even more tangible memory, and the stone needs to be taken back.

15: THE CROSS THAT WOULD FRIGHTEN GIANTS: PABBAY & KILLEGRAY

THE isle of Pabbay, in the Sound of Harris, seemed to be an island that didn't like to be visited. I had three frustrating close encounters.

The first was in the spring of 1999. The yacht *Annag*, retreating from a gale-lashed St Kilda, had anchored in the lee of Pabbay. We dried our rain- and sea-soaked gear on deck while waiting for the rising tide to give enough clearance to sail through the shallow Sound of Harris. A paltry fifty feet away a field of lazy-beds striped the slopes above the Pabbay shore. I could hear the island calling: 'Here I am.' Oh how I wanted to tread those shores, but there was no time. As soon as the tide rose we set sail for Berneray Harbour.

An even more depressing close call occurred two years later. I planned a four-day stay with the Mackillops on Berneray, thinking the weather, and the sea, would cooperate on at least one day to allow a visit to Pabbay. On our first three days they didn't. Then, on the last day, Pabbay decided to tease me once more. The rain slackened, the wind calmed, and hope rose that I might get there after all. Donald Alick (Splash) made arrangements with Neil MacAskill, a local fisherman, to take me over. But an hour before our scheduled departure Pabbay rendered the killing blow; plunging her dagger deep into my spirit. Like Norna of Fitful Head, she did this by calling forth spirits from the well of the south wind, and in a matter of minutes wild white horses were stampeding across the sound.

Wind howling from the south I made my way to Berneray Harbour, where I found Neil standing on the deck of his boat.

"You *still* want to go?" He asked, in a surprised tone.

Silly question (I thought). "Yes!"

Silly answer (he thought).

Berthed across from Neil's boat was *Annag*, which had taken me to St Kilda, and that first close encounter with Pabbay. Donald Wilke rose from the cockpit, and voiced his opinion that it would be a hard, if not impossible, landing. They both wanted me to be the one to call off the trip, and were letting me down in the most polite way imaginable. I did not want to face reality. But I knew in my heart it was not to be.

The third near-miss came three years later, during a cruise to Kilda that passed through the Sound of Harris. In the shadow of the *Castaway* television show the island of Taransay was the port-of-call the other passengers aboard wanted, so Taransay it was. Our course the following day took us to the Flannans. And as we motored west I could see the pyramid of Beinn a Charnain, Pabbay's distinctive peak, recede astern.

Pabbay. I was getting tired of wooing her, tired of having every advance brushed off. I decided the time had come to make an all out assault. I would dedicate an entire vacation to setting foot on the Isle of the Priest.

And so arrangements were made for a week-long let of Boreray Cottage, a restored croft-house in Clachan Sands, at the northern tip of North Uist. It lay seven miles from Pabbay, and a better spot for island hopping could not be found. Pabbay, Berneray, Ensay, Killegray, and Boreray were all within reach. And on days when sea conditions were bad I'd have options such as wading to Vallay, or climbing the Uist Hills.

During our first three days at Clachan the rain spat and the wind howled. But even so, they were days filled with gloriously wet walks on North Uist and Vallay. One long trek took us out to Àird a Mhòrain.

The causewayed duns of Loch Hunder

And as we ate our lunch near the old burial ground we watched a sea otter eating his lunch on the beach. A walk on another breezy day took me deep into the bogs south of Lochmaddy, weaving three miles through a maze of lochs to the base of South Lee and the amazing causewayed duns of Loch Hunder (NF 905 652).

From the south-east shore of Loch Hunder a three-foot-wide causeway curved a hundred feet into the loch. At its end sat an island broch. The fort was thirty-five feet in diameter, and its circular stone walls stood six feet high. From the broch the causeway continued for sixty feet into the loch to a point where it forked; the submerged right branch going out towards Dùn Bàn, another fort in the centre of the loch. The left branch went to a nearby island, one that was once fortified. The south side of this island was then, in turn, connected back to the mainland by a causeway with a ninety-degree kink at its centre.

I had hoped to circumnavigate this loop of causeways, fort, and island. But the middle causeway lay under a foot of water, and there was no traction on the submerged stones. Not in the mood for a swim I backtracked to the mainland and, leaving the dun-complex behind, climbed to the occasionally mist-shrouded summit of North Lee. There

I found a windy viewpoint that looked out over the loch-spattered interior of North Uist, and across the Little Minch to the headland of Waternish on Skye.

Then, on the fourth day, the Lord said "Let there be light." The sun complied, and a day of magic was in store.

Pabbay

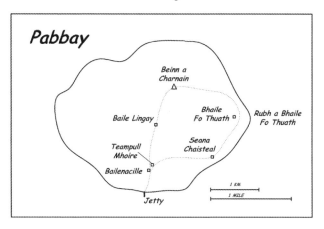

Map Reference: Ordnance Survey Landranger 18

The RIB (Rigid Inflatable Boat) bounced across the sea at thirty knots, her bow pointed at Pabbay. Pointed at Pabbay at last! I had made arrangements with Niall Johnson of the Uist Outdoor Centre in Lochmaddy for a day charter. With his RIB loaded on a trailer, Niall hauled it from Lochmaddy to the slip-way at An Leac Bhàn, near the south end of Berneray causeway.

It was appropriate to meet him there, for *An Leac Bhàn* (the white slab) had been the traditional ferry-point for these islands. A large boulder here once marked the spot where, if you made yourself visible, the ferryman on Berneray would come fetch you. The stone is pictured in Alasdair Alpin MacGregor's *Searching the Hebrides with a Camera*, and the caption under that photo had cast a spell upon me long ago.

Down through the silverweed and the iris-flags I linger to the foreshore at the Leac Bhàn, and seat myself upon a boulder that has known me for some years now. This boulder and I seem to recognize each other. It invites my weight with an intimacy convincing me that even the things men describe as inanimate object may have personality.

During the spring of 1997 I had found and sat upon MacGregor's boulder. If I'd looked a year later I'd have been out of luck, for it became part of the Berneray causeway in 1998, buried under tons of quarried stone, never to be seen again. It did have a personality. And when I sat on it, waiting for the Berneray ferry the causeway would soon replace, the memories captured in my mind from reading MacGregor's book came alive, and I was taken back sixty years to that day of wandering he so well described, a day when he sat at An Leac Bhàn awaiting the ferryman.

It took a quarter hour for the RIB to cover the six miles to Pabbay. As we approached the island Niall slowed down sooner than I thought he would, and indicated why by pointing straight down. The seafloor was only a few feet below water level, and we were still several hundred feet offshore. Naill let the boat crawl forward, keeping an eye out for the myriad rocks and kelp beds that could cause havoc with the prop.

As we neared the shore a small stone jetty came into view. We crept up to it and, grabbing it with one hand, Nail stopped the boat's forward motion. I reached out too, to finally touch Pabbay.

On the hillside above the landing I found the ruins of Balnacille (church town). Most of its stones have been robbed over the years to build the many field enclosures that cover the area. The only original

Teampull Mhoire

house still standing is the shepherd's, whitewashed and trim, and still used by the tenant. Just beyond the house lay the ruin of Teampull Mhoire, usually called St Mary's Church. A name similar to that of Teampull Mhuire on nearby Vallay, and Eilean Mhuire of the Shiants; a confusing set of names, dedications to either Mary, Moluag, or Maelrubha.

The original Pabbay church is thought to have been dedicated to St Moluag of Lismore. Its scant remains, dotted with old tombstones, lay to the west of the more substantial 600-year-old ruin of Teampull Mhoire. The west gable of Teampull Mhoire stands, as does most of the south wall, although it is falling outward. In amongst the tombstones and nettles that covered the interior of the church stood a five-foot-tall, almost human shaped, cross.

This cross is mentioned in a booklet about Pabbay by Bill Lawson (*The Teampull on the Isle of Pabbay*). In it he mentions that the cross is referred to in Oran an Eagail, *A Song of Fear*, by the Pabbay Bard, Neil Morrison, as *chrois Phapanaich*, the Catholic cross. The song, one of superstition, calls the 'Priest's Temple' a fearful thing with its cross that 'would frighten the very giants.'

East of the church I came across the ruin of a grain drying kiln. Fertile Pabbay had once been known as the granary of Harris, but it also had a good number of its own people to support. In the nineteenth century the population exceeded 300; most evicted when the island was cleared for sheep in the 1840s. Continuing eastward from the kiln I crossed a series of grassy sand dunes that covered what had once been Baile Meadhanach, a village buried during a severe sandstorm

The cross that would frighten giants

300 years ago. Just beyond it stood a sandy mound surrounded by low stone walls. At its top sat the scattered ruin of Seana Chaisteal, the Old Castle.

Dean Munro, writing in the mid 1500s, reported that MacLeod of Lewis came to this castle when he wished for peace and quiet, or was 'fearit'. It must have been quite a substantial structure in its day for MacLeod to have holed up here in times of trouble. An evocative cairn, a grave marker of sorts for the castle-that-was, capped the top of the mound. The cairn was hollow, and the gull chicks nesting inside made a ruckus until I left.

I then wandered around the east end of the island to a cluster of lazy-beds above *Rubha Baile Fo Thuath* (the headland of North Town). Somewhere here lived the MacLeod tacksman who set sail once a year for the fifty-mile journey to collect the Kildan rents. There is nothing much left of the village, but there was a spot in the sea, fifty feet offshore, that drew my eye. It was a spot that brought back memories of a day six-years before; a windy day when *Annag* lay at anchor; a day when I'd been almost close enough to touch Pabbay, only to have her slip away.

A six-hundred-foot climb took me up the soggy slopes of Beinn a Charnain. At the summit I sat atop the trig-pillar that stood nestled inside a circular stone wind-break. Far off in the sea-haze the hump of Scarp marked the western extent of the big islands to the north. Much closer, and looking like a sea-ray on the prowl, was Shillay of the seals. Two other islands that also must be visited sang their siren-songs from the isle-studded sea: Boreray of the monks to the south-west, and Killegray of the teampull to the south-east.

Sitting atop the pillar I cracked open a red can of MacEwens. Then, in honour of all the isles in view, recited an island poem-song I'd said atop several dozen islands by that time, one that dates to World War I. Its third verse starts: 'It's the blue Islands that are pullin' me away…'

Baile Lingay

With the poem said, and the beer gone, I slid off the pillar and started down to the village of Baile Lingay. The village ruins straddle a small stream, the Abhainn Lingay. One ruin stood out from the rest. The stone frame of its doorway supported a large lintel, which rose above the pillaged walls, and atop the lintel grew a thick clump of lush turf. I passed under this stone and earthen altar to enter the roofless house.

Spread out before me on the grassland between the house and sea sat the shells of a dozen similar ruins, and beyond them, across the waters of the sound, the white sands of Boreray, Berneray, and Àird a Mhòrain sparkled in the sun. Over 300 people, in 65 households, lived on Pabbay in 1841. And what a splendid view these long gone people had. On a summer day like this it was like a Caribbean seascape, turquoise water and azure sky. For most of the year conditions are far worse, but it would have been days like this, the long days of summer sun, that would have made the leaving so grievous for the last residents of this home when they were forced out in 1843.

A few minutes later I was back in Balnacille. The tide had dropped several feet and Niall had taken the RIB offshore to wait. I waded out to where he floated on the calm sea and climbed aboard. The outboard sprang to life and we started back to An Leac Bhàn.

With Pabbay receding behind I wondered what the next day would hold. Would it be pushing my luck to try for another island? And if I did, which would it be? As we jetted south the sands of Boreray glowed at us from the west, and looking to the east I got a brief glimpse of Graveyard Point on Killegray. In the few seconds before Killegray was eclipsed by the sandy shores of Berneray a decision was made.

The evening after returning from Pabbay was cloudless, and the forecast for the following day indicated more of the same. So I walked from our cottage to the red phone box that sits on the verge of the B893. After investing 80 pence in phone calls I'd made tentative arrangements for someone to take me to Killegray the next day; *if*, that is, the weather was good. But it would not be another RIB ride. That venture had blown the budget.

On the morning of the fifth day the Lord said "Let there be more light." The sun, on a run, complied. Another day of magic was in store.

Killegray

At 7.30am the following morning I walked onto the 100-foot *MV Loch Bhrusda*, the Berneray-Harris car-ferry. After departing the terminal at *Aird Mo-Rubha* (possibly the headland of St Maelrubha) the ferry motored four miles to the south-east and then made a ninety-degree turn to port. After four miles of zigzagging our way through

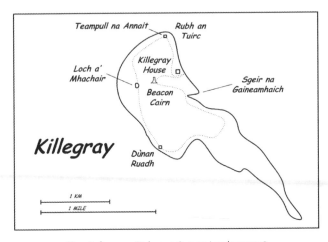

Map Reference: Ordnance Survey Landranger 18

Killegray House

skerries galore, the ship made a sharp turn to the left, the south tip of Killegray only a half mile to the west. I was close, but still had one more boat ride before I could set foot on the island. Twenty minutes later the ferry's ramp dropped down, the harsh grating of iron on cement announcing landfall on Harris.

I walked down the slick metal ramp and climbed the slipway. After waiting for a while at the end of the pier, bits of which date to Lord Leverhulme's failed efforts to develop the port in the 1920s, I saw a small boat approach. After shaking hands with its skipper I stepped aboard and we set out for the three-mile crossing to Killegray. The engine was switched off once we reached the small bay below Killegray House, and I was taken ashore in an inflatable.

Parts of Killegray House date to the eighteenth century, and dormers in the roof hinted at a small third storey. A new wing, faced with matching stone, had recently been added to its north-west side. Similar to the sea-gate pillars on nearby Ensay, two stone-ball-topped pillars framed the gate that gave access to the rear grounds of the house. I opened the gate's recently greased metal latch, smearing my hands with black goo, crossed behind the house, and then set out for Graveyard Point.

Like Ensay, Killegray must have once supported a substantial population, for the terrain showed extensive evidence of old cultivation ridges. Just north of the house I crossed the sandy terrain of *Rubh an Tuirc* (point of the boar) and soon came to the northern tip of the island. There, on a small level patch of ground above the beach at *Rubha Cladh* (graveyard point), sat Teampull na Annait, Tobar na Annait, and the burial ground of Cladh Aruinn. I couldn't find *Tobar na Annait* (the holy well of the mother church), but the site of the *teampull* (chapel) was outlined by the low hump of a foundation under the turf. Next to it a solitary tombstone—perhaps a small standing stone—rose from the long abandoned burial ground.

Killegray means Burial Place Island, and the term *Annait* usually designates the church of the greatest antiquity in an area. So perhaps Moluag or Maelrubha once had an outpost here, which later became a popular place to be buried. When one of the graves was exposed by the battering sea a century ago, its occupant was found well equipped to meet their maker with a hammer and scales; the hammer for the dear-departed to knock at the door of heaven, and the scales so that the weight of their soul could be judged at the Weighing-In.

Walking down the west side of the island I passed small reed-fringed *Loch a' Mhachair*, the loch of the grassland. My next destination was *Dùnan Ruadh*, the red (or perhaps scorched, meaning vitrified) fort. A half-mile south of the loch I came to a section of thirty-foot cliffs where a narrow gully, floored with sloping slabs of crumbling rock,

Beacon Cairn atop Killegray

154

led down to the sea. The tide was low, and I crept out across a section of slick, tangle-covered rock to the base of a twenty-foot-high stack, which during high tide would be an island in its own right.

On the top of the stack I found a grassy, flat-topped mound, with relics of the fort's stone walls hidden under the short turf. Dùnan Ruadh had been located at a strategic choke-point, the narrowest constriction of the seaway through the sound. Based on its location, perhaps its occupants charged tolls, or pirated ships. Or it could have been a retreat, a place for the residents of Killegray to come to when *they* were 'fearit'.

I wandered the island for another two hours, crossing to the eastern shore to find a massive stone bridge over a creek that drains a nearly land-locked section of beach near *Sgeir na Gaineamhaich*, the rock of the sands. A stone walkway below the bridge led to a drop-off above the sea, where the island's sheep are loaded onto boats. From there a steady climb to the north-west took me to my final destination, the large beacon cairn that crowns the island.

The beacon stands six feet high atop a rock at the island's highest point. It is a tapering tower of stone, four feet square at its base, narrowing to one foot square at the top. At its base is a small fireplace with a low, foot-long opening. The cairn does not appear ancient by any means, and is not a triangulation pillar. I can only guess it had once been used as an aid to navigation in these dangerous rock-studded waters.

As much as I wanted to, there was no safe way to sit atop the cairn. So I sat on the bedrock next to it and groped around the inside of my pack, finding that what I was looking for had sunk to the bottom. Before opening the beer I took a clockwise look at all islands around me. I was surrounded by history, and realised how fortunate I'd been to have set foot on five of the six holy isles in the Sound of Harris: Vallay, Berneray, Ensay, Pabbay, and now Killegray. But the sixth, Boreray of the monks, still remained a mystery.

Teampull na Annait at Rubha Cladh – Pabbay in the distance

It was time to go. I took a last swallow of beer, and then started down to the beach. Two hours later, as I rode the ferry back to Berneray, I wondered if I dared hope for more. Should I push my luck again, and try for Boreray tomorrow?

But on the sixth day the Lord said "Let there be no more light." The sun, finishing its run, took a rest, and sheltered from the wind and rain behind a blanket of clouds. There would be no more islands that trip. It took five years, but I would come back to these isles in the sound to see The Monks' Field of Boreray, where many of the monks who toiled in the Western Isles are buried; and it was indeed, another day of magic.

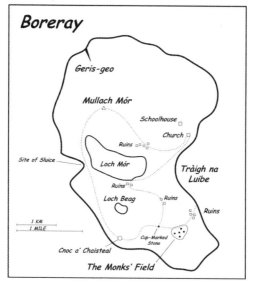

Boreray

Geris-geo

Mullach Mór

Schoolhouse

Church

Ruins

Site of Sluice

Loch Mór

Tràigh na Luibe

Ruins

Loch Beag

Ruins

Ruins

1 KM
1 MILE

Cnoc a' Chaisteal

Cup-Marked Stone

The Monks' Field

Map Reference: Ordnance Survey Landranger 18

Boirearaigh Uaighean nam Manaich, Boreray of the Monks' Field, is said to have been the burial isle for all the monks who worked north of Eigg, and the patch of ground where they are buried is called The Monks' Field. The monks who worked south of Eigg were buried on Iona; which is a special place, if you can escape the crowds that plague it. I had always wanted to see if Boreray had that same feeling—minus the crowds. And so, five years after that visit to Pabbay, when I'd seen the glowing sands of Boreray, I decided to make an all out effort to set foot on the island.

When looking into ways to get to Boreray it was suggested I contact Ruari Beaton. Ruari ran Am Bothan, a hostel in Leverburgh, and also offered trips on his boat *Free Spirit*. When I emailed him about it he replied a charter could be done, but it would not be cheap, and perhaps I could find someone to share the cost. But in the end I could not find anyone else interested in going, so I had to foot the bill on my own.

On the appointed day, a brilliant Saturday in late May, I met Ruari at Leverburgh Pier. The tide was low which, in the shallow waters of the Sound of Harris, meant taking an indirect route. Under clear skies, and over a calm sea, we motored around the north end of Ensay, and then set course towards Boreray.

As we motored west, the low silhouette of the island slowly rose from the sea. We had covered eleven sea miles when Ruari dropped anchor in the bay off *Tràigh na Luibe* (the curved beach), on the east side of the island. Just then another boat jetted behind us to make landfall on the sandy beach. It was Jerry Cox, Boreray's only resident. I'd be meeting him in a few hours.

Ruari set me ashore at *Sgeir an Tairbh* (bull rock), where just above the beach stood the ruins of a village that had been occupied until 1923. It was here the last Macleans of Boreray lived. The Macleans came in 1460, living in a fort atop nearby Cnoc a' Chaisteil, and in more settled times in the village. The ground was fertile, and the island flourished. The population peaked at 181 in 1841, but had dropped to 150 in 1879 when the schoolhouse and church were built.

The population was down to sixty-four in 1920, when the islanders asked to be relocated on North Uist. They were all gone by 1925, but one former resident, Colin Maclean, decided to return. After Colin

Village at Cladh nam Mhanaich

died in the 1960s, Boreray remained uninhabited until 1999, when its current (and only) inhabitant moved in.

Next to the village lay *Cladh nam Mhanaich*, The Monks' Field. At its northern boundary lay a small rock outcropping with several cup-marks scooped out of its surface. I stood on the ritually carved bedrock and looked to the south, where a dozen grass-grown mounds rose from the lush grassland. These are traditionally the monks' graves. They may in fact be overgrown burial cairns, but some may be collections of stones from when the fields were cleared for cultivation.

Even with its tradition as a burial ground, the field was not used by the people of Boreray as a cemetery. For that honour they chose a patch of ground near the Well of the Cross on the headland of Àird a' Mhòrain, a mile away on North Uist. The small burial ground there has a hundred unmarked tombstones, and amongst them stands a large enclosure built for the Macleans of Boreray. If you ever make the long walk there from Sollas, and you should, you will find several memorial

The Monks' Field

stones. The largest is a moss-grown marble tombstone made for the 13th, and last, Maclean of Boreray.

> *JOHN MACLEAN*
> *OF BORERAY*
> *WHO DIED ON THE ? DAY OF APRIL 1821*
> *IN THE 62ND YEAR OF HIS AGE*
> *AND WHOSE REMAINS WERE LAID*
> *IN THIS PLACE WITH THOSE*
> *OF HIS ANCESTORS*

Why the Macleans were not buried on Boreray is a mystery. One could guess the limited acreage was too precious for such usage. Either that, or there was a close connection to the saint who had a cell at Àird a' Mhòrain, and incised the cross in the rock above its holy well. As for Boreray's use as a monks' cemetery, the following is a paraphrased version of Martin Martin's description from 1695.

> *The burial place is called the Monks-Field, for all the monks that dyed in the islands north of Egg. Each grave has a stone at both ends, some of which are 3 and others 4 foot high. There are big stones without the burial place, several have little vacuities in them as if made by art; the tradition is, that these vacuities were dug for receiving the monks knees, when they prayed upon them.*

Martin's report has an interesting interpretation of the cup-marked stones—the vacuities being made to receive the knees of kneeling monks. If a true explanation is ever found for these mysterious carvings, which are found in several places on the islands, including near the well on Àird a' Mhòrain, it will probably be just as fantastic.

A half mile west of the field I reached *Cnoc a' Chaisteil* (Castle Hill). This was where the Norse, and the Macleans, had a fortified dwelling, but all that remains is the vague circular outline of a foundation, sixty feet in diameter. It was a good viewpoint out over the isles, and a place where watchmen once stood guard.

From Cnoc a' Chaisteil a short walk led to the shore of Loch Mòr, the big loch, which nearly splits Boreray in two. Several ruins dotted

Cnoc a' Chaisteil

the terrain, many occupied by nesting fulmars. Martin Martin had this to say of Loch Mòr:

> ...*a freshwater lake well stocked with eels... there is a passage under the stony ground, which is between the sea and the lake, through which it is supposed the eels come in with the spring tides; one of the inhabitants called Mack-Vanish (the Monk's Son) had the curiosity to creep naked through this passage.*

One wonders if a natural tunnel once linked the loch to the sea, let alone one big enough to crawl through. But what *is* true, is that a sluice had been built in 1885. A 300-foot channel to the sea was blasted through the rock, and the loch drained. With a flood gate in place, any seawater that got in could be drained at low tide. Although this effort reclaimed some ground for cultivation, the sluice was abandoned.

Stone beach between Loch Mòr and the sea

A high narrow causeway of pebbles separated the loch from the sea. And after crossing it I started the easy climb up Mullach Mòr to the highest point of the island.

The weather was bright and dry, and the view from the top inspiring. To the east lay the long white sands of Berneray, and nearer at hand stood the low, round isle of Lingay, where the Boighreachs once dug their peat. From that high vantage point you can clearly see how Boreray is nearly cut in two by Loch Mòr—to the east only a narrow section of sand-dunes separated the loch from the sea, and the pebble-beach causeway barely kept it at bay to the west. Something else amazing caught my eye. The two main islands of St Kilda, Hirta and Boreray, could be seen forty miles away on the horizon. It was a unique sight, seeing Boreray from Boreray.

View from atop Boreray

At the foot of the slopes lay a string of ruined houses, most of their stones taken for other uses. Amongst them stood the only two modern dwellings on the island; one a holiday home, the other the restored schoolhouse, where the current resident lives. Beyond the houses lay the derelict church, with what remained of its slate roof cloaked with yellow lichen.

I wanted to take a closer look at the church. I also wanted to respect the privacy of Boreray's resident. So a roundabout approach was made, keeping well away from the house. But while doing this the sound of barking made me look towards the house. A yapping dog was approaching, and behind it sauntered a tall man in blue overalls and yellow wellies.

I had just reached the church when he asked "Are you Martin?"

"No, I'm Marc."

"Oh... I thought you were Martin. Martin from the RSPB, here to count birds."

Boreray Church

My fears as to being warned off soon vanished, as Jerry Cox, Boreray's only full time resident, said hello. He then introduced me to Molly who, seeing I was not a threat, stopped barking.

Jerry lives in the schoolhouse, which he started renovating in 1999. The church, however, is not in such good shape. The walls and gable ends looked structurally intact, as did the central chimney, but the windows and doors were missing, birds were roosting in the rafters, and Jerry mentioned he has battled rats in the structure over the years.

By now Molly had warmed to me. So after exploring the church I sat on turf to pet her. It is hard to say how long I could live on my own like Jerry, but he wasn't truly alone, Molly saw to that. Jerry suggested taking a look at Geris Geo, an impressive slot in the rocks on the north coast where seabirds galore roost. But only a little time was left, and that time would be spent back in the Monks' Field.

I said goodbye to Jerry, then headed south. On the way several clusters of ruined houses were encountered, indications of Boreray's once crowded condition. A half hour later I stood again atop the cup-marked rock, looking out over The Monks' Field. Were all those gentle, grass grown mounds, really tumuli; burial mounds of generations of monks? Old maps and tradition say they are. Oral history is the root of Gaelic culture, so there must be some basis in fact. I said goodbye to the spirits of all those monks, then walked down to the shore as Ruari motored over in the inflatable.

Postscript

Looking back on my time on Boreray I understand why the monks chose it for their burial isle. Its gentle terrain, its low green hills, give anyone treading its grassland an Iona feeling—a feeling known by all who have spent any time there. Iona is what some call a thin place, a place with a spiritual presence: it's a place you want to be. Boreray has that same spirit: it's a place one could easily rest forever.

Boreray's two residents stroll on the beach

Molly of Boreray

PART V:

WANDERINGS IN HARRIS & LEWIS

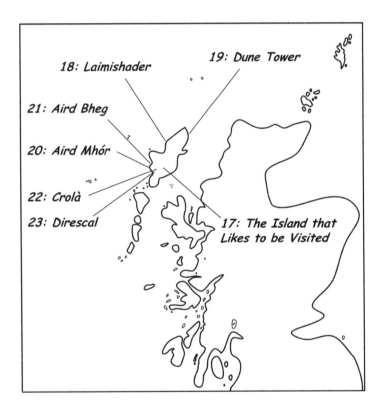

18: Laimishader

19: Dune Tower

21: Aird Bheg

20: Aird Mhór

22: Crolà

23: Direscal

17: The Island that Likes to be Visited

17: The Island that Likes to be Visited: Harris

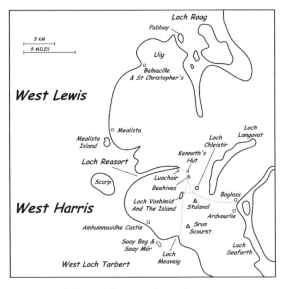

Map Reference: Ordnance Survey Landranger 13

One of the best walks in the Western Isles starts on the shore of Loch Seaforth near the Lewis-Harris border, and ends on the other side of the island at Loch Meavaig, an inlet off West Loch Tarbert. This fifteen-mile hike travels through the deserted expanses of the Harris interior, and chances are you'll not see another soul all day. The middle third of the hike is the hard part, as it crosses rough, trackless moorland. But the rest is along easy-to-follow paths.

During this walk you'll see the most intact beehive cells in the islands, explore the remains of the last black houses to be occupied, and visit the site of an incident in the feud between the MacLeods and Macaulays of Uig—one event in a long tale of murder and revenge. Then, to top off the walk, you'll have a chance to look for the most mysterious island in the Hebrides: the Island of Mary Rose.

I started the hike at Bogha Glas, on the shores of Loch Seaforth (NB 186 115). From there an old track led west up to *Bealach na Uamh* (the pass of the cave). Once the pass was reached, 650 feet above the sea, the vast expanse of Glen Langadale appeared far below, slicing its way through the Harris interior. From there the track quickly dropped 500 feet to the Langadale River. The map showed stepping-stones, but I had to go upstream for a few minutes before I found some.

As quickly as it had dropped, the path climbed the west side of the glen to a pass below the summit of Stulaval. I had just reached the highest point of the walk, almost 1100 feet, when another rapid descent took me to the shore of Loch Chleistir. The time had come to quit the path and go cross-country. So I turned to the north-west to follow a grassy ridge that gently descended to the trickling waters of *Abhainn a Chlàir Bhig* (river of the small plain). After crossing a section of peat hags, I forded the stream and came to a pair of beehive huts in remarkable shape.

The two beehives stood side-by-side above the riverbed (NB 117 148). With their turf coverings still partially intact, they blended so well into the surrounding terrain that they looked as if they had grown there. The corbelled stone roof of the smaller beehive is whole, and the only damage to the larger is a small hole in its roof. Getting down on all fours I crawled through the entrance of the larger cell into its dim interior.

Beehive cells at Abhainn a Chlàir Bhig

Beehive cells are mysterious structures. Some are built partly underground, but these are completely above ground, and some of the best surviving examples in the Hebrides. Could they be early Christian dwellings, like the two side-by-side cells in the Garvellachs? Possibly, but the walls of these two are not nearly as thick; a few layers of stone, versus the three feet of densely packed rock that make up the Garvellach cells. I squatted in the gloom of the cramped chamber for a few minutes, the air thick with the smell of dirt and decay. Deciding the life of a hermit would not have been for me, I crawled back out to the light of day.

I left the beehives and followed the Abhainn a' Chlàir Bhig for a mile to where it met the Kinlochresort River. Here I came to Tota Choinnich, Kenneth's hut (NB 112 164). Some 500 years ago an act of treachery, and heroism, occurred when a teenage boy was left here to die.

In WC Mackenzie's 1932 book *The Western Isles* there is a chapter written by John Morrison entitled *The Adventures of John Roy Macaulay*. These adventures occurred in the fifteenth century, when the sons of MacLeod of Pabay Mòr, an island in Loch Roag, murdered the family of Iain (John) Roy Macaulay, following a dispute over the ownership of a cow. Thirteen-year-old John Roy had been away at the time, living with his foster-father in Mealista, on the west coast of Lewis. MacLeod of Lewis, not happy with the behaviour of the Pabay MacLeods, ordered that in recompense they take young John Roy into their custody with a promise to keep him safe.

But his period of safekeeping would not last long. On a snowy November day the MacLeods took him on a hunting trip, and here at Kenneth's hut, an old shelter, they showed their true colours. He was tied to rocks in the snow and left to the elements.

John Roy's foster-father had a premonition something was amiss. He hiked to Kenneth's hut and found the near-dead boy. After resuscitating him with some warm milk, he carried him over seven miles of hills and bog to Mealista. Several years later John Roy would have his revenge when he pursued the eldest son of MacLeod to the shores of Uig Bay, killing him just before he could reach the sanctuary of St Christopher's chapel.

I had lunch amid the ruin of Kenneth's hut, a turf grown jumble of stones, ten by eight feet in size. With the sun straight overhead in a partly cloudy sky, conditions were far different from when John Roy was left here in the snow. But his adventures had a happy ending. MacLeod of Lewis, in compensation for all John Roy had suffered, granted him some of the lands of Uig that belonged to the Pabay MacLeods. This included Balnacille, which surrounds the holy ground of St Christopher's Chapel, where John Roy had slain that eldest MacLeod son who'd left him to die. I myself have spent many enjoyable days and nights at Balnacille, for it has one of the best guesthouses in the islands, with an unforgettable view out over the Uig sands and the burial ground of St Christopher's. (The true name for that burial ground may be *Cille Chriosd*, meaning Christ Church.)

From Kenneth's hut I followed the river to its end at Kinlochresort. The OS map shows a footbridge over the river here, and decades ago there was a substantial one. But it has washed away. The only remnants of it are two cement footings on either side of the stream. So I continued downstream, splashed through the shallow water near its mouth to the other side, and then made my way to a group of four roofless black houses. I had reached the deserted clachan of *Luachair* (the place of rushes).

Alasdair Alpin MacGregor's *The Haunted Isles* has a picture of Luachair when it was inhabited. His photo of the black houses shows peat smoke rising from a chimney-bucket in the thatched roof of one

Luachair – the place of rushes – as it was. Photo: AA MacGregor
© National Museums Scotland. Licensor www.scran.ac.uk

house, and a dark stack of peat piled against the wall of another. A row of white nightshirts hanging over a fence to dry adds more signs of life to the scene. These were some of the last black houses to be occupied in the Hebrides, and one had been home to the postman who carried the mail to Kinlochresort. But where there was once life, there is now only stone. The thatched roofs are gone, and the empty window openings stare like sightless eyes out over the waters of Loch Reasort. I explored the forlorn ruins for a while, their interiors overgrown and littered with fishing nets and floats.

So far the day had been filled with relics of things ancient and dead. The time had come to look for something different. The time had come to look for the portal to Tìr nan Òg, the land of everlasting youth, the Island of Mary Rose.

JM Barrie wrote *Mary Rose* between 1912 and 1920. He conceived the idea for the play—which is based on Celtic legends of faeries

Luachair – as it is

174

and Tìr nan Òg, the Land of Everlasting Youth—while staying at Amhuinnsuidhe Castle on the shore of West Loch Tarbert. The story concerns the two strange disappearances of Mary Rose from The Island that Likes to be Visited. At age eleven Mary is left on this small island while her father is fishing. When he returns she's nowhere to be found. Several weeks later she reappears with absolutely no memory of where she's been, and no sense that any time has passed. Later in the story we learn a similar event had happened before, when a two-year-old boy had disappeared from the island; a boy who had yet to be found.

Eleven years later Mary Rose visits the Hebrides with her husband and two-year-old son, a son supposedly born while her husband was away. Could the boy have been a changeling, a playmate she'd found among the faeries? The island calls again 'but no one can hear it but those for whom it is meant.' It is meant for her, and this time she disappears for twenty-five years. When she returns from that long absence we find she has not aged, and it seems to her as if only an hour has passed.

So where did Mary go? There are dark and light sides to the tale, revealed at the end of the story when we see the struggle between the faeries, who'd taken her twice to their subterranean world where time stands still; and Tìr nan Òg, the paradise of everlasting youth. *Mary Rose* is a chilling tale, and one that Alfred Hitchcock wanted to make into a movie. Unfortunately, it was a project that never came to be.

In the Harris interior, four miles north of Amhuinnsuidhe, lies Loch Voshimid. The tradition on Harris is that an island in this loch had been the inspiration for Barrie's mystical island. In the play the island has two trees, a pond, and a small hill—perhaps one of the faerie knolls of legend? And it is also said to be an island that comes and goes. Here again we have an item from mythology, the floating island. At the end of the story, a final bit of legend appears, when a piece of iron holds open the trap to the faerie world.

From Kinlochresort I retraced my steps to Kenneth's hut and then turned right to follow the Kinlochresort River. This is the hardest part of the hike. You have to climb over endless hummocks of soft earth, and you need to pay close attention to every step or you'll sink to the knees in black, boot-sucking bog. After a tiring hour of hard going I reached Loch Voshimid.

There were several small islands in the loch, one of them possibly the Isle of Mary Rose. I followed the east shore of the loch to a point opposite one of the islands. The water level was low, and a string of stepping-stones linked the island to the shore. To get to any of the other islands would require a boat—or a cold swim—so I christened this one the Isle of Mary Rose.

I tiptoed across a stretch of mud and, after a bit of stone-hopping, stepped onto the island. It had been visited before, for a slight trail led past a small tree to the top of a heather clad knoll. I sat on top and looked out over the waters of the loch. It was quiet. No wind or birdsong broke the silence, and it indeed matched one of the descriptions of The Island that Likes to be Visited, for it was as still as an empty church.

I thought about the end of the play. It is one of those scenes that stay with you forever. Mary Rose's son hadn't seen his mother since she had vanished when he was two. By the time she returns from a twenty-five year absence he has grown and left for parts unknown. It had been a deep yearning to see him that allowed her to return to the land of the living—perhaps because those yearnings upset the jealous faeries. When she returns, however, he is nowhere to be found. She can't go back to the other-world without finding him, and, years later, when she dies, her spirit remains trapped.

After her death, Harry, the long lost child, visits the home of his youth. While there, he sticks his penknife into a wooden box, seemingly a strange action. He then has a spirit visitation, and, in an instant where time stands still, we learn his mother's story. Then her ghost appears.

An island in Loch Voshimid

At first she does not recognize her grown child. It has been so long that she's 'forgotten who she seeks,' but her trapped soul eventually recognizes him, and her spirit can finally be set free. But where to go? Not to the faeries … for with her son's knife in hand, a bit of iron to keep the faeries from trapping her, she's released to the empyrean—the heavenly paradise of everlasting youth, Tìr nan Òg.

I heard no call on the little island other than that of Barrie's play. My youth would not be with me forever, so before my sore legs fell asleep for twenty years, I stood up and forced myself to leave the island of the faerie knoll.

I crossed back to the shore of the loch and found the start of the track to the coast. Ninety minutes later I reached the road above the shore of Loch Meavaig. Just offshore the islands of Soay Beg and Soay Mòr lay surrounded by the noisy white horses of a turbulent sea. There is some thought that Barrie may have used one of these islands as inspiration for The Island of Mary Rose, but not as far as I'm concerned. For that quiet little island in Loch Voshimid, with its soft covering of heather, where I'd sat in peace for minutes that seemed like hours, was indeed an enchanted place where time could stand still. It was a place that liked too much to be visited. And if you weren't careful, it was a place that might capture you forever.

18: Somewhere in the Hebrides: Laimisiader of Lewis

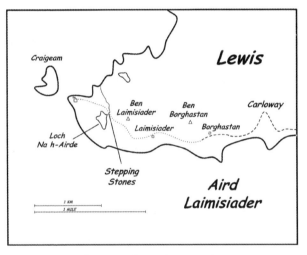

Map Reference: Ordnance Survey Landranger 13

One of the most memorable passages of Scottish island-writing is the prologue to Alasdair Alpin MacGregor's *The Haunted Isles*. It is entitled *Somewhere in the Hebrides*, and takes the reader on a wander across the stepping-stones of Aird Laimisiader, a headland on the west coast of Lewis. This wander starts by following a mountain track to its end, where we descend to a fertile hollow. Here we cross stepping-stones to the moorland where, at what is still an unknown location to the reader, we're bestowed with a view west to the Pirate's Isle of Bearasay, and beyond to where the sun sets on the lighthouse of the Seven Hunters, whose keepers mysteriously disappeared one December day over a century ago. MacGregor's prologue ends with:

And all these strange places are situated somewhere in the Haunted Isles—somewhere on the terrestrial bourne of the sunset, on the threshold of Tir nan Òg.

At 6am on a clear spring morning I stepped out the door of the Doune Braes Hotel, intent on following in the footsteps of MacGregor's wander. A two-mile drive took me to Carloway, where I turned west and drove a mile to Borghastan. Here the pavement ended, and I set out on foot down a dirt track to the west. The track gradually deteriorated into a footpath that wound around the southern flank of Ben Borghastan, and then came to an end at the edge of a forty-foot cliff. I found a way down a cleft in the rock, and then crossed a bit of boggy moorland, where the small settlement of Laimisiader had once been home to several families (and possibly a monastery), and is now home to grazing sheep.

After crossing the southern shoulder of Ben Laimisiader I found myself amongst the abandoned peat cuttings that surround Loch na-h Airde. Here I found MacGregor's stepping-stones, one of the two things that had brought me to this deserted headland. The soft ground was dry, so I didn't need the stones to cross. But I stepped on them anyway and continued on to the moors beyond. After another third of a mile I reached a small light-beacon that stood atop the headland of Aird Laimisiader.

The beacon flashes every twelve seconds over the islands that dapple the mouth of East Loch Roag. One of those islands, Craigeam, floated just offshore, its short cliffs dotted with guano. Three other islands drew my eye, three that demanded a visit someday. To the south-west I could see Little Bernera, the final resting place of the Princess of Thule. To the west lay the Pirate's Isle of Bearasay, where Neil MacLeod had a

The Stepping Stones at Laimisiader

stronghold in the seventeenth century. And last, but definitely not least, a tiny isle was barely visible in the open sea far to the west, Eilean Mòr of the Flannans, with its infamous lighthouse.

I lingered for a while, and then turned my back to the sea to recross the stepping-stones and climb to the top of Ben Laimisiader. I took a seat there, high above the sea, somewhere in the Hebrides, and found the second thing I'd come for. To think on those four memorable pages that start MacGregor's *Haunted Isles* in the place that gave them birth. Four pages I've read countless times, as should you; four pages that will lead you to the very threshold of Tir nan Òg.

In time of winter the stepping-stones, that in summer one can barely find because of tall, green rushes and marsh-mallows and buttercups, just show their faces above the surface of the soft ground, across which they bear those who wander to and from the moors beyond, and those who delight to linger by the margin of the open sea.

181

19: Dune Tower and the Stone of the Peats: Lewis

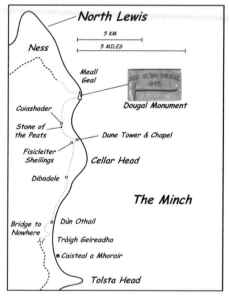

North Lewis

5 KM
5 MILES

Ness

Meall Geal

Dougal Monument

Cuiashader

Stone of the Peats

Fisicleiter Sheilings

Dune Tower & Chapel

Cellar Head

Dibadale

The Minch

Bridge to Nowhere

Dùn Othail

Tràigh Geireadha

Caisteal a Mhorair

Tolsta Head

Map Reference: Ordnance Survey Landranger 8

DESPITE its name, the Bridge to Nowhere leads somewhere. Built in 1920, this bridge on Lewis was to be the beginning of a new road up the east side of the island, providing a direct connection from Stornoway to Ness. The road had been completed for a mile beyond the bridge but, with the collapse of Leverholme's plans in the 1920s, it was never finished.

During my first visit to Lewis I stood on the Bridge to Nowhere and looked with disappointment to the north. There wasn't time to make the full day hike along the route this never-to-be road would have taken. The route takes you by Dùn Othail, where the Morrisons of Ness had a stronghold. You then pass deserted Dhìobadail, and cross Cellar Head to the abandoned shielings of Filiscleitir. From Filiscleitir you could turn right to visit the ruins of Dune Tower and its chapel, perched high atop the sea-cliffs, standing roofless to the sky.

Then another old shieling site could then be visited, Chuidhsiadair, where you'd step on the Stone of the Peats to cross the Black River at the Peat Stone Ford. And finally, before you left the grass and heather of the moorland for solid ground, you would be tempted to make a detour across a mile of boggy terrain to the headland of Meall Geal. Because even though you've already tramped ten hard miles, and your legs feel like mincemeat, an obelisk on the cliff tops above the sea must be visited. It is a memorial to someone whose collected stories of island memories, published over seventy years ago, left a lasting impression on you.

But sadly I didn't have time to make the walk. So I turned the car around and drove away. A year later, to the very day, I came back.

On the morning of what would turn out to be a brilliant day of sunshine my wife dropped me off at the Bridge to Nowhere. I was not sure how long the trek would take, so the plan was to find a phone box in Ness, at the end of the walk, and give her a ring to come pick me up. The bridge stands above Gearadha Bay, where the hundred-foot-tall rock stack of *Caisteal a' Mhorair*, the Nobleman's Castle, capped with the ruin of a small fort, rises from the grey-white sands. Once over the bridge the road bends to the north above the sea. My steps were light, and as I walked along I enjoyed the unlimited vista of sea to the east, and the profile of Cellar Head to the north. But after twenty minutes this carefree stroll was interrupted when the road ended at *Amhuinn na Cloich*, the river of stones.

I crossed the river and started out over the grassy moorland. Even though marker-posts have been planted here and there to show the way, I occasionally lost sight of them as I followed the undulating terrain to the north. The grass was tall and thick, the ground soft and wet, and I soon discovered a walking technique that made the going easier. Raising high each foot in turn, I marched along, like a soldier on parade.

It was exhausting terrain, harder than sand walking, and stretches of evil-looking bog required a bit of heather hopping. After a mile I came to Dùn Othail, a large promontory stack jutting out from the cliffs. There had been a fort here at one time, manned by the Morrisons of Ness, and the rocky summit was surrounded by sheer drops on three sides. To get a closer look I dropped part way down the ridge of rock that connected the stack to the mainland cliffs. But not wanting my wife to become a widow on vacation, I decided not to climb the stack.

Here at Dùn Othail one of the many leap tales of Hebridean folklore occurred, that of *Leum Mhic Neacail*, MacNicol's Leap. Here is one version of the tale, which is identical to the story of Gorrie's Leap on Mull.

A MacNicol was castrated for some misdeed. Seeking revenge, he kidnapped the infant son of the chief who had sentenced him to this punishment. His pursuers almost had him in their grasp when he managed to get up onto Dùn Othail. Dangling the child over the sea, MacNicol had some bargaining power. So he demanded that the chief castrate himself; otherwise he would drop the child on the rocks. The chief did as demanded, and once MacNicol saw the bloody proof, he shouted "I will have no heir, and neither will you." He then jumped off the rock, killing himself and the infant.

Instead of jumping (or severing any body parts) I made my way back to the cliff top and headed inland. After two miles I reached the shielings of Dibadale, the deep dale. Dropping down into the ravine of the Dibadale River I stopped to rest and top off my bottle with some fresh water. Continuing on across the lonely moorland a lapse of concentration caused a mis-step, and I sank to the knees in bog. But the sun and tall grass soon dried the black mud from my legs.

Small lochans dotted the terrain. I was at peace, enjoying the silence of the yellow-green countryside as I walked along. Then I scared up a golden plover roosting in the tall grass. As it took flight the sudden fluttering of its wings sounded like a helicopter taking off. My heartbeat took off as well, so I paused to let it slow.

A solitary ruin appeared off in the distance, and I made a slight course adjustment towards it. On the map it's named Dùn Bilascleiter, after a Norse watchtower that once stood there. Some ninety years ago a house had been built that incorporated some of the tower's stones. It was known as Dune Tower, and is mentioned in several old books about Lewis: most notably Alasdair Alpin MacGregor's *The Haunted Isles*, and *Island Memories*, a posthumously published collection of the writings of JW Dougal (whom we'll hear more of later). Dune Tower seems to have been a favoured place to stay for people exploring this remote coastline. And it's no wonder. Perched on the cliff top, the house has an amazing view to the far mainland; the sea in between haunted by *Na Fir Ghorm*, the Blue Men of the Minch who, along with the Merry Dancers, *Na Fir Chlis*, are said to be the angels cast out of heaven with Lucifer.

It had been quite an undertaking to build Dune Tower. Sometime between 1907 and 1920, John Nicolson, who had been a Baptist preacher in America, had the house (and the nearby chapel we'll be visiting shortly) built. Nicolson dreamed for years of having a home and chapel near where his father had a summer shieling. Nine tons of

185

Dune Tower

sand were brought in by boat and carried up the 200-foot cliffs. And several tons of cement, along with all necessary lumber and fixtures, were carried across the moors from Ness, six miles away.

Dune Tower is in sad shape. One gable is complete, but the northern one lies half-crumbled. I entered the ruin through the doorway facing the moorland, and saw that each gable had a fireplace set between two large windows. Three windows in the east wall once looked out to the sea. And what a view they had. I wish I'd brought a sleeping bag to spend the night. I could have watched the sky dim, and the distant lighthouses come to life: Stoerhead, with its single flash to the west; Tiumpan Head, a double flash to the south; and Cape Wrath, its quadruple flash marking the corner of Scotland every thirty seconds.

I left the house and walked over a rise to find the small chapel Nicolson built for the people who inhabited the Filiscleitir shielings in the summer; shielings that have lain empty now for over fifty years. The chapel is in better shape than the house, all four walls stand complete, and two lancet window openings grace its western gable. Entering through the vacant doorway I saw a tumbled fireplace to one side, but nothing else remained inside other than the bare cement floor. It must have been a wonderful place to worship, overlooking the small bay where the Leum Langa River tumbles from the cliff to the rough waters of the Minch.

I left Dune Tower and its chapel to their ghosts and walked north to Chuidhsiadair, where scattered clusters of old shielings line the Abhainn Dubh, the Black River. Somewhere in the river lies a boulder called Stone of the Peats. It is mentioned in MacGregor's *The Haunted Isles*, and was used as a stepping stone to cross the river when people went out to the moorland to gather peat. I wanted to find the stone because it was described as having human footprints carved on it.

A small bridge now spans the Black River. I was not sure if the large rock below it was the stone, but this had certainly been an old ford. There were two worn marks on the surface of the stone that I convinced myself were footprints; they certainly looked foot-print-ish; but they were extremely small, like those of a child. Even though the bridge was handy, wanting to keep in the spirit of the walk I stepped on the stone to cross the stream.

I now had ten squishy miles under my belt, and could see the solid ground of a paved road a mile off. I was tempted to walk to it. But off to the right was something that looked like a rocket ready to blast-off from the cliffs. Knowing what it was, I headed in that direction.

As I walked towards the cliffs an evil looking skua wheeled smoothly overhead. Like a Luftwaffe fighter on patrol, its spread wings exuded pure menace. A few minutes later I'd forgotten all about the skua when it suddenly swooped down from behind. A sudden whoosh of air tingled my scalp—a shot of adrenaline tingled the rest of me—as it passed overhead by inches. I thrust a fist defiantly in the air, so that

The Dougal monument

on its next two strafing runs it had to pass higher up. I have an intense dislike for skuas, as I've seen them kill puffins at sea, and then munch away. When I reached the cliffs the skua soared away in search of smaller prey.

At the edge of the cliff a ten-foot pillar rose from a two-tiered pedestal. Its white paint was well worn, and it had a metal plaque embedded high up on one side. The plaque had an engraving of a rock-hammer, along with the words *John Wilson Dougal* and the date *1905*. It was in 1905 that JW Dougal noted the flinty-crush bands of the Outer Hebrides.

Dougal was the founder of a chemical company in Edinburgh, and in his spare time an amateur geologist. For many years he explored the geology of the Outer Hebrides, and had been the first to describe their flinty-crush rock formations. You're asking what flinty-crush is, aren't you? Here is one definition I found: 'It is an ultracrushed variety of mylonite, in which the primary structures and porphyroclasts are obliterated so that the rock becomes homogeneous and dense with little parallel structure.' How is that for geologic jargon? Couldn't be any simpler, could it. No? Well in layman's terms: it's very hard rock.

Dougal, who died in 1935, thought it was a band of this tough material stretching the length of the Western Isles that helped them survive glacial erosion. In other words, the islands might not be here today without it. (Thank-you, flinty-crush.)

Dougal wrote up many of his adventures in the Hebrides. After his death they were published in *Island Memories*, a jewel of a book for anyone interested in the islands. His walks around the Lewis coast

John Wilson Dougal on Lewis, rock-hammer hanging from his belt
Courtesy of his granddaughter, Valerie O'Grady

while staying at Dune Tower, and in the Uig hills on the west side, inspired me to explore these remote places for myself.

My legs had had it. No more detours. So I took a bearing on the shortest distance to solid ground, a gate off in the distance that marked the beginning of a paved road. But before heading in that direction I looked out to the sea. Somewhere beyond the northern horizon lay the remotest of the Hebrides: Sùlaisgeir and North Rona. Dougal visited and wrote about both of those far-flung isles.

I turned my back on that marvellous view and headed inland. A mile later I came to a road and sat on the tarmac to rest. To celebrate completing the hike I cracked open a whisky miniature I'd brought for the occasion. I swallowed it in one gulp. It burned my throat, and I coughed for five minutes, scaring all the sheep away from a nearby field.

Normal breathing restored, I decided to walk to the guesthouse we were staying at, seven miles down the road in Galson. So when I saw

The chapel

a phone box I resisted calling my wife for a pickup. It was easy going for a while. I was on solid ground and didn't have to navigate. But, two miles later, as I passed through Habost, my ankles were screaming for a rest. After all those hours on soft terrain the hard cement sent a shock wave up them with every step. Then the true test of my resolve occurred. I came to another phone box. According to the map it would be the last one. This was the point of no return. Could I keep going for another five miles? No. I gave BT twenty pence and called my wife for rescue.

Take my advice, a more fascinating island hike than the Tolsta-Ness coast is hard to find. As island jaunts go, it rates up there with a walk around Rum, or any of the walks in the Lewis interior that visit Kinlochresort. It is a walk you will never forget, as you follow in the footsteps of John Wilson Dougal to pay your respects to the memory of the people that once lived along this spectacular coastline. It is a hard walk, but the directions are simple—just take the Bridge to Nowhere.

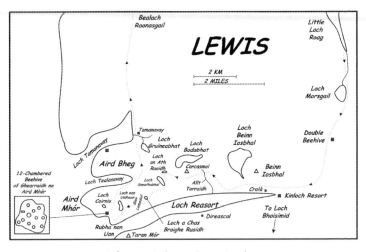

Map Reference: Ordnance Survey Landranger 13

When discussing walks on Lewis and Harris, the term 'the big one' usually means one thing; the trek from Morsgail to Kinlochresort, then south past Loch Voshimid (and a certain island that likes to be visited) to the sea at West Loch Tarbert. It is twelve long miles of bog hopping. But the seed of an even longer walk on Lewis had been planted in my mind when I first read Daphne Pochin Mould's wonderful book *West Over Sea* (1953). It would be a walk to make 'the big one' pale in comparison.

In *West Over Sea* the author describes a visit to the twelve-chambered beehive of Ghearraidh na Aird Mhòr, a dozen stone cells linked together into a sort of prehistoric apartment house (NA 0245 1660). It is not known whether this unique structure dates to pre-Christian times, was a Celtic Christian settlement, or an old shieling village. I've only come across one other reference to it, this frustratingly brief mention in Seton Gordon's *Afoot in the Hebrides*:

> *Here are the ruins of a cluster of very old dwellings built of stone. Little remains of these dwellings, which are smaller than summer shielings, and may have been used by the Picts in the ancient past.*

The description of the big beehive in *West Over Sea* is tantalisingly detailed. It mentions its last use was as a shieling in 1823, and includes a diagram drawn in the 1850s. I had to see this relic, but it would not be a trivial undertaking. A walk there and back would cover twenty rough miles, for *Ghearraidh na Aird Mhòr* (the summer grazing headland) lies on a bleak corner of Lewis, miles from any road, where Loch Reasort meets the open waters of the Atlantic.

In the year 2000 I managed to convince two friends to accompany me on this long walk. Diana and Andrew Smith are veteran visitors to Lewis, and especially the Uig area. My enthusiasm for this unusual adventure convinced them to come along; either that or they wanted to make sure I wouldn't disappear in the Lewis bogs without a trace.

I carried camping gear across the Atlantic and we met up on Lewis. My wife is not a big fan of long bog hops (in other words, she's sane) and Andrew had to cancel out at the last minute. This left Diana and me on our own to make the long trek. Our packs were loaded with tents, sleeping bags, and enough food for two days, as we set out on foot down the private road to Morsgail Lodge.

The first part of the walk consisted of an easy stroll along the paved road. After a mile a sign directed us to a footbridge spanning the Morsgail River. From there the path skirted the east shore of Loch Morsgail, and then led out onto the soggy moorland. Squelchy step after squelchy step we marched through oozing bog, hopping from one heather clump to the next to keep out of the muck. After an hour we came upon a double beehive dwelling in a shallow valley. Their corbelled stone roofs were mostly intact, and a rotting sheep carcass lay in one of the dark chambers.

From the beehives we turned west and crossed a very long stretch of bog to a viewpoint above Loch Reasort. (Sadly, we totally missed the Postman's Stones which lead the way across the bog to Kinresort. But don't worry, we'll be back to look for them in chapter 22.)

The entire length of the loch now lay in front of us, a narrow fiord of blue water leading to the sea. We had come five miles, but Aird Mhòr was another five to the west. A little farther on we had a distant view of Crolà, in its day one of the most isolated crofts in the Hebrides. In Alasdair Alpin MacGregor's *Behold the Hebrides* there is a picture of

Crolà and the head of Loch Reasort

Crolà as it was eighty years ago. The picture shows two thatched houses nestled above the shore, a cultivated field on the hillside behind, and chickens roaming in front of the main cottage. The old houses are now just shells, their thatch roofs gone with the wind. And the once fertile field is now an overgrown patch of green on the brown heather hillside.

I had planned to take a direct route along the north shore of Loch Reasort. But it was not to be. Several headlands blocked the way, and the endless ups and downs to follow that course were just too daunting to consider. So Diana and I wound our way north to Loch Beinn Iosbhal. From there we turned back towards Loch Reasort, all the while trying (mostly in vain) to maintain elevation as we travelled west. In order to avoid the deep glen of the Allt Torraidh we rounded the head of another glen, and then stopped for an hour-long snooze in the sun.

Energy restored, we continued on. Another soggy glen blocked our way, so we rounded its head near the 384-foot summit of Corcasmol. From there we curved around the south shore of Loch an Ath Ruaidh and found ourselves standing on the small sandy beach of Loch Sneathabhal. The firm grey sand the only solid ground we'd stood on for hours. We were bog and loch hopping, our zigzag progress on the map marked by the number of small dark lochans we passed. We'd been marching for eight hours when we rounded the headland of *Rubha nan Uan* (the point of the lamb), where we came across three jumbled shielings on a hillside. Unless we were truly lost we'd reached Ghearraidh na Aird Mhòr. But the much anticipated twelve-chambered beehive was nowhere to be seen.

We were too exhausted to be disappointed. It was threatening to rain, so setting up tents became the first order of business. The second would be to find water, so I walked over to the small stream that drains the glen, the Allt Gleann na Aird Mhòr. It was a trickle of brown peaty water flowing through a shallow trench to the sea, and wasn't going to quench our thirst. But as I squatted next to it I noticed nettles growing from stony mounds on the far side of the stream. Mounds that were draped with dried up seaware and littered with jetsam. Thinking we might have found something we cleared away fish nets, floats, and plastic bins. Soon the outline of several cells became apparent, and we realised that this was what we'd been searching for.

The beehive had eight definite chambers and, with some imagination, a few other spaces could be included in the count. The walls stood anywhere from a few inches to a couple of feet high, and several connecting passages were discernable. On the seaward side five chambers appeared to be connected; in the middle, four were linked; and on the inland side there were a few single cells. The whole structure was thirty feet wide, and covered 800 square feet. In an 1850s drawing of the site, made three decades after the cells were last inhabited, four

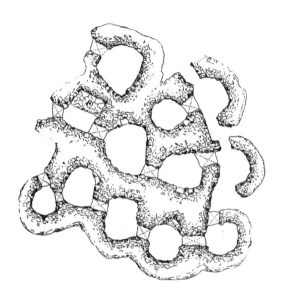

Diagram of the 12-Chambered Beehive, Capt. Thomas R.N.
Proceedings of the Society of Antiquaries of Scotland, Vol. III (1857–60)

of the circular spaces are indicated as sheltered porches. So there were a total of eight living rooms. They were all tiny, and each could have held one person at most.

This amazing building sat just above sea level, the crashing surf only feet away, and had probably been covered with turf at one time. It is strange that they built it so close to the water. Could it have been made when the sea was lower? Could it have been a Celtic Christian settlement, a mini-monastery of sorts? It was certainly located along the sea-lanes that connect the remote Christian sites on the seaboard of the Western Isles. Lots of questions, but I have none of the answers. Although one thing is certain; this little valley had been able to support quite a number of people at one time, for the ground of Ghearraidh na Aird Mhòr lay wrinkled with acres of overgrown cultivation ridges.

In June, at these high latitudes, the night sky never fully darkens. But sleep came easy after our hard day's work. It drizzled on and off during the night, and a light rain fell in the morning as we started the ten-mile hike north to Uig. We followed the glen to the north coast of

The surf-battered ruin of the 12-Chambered Beehive

Aird Mhòr, and then descended a steep grassy slope to the shores of Loch Tealasvay. There we thought we'd have an easy beach walk. But with the tide high we had to clamber over a boulder strewn shoreline to the head of the loch. After climbing to the top of Glen Tealasvay we rounded Loch Gruineabhat and came to a point overlooking Loch Tamnavay.

From Tamnavay I dearly wanted to make a detour to the west, and pay a visit to the deserted clachan of Aird Bheag. But that would have meant an extra two hours of hard hiking, in addition to the eight miles we still had in front of us. So I promised myself to come back to visit Aird Bheag, and we continued down to the footbridge over the Tamnavay River.

Once over the river we started up the long road to Uig, a seven-mile track that had been recently hacked out of the hills between Uig and Tamnavay. It is an extremely ugly scar on the hillside. But, that said, we were happy to stop navigating and follow the road as it zigzagged up a series of switchbacks to the cloud-shrouded pass. When we were halfway to the top an estate Land Rover slowly passed us going in the opposite direction, the driver giving a friendly wave as he drove by. We had heard stories of hikers having their packs searched here, but we must not have looked like the poaching type.

Three miles later, and 900 feet higher, we reached the wind blown summit of Bealach Raonasgail. From there we still had four miles to go on the stony road as it snaked its way through the hills. As we continued north, Mealisval, the highest of the Uig Alps, rose up on our left. And to our right, Teinneasabhal, Tahabhal and Tarain filled the skyline. These mountain names should have inspired us to pen poetry. But at the moment it was all we could do to put one foot in front of the other. After what seemed an eternity we came to the locked gate that prevents anyone without permission from driving a vehicle down the Burma Road to Tamnavay.

Taran Mòr rises across Loch Reasort from Ghearraidh na Aird Mhòr

Postscript

The twelve-chambered beehive of Ghearraidh na Aird Mhòr is so out of the way that it is not in any danger of vandalism. But this fantastic relic is falling apart, stone by stone, with every winter storm it sees. It is a shame such an incredible piece of history is allowed to wash away with the surf—which it no doubt will.

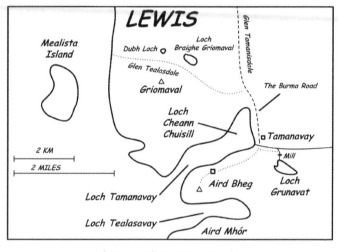

Map Reference: Ordnance Survey Landranger 13

IN ALASDAIR Alpin MacGregor's *The Haunted Isles* (1933) there is a chapter entitled *The Back of Beyond*, which tells of the people who, some eighty years ago, called the small Lewis peninsula of Aird Bheag home. It was one of the most remote settlements in the Hebrides, consisting of two black houses; one occupied by the MacLennan brothers, the other by the MacDonald family. In *The Haunted Isles* there is a picture that shows the two houses, a walled garden, and a wide path that follows a strange S-shaped course between the houses. MacGregor's endearing story, and that enigmatic picture, kept calling out to me. So I decided to answer that call. I decided to find out what remained of Aird Bheag.

There are only a few ways to get to Aird Bheag. None are easy. You can go by water. But that requires a boat and calm seas. You can go on foot, either crossing miles of bog from the east, or crossing the hills of the gloomy pass from the west. Or you can go part way by car. Eighty years ago no roads came anywhere near Aird Bheag. But in the late 1990s a seven mile private track was gouged out of the bogs and hills between Uig and the head of Loch Tamnavay, a mile east of Aird Bheag. But to drive this road required two items not at my disposal: a Land Rover and a key. You need a Land Rover because the road is steep and rocky. And you need a key as the road has a strategically placed gate. When constructed, a short section of the road was routed over a swampy bog (something not hard to find on Lewis). A narrow, ten-foot-high causeway carries the road over the bog at this point. And a locked gate, strategically placed in the middle of the causeway, is a vehicle barrier that can not be bypassed.

A year had passed since Diana Smith and I had walked around that barrier on our way back from a hike to the twelve-chambered beehive at Ghearraidh na Aird Mhòr. Over that year I'd convinced Diana and her husband Andrew to join me on another long bog-hop, and we decided our route to Aird Bheag would be via the gloomy pass.

So on a bright June morning we drove the coast road south from Uig to where it abruptly ends near the ruins of an old nunnery, *Tigh nan Cailleachan Dubh* (the house of the women in black). A half-mile offshore the small hills of Mealista rose from the sea, a deserted island I must visit someday. With the beach on Mealista shining gold in the sun, we climbed east into Glen Tealasdale.

We soon reached Dubh Loch, a sterile cauldron of black water on the stony hillside. Passing the loch we hugged the rock-strewn base of the cliffs below Griomaval, the gloomy mountain, and soon reached the top of the pass, 1000 feet above the sea. From there the wide deserted expanse of Glen Tamanisdale appeared far below. And as we hiked down into the glen we came upon a series of small cairns, set up a century ago, that mark the way over the pass. We slogged on down the slippery hillside until we reached the sea at the head of Loch Cheann Chuisil.

After following the shore track for a mile we came to the head of Loch Tamnavay (Haven Bay), where we passed the old keeper's cottage and the shuttered up estate lodge. Then the track ended at the wooden footbridge over the Tamanavay River. Rock shelters on the hillside above, some with skeletons it is said, tempted a detour, but we carried on.

Aird Bheag lay another hard mile away. It was at this point that Diana and Andrew decided to turn back. They had to return to Uig and the hospitality of the guesthouse at Balnacille, so they needed to be out of the bogs before dark. But I had decided to spend the night in Aird Bheag. So I walked on alone across the soggy hills until the shells of two black houses appeared. With exhilaration I realised these were the old dwellings in MacGregor's photo.

The wind had kicked up, and it started to rain. For shelter I thought about setting my tent up in one of the houses, and went into the larger one to have a look around. This must have been the home of the MacDonald family eighty years ago. Two fireplaces stood inside, one with a metal barrel inserted as a makeshift stove. The thought of sleeping there felt strange, like I would be intruding on ghosts.

As I walked over to take a look at the second house I discovered something wonderful. Remember that S-shaped path in MacGregor's photo? Well, it was not a path at all. It was a stream flowing with clear icy water that wound around each of the houses, portions of its course covered with flagstones. The folks of Aird Bheag had running water at their doorsteps. They also had fresh food, for near the houses lay the ruin of a walled garden.

Aird Bheag – as it was. Photo: AA MacGregor. (Permission sought)

In the end I couldn't bring myself to sleep in either house. So I used a stone enclosure next to the MacDonald home as a windbreak for the tent. With shelter taken care of I thought about paying a return visit to the twelve-chambered beehive. But as that would involve a hard, five mile round trip in the pouring rain, I decided not to go so far.

Instead I climbed to the top of the peninsula, Mullach na Aird Bheg. And from its high ground, 600 feet above the sea, all of Aird Bheag could be seen: the black houses, my tent in the enclosure, and the walled garden. I could also see an overgrown track that led down to a stone jetty on Loch Tamnavay. Stacks of lobster pots sat on the jetty, and just offshore several rows of mussel ropes floated on the dark loch. I then looked to the south-west, and even though it was only three miles away, the island of Scarp could barely be seen through the pouring rain.

Although the weather was miserable, I was anything but miserable. I gloried in the isolation, in possessing, although for only a very short time, the entire peninsula. Thanks to the writings of Alasdair Alpin MacGregor, the ghost village below lived on. My being there, in some sense, had brought it back to life for a day. Please go there yourself someday, so that it will live yet again.

Back down in camp I resisted the thought of poaching some fresh mussels for dinner, and settled instead for a US Army MRE (Meal Ready to Eat). It wasn't too bad, a vacuum packed omelette with ham—the mussels would have been better. Fresh vegetables were not on the menu either, as the walled garden has been overgrown for decades.

It was still light out, but sore legs had me in bed by nine-thirty. A cuckoo tried its best to keep me awake. Then, as I started to doze off, I heard loud barking. I sat up, peered out the tent, but saw nothing in the dusk. Had I been dreaming? I started to get a little paranoid. I had not asked for permission to camp here, and envisioned the estate police unleashing rabid Alsatians on any potential poacher who dared trespass. (Note: This walk was in the year 2001.)

I heard more barks. There are old tales in the islands of the *each-uisge*, the water-horse, which rises from its loch at night to devour unwary victims. But I'd never heard that they barked. Then I saw the source of the noise. On the hillside above, a half dozen red deer were staring intently at my tent. Back home I'd camped in the high-country, where during rutting season the bony nasal sounds of bugling bull elks echo through the valleys. But I'd never heard anything like this. These deer were barking like dogs. Then they saw my movement (either that or they smelled me, for I was a bit smelly) and loped away into the twilight. Around 4am the cuckoo decided I'd slept enough, and began to 'tell his name to all the hills around.'

At dawn I said good-bye to Aird Bheag, filled my jug with icy-cold water from the stream, and then set off back to the head of Loch Tamnavay. At the footbridge I set my pack down and walked up-river for a hundred yards to the stream that drains down from Loch

Aird Bheag – as it is

Grunavat. I was looking for the mill that crushed the grain of the folks of Tamanavay and Aird Bheag.

The mill, described in Daphne Pochin Mould's *West Over Sea*, occupies a small island in the stream. And as I climbed through the wet grass I came to a spot where the stream split in two. Here sat an island of sorts, but no sign of a mill. Then, as I climbed higher, the walls of a stone structure seemed to rise from the water. It looked like the front of a house, water spilling out its door. It was the ruin of a mill, and it did indeed stand on a small island (NB 043 199).

Three feet down in the central pit of the mill lay a millstone. It had a hole at its centre, and when the mill was working this stone would have remained stationary, and another would have been connected to an iron spindle with paddles on one end. The paddles, turned by the force of the stream, would have rotated the spindle and the mill stone. Water still poured through the mill, but its stones were no longer harnessed to grind.

Then my resolve to keep exploring failed. On the slopes to the north were rock shelters. One story claims a man had been murdered in one of them for the Lewis chessmen. Carved from walrus ivory, the chessmen are a collection of seventy-eight pieces that date to the twelfth century. In 1831 they were uncovered in the sands of Uig, seven miles to the north. How they originally got to Lewis is uncertain. As one tale goes, a man absconded with a bag of loot from a ship anchored in Loch Tealasvay, a mile to the south. He was followed here to Tamanavay, and then his treasure and his life taken. His skeleton is said to be in one of these rock shelters. But I decided not to look for it, as I needed to save something for next time.

As it had rained during the night the streams draining the pass below Griomaval were in spate, so it would be a hard, soggy slog to return the way I'd come. A mindless eight-mile tramp up the stony track to Uig was just the ticket; no thinking involved, just put one foot in front of the other. This would be my second climb up this hellish road, with its seemingly endless series of false summits.

A thousand feet later, in the vertical sense, I reached Bealach Raonasgail, the top of the pass. Before starting the descent to Loch Raonasgail I sent up a prayer of thanks to Alasdair Alpin MacGregor for keeping alive the story of Aird Bheag, and the folks who called it home so long ago. An hour later I came to that locked gate, and the public road, high above the gold sands of Uig.

22: A Night in Crolà & The Postman's Stones: Lewis

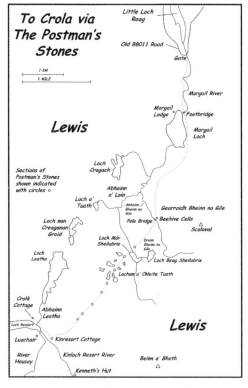

To Crola via
The Postman's
Stones

1 KM
1 MILE

Little Loch
Roag

Old B8011 Road

Gate

Morgail River

Morgail
Lodge   Footbridge

Lewis

Morgail
Loch

Loch
Cragach

Sections of
Postman's Stones
shown indicated
with circles o

Abhainn
a' Loin

Loch a'
Tuath

Abhainn
Bheinn na
Gile

Gearraidh Bheinn na Gile

Pole Bridge   Beehive Cells

Loch nan
Creaganan
Groid

Scalaval

Loch Mór
Sheilabrie

Druim
Bheinn na
Gile

Loch
Leatha

Loch Beag Sheilabrie

Lochan a' Chleite Tuath

Crolà
Cottage

Abhainn
Leatha

Loch Resort

Lewis

Luachair   Kinresort Cottage

River
Housay

Kinloch Resort River

Beinn a' Bhoth

Kenneth's Hut

Map Reference: Ordnance Survey Landranger 13

For many years I'd wanted to follow the Postman's Stones to Crolà and spend the night. Aside from Direascal, Crolà is about as remote a place as you'll find in the Hebrides: near the head of Loch Reasort on the island of Lewis, and miles from any road. Crolà had fascinated me ever since I saw a photo of it taken by Alasdair Alpin MacGregor.

The photo, in the 1948 edition of *Behold the Hebrides*, shows a solitary croft house set next to a small byre; each with a thatched roof held down by rope netting. A triangular patch of rushes grows in front of the house, and next to them a chicken struts around, looking for tasty tit-bits to eat. The hills of Harris rise in the far distance, the top of Clisham hidden in cloud. Between the house and the hills lie the calm waters of Loch Reasort, and across the loch you can see the black house village of Luachair. It is a photo full of life, although not a person is to be seen.

Having had memorable nights of camping in Aird Bheag and Aird Mhòr, I decided I wanted to spend a night in Crolà, camping near the house in MacGregor's photo. I also decided I would get there by following the historic Postman's Stones to Kinlochresort. These stones, set in place in the early twentieth century, allowed the bogs to be safely crossed in all weather, easing the postman's job, as he had to make the journey year round.

So in 2010 a week-long stay on Lewis was made, with hopes good weather would allow for an overnight visit to Crolà. On a sunny Sunday morning, a quiet time on sabbatarian Lewis, I found myself with a pack on my back standing next to the gate of the road to Morsgail Lodge. My wife was, as usual, worried about me hiking on my own. There is little spare wood to be found on Lewis, so she gathered a few sticks and asked me to take them in case I needed to build a fire. After sliding the sticks into the pack, I gave her a kiss, and then set out down the road to Loch Morsgail.

I had been this way before, on a walk to the twelve-chambered beehive ten years before. So the first part of the walk would be familiar.

A mile of road-walking led to the footbridge across the Morsgail River. Once over the bridge the going got wet, and here and there old tyres had been set down as stepping stones. I made the mistake of stepping on one. Both it and my foot sank deep down into black, murky muck.

The path went past the south end of the loch, turned west, and then petered out. I carried on in the same general direction, but soon realised I'd gone too far west. After a bit of backtracking, and a turn to the south, I regained the path. The way was obvious here, as deep ruts from quad bikes had made two straight lines across the moor. The ruts led directly to the double beehive cells I'd seen on my last walk here. But this time no dead sheep lay inside the larger of the two cells, and I paused for a drink of water to cool down from the mid-day heat.

Beehive Cell south of Loch Morsgail

A nearby bridge of old telegraph-poles, held together by fence wire, made for an easy crossing of Abhainn Bheinn na Gile. After crossing the bridge no path marked the way, so the time had come to search for the Postman's Stones. After a while I realised I'd once again wandered too far west, and a few minutes after turning back east a standing stone came into view. It was not a big monolith, a foot high at most. To the south stood a similar stone, and beyond that another, and another... I had found the Postman's Stones to Kinlochresort.

I passed five more stones over the next ten minutes, and then seemed to lose them. But continuing in the same general direction another string of stones soon appeared. I crossed the shoulder of Druim Bheinn na Gile to reach the shore of Loch Mòr Sheilabrie. From there another set of stones led me through a cluster of six little lochs set closely together. After that came an endless sea of peat hags: three to four-foot-high islands of turf surrounded by black bog. No guiding stones stood there, and I wondered if they had been swallowed by the swamp. It was slow going. Several times I would reach the end of an island of turf only to find myself surrounded on three sides by an evil looking dark miasma of goo; or, as Nigel Tranter described it in one of his novels, black treachery. If I stepped in that treachery I'd never be seen again.

Making a dozen detours, I plowtered on through the quagmire. At one point I thought I'd gone astray again, but then happily noticed a standing stone on the southern horizon. When I reached it I found it to be a pillar stone embedded high atop a large mound. This was the supreme, and last, Postman's Stone. From there Kinlochresort could be seen. (I have read that another series of stones mark the route to Hamanavay, five long miles to the west—a journey for the future.)

I came to Kinresort House, which had been built in 1850 for the estate gamekeeper. On the front of the house a corrugated iron door was secured by a sturdy padlock. The roof, too, was a flat, ugly,

The Postman's Stones to Kinlochresort

The last Postman's Stone above Kinresort

corrugated thing; a far cry from the double dormered slate roof shown in pictures taken in the 1960s, and in a picture I took of it on my walk to Loch Voshimid in 1998. From the house I walked down to the Kinlochresort River, which was followed to Loch Reasort. From there I continued along the north shore of the loch to find the reason I'd come all this way. After rounding a small point, that reason stood before me: the cottage of Crolà.

It was a beautiful spot, but marred by tons of jetsam. The site appeared to be a natural tide trap. While looking at all the junk I recalled what someone once told me about some of the fishermen that ply these waters: rarely did a boat return to port with any garbage; they toss it all overboard. And there at remote Crolà, proof of that was all too evident.

Before setting up camp I spent an hour gathering jetsam and moving it away from the cottage. Some of it lay half buried in mud, and rushes had grown through the rope-holes of many of the heavy plastic floats, anchoring them firmly to the ground. One after the other, floats of all sizes were pulled out, and tossed as far away as possible. In addition to floats, thick plastic sheets—the bottoms of mouldering fish crates—had to be dug up before they'd come free. A small stream trickled down to the loch beside the cottage. In it sat a large, rusting barrel, half filled with something unknown. I managed to release the barrel from its mud-embrace and roll it away.

The day was warm, and all that work tiring, but after an hour most of the debris had been cleared away. With the site cleaned up, I climbed the hillside to re-create MacGregor's photo. I found where he had taken the picture by lining up the cottage with the peaks of the distant Harris hills and several large rocks in the loch.

Unlike MacGregor's picture, mine would have no signs of human presence; no thatched roofs, tilled fields, or wandering chickens. So after taking a few photos, I pitched my tent next to the ruin, and then climbed back up the hill to take more pictures. Crolà looked occupied once again, and it would be, for a little while, anyway.

I made myself comfortable, cracked open a small bottle of Bell's, and then whiled away the hours; watching as the falling sun lengthened the shadows of the lazy beds that rippled the hillside across the loch. And as I lay there in the waning sunlight, a gentle breeze kept the midges away. In short, it was paradise.

There is little written history about Crolà. Although Alasdair Alpin MacGregor's photo made it immortal, he did not write much about it. All I have come across is a brief mention in Bill Lawson's *Lewis: The West Coast*, and a magazine article written in 1993 by Ian Mitchell. The magazine article tells how a family of MacDonalds, cleared from the island of Scarp, lived here from 1861 to 1961. The last generation here included Kate MacDonald and her brother Murdo. Kate was a teacher in the little school over in Luachair, and Murdo was the Postman who had the Crolà to Aird Bheag route, and the last person born in Kinresort.

In their later years Murdo and Kate abandoned Crolà and lived in the Luachair schoolhouse that had been built in the 1880s, and also served as a church. Looking across the loch I could see the ruin of the schoolhouse, and on the shore below it the Luachair blackhouses. In those houses lived more cleared Scarpachs; another family of MacDonalds, and the Macaskills. Malcolm Macaskill became the postman for the Kinresort to Morsgail route I had followed. Malcolm had set up the Postman's Stones, and he is said to have had a stash of whisky near one of them if some refreshment was needed. Making that rough walk on a regular basis—and the occasional dram—was good for his health, as Malcolm lived to be 88.

Another brief glimpse of life here is found in Daphne Pochin Mould's *West Over Sea*, where she mentions the postman while writing of a walk made in the 1950s:

I went down to the Kinloch Resort River, splashed across above its junction with the stream from Voshimid, and went slowly on to Kinlochresort... Loch Resort is a very fine fiord....at its head is the clachan of Kinloch Resort, a huddle of a few houses and some croft fields... The folk who live at Kinloch Resort think themselves much more in the world than the keeper and the postman-crofter who stay at Tamnavay, for at Kinloch Resort the postman walks every day five miles across the moors to link up with the Uig bus-route at Morsgail. A mere five miles from the road – indeed they are in the world!

They were indeed in the world, relatively speaking. But today Crolà is far out of the world, blessedly far out.

As the sun set, the high prow of Sron Ulladale took on a reddish glow. Although it lay three miles away, its height made it a prominent landmark on my walk. It rises to nearly 1500 feet, and on its eastern flank is the strone, an overhanging cliff. In a few weeks climbers would be converging there in order to scale what is described in the *Scottish Mountaineering Guide* as one of the most awe inspiring rock towers in the whole of the British Isles. But I was glad they were not here now, on this quiet, Sunday night. I was probably the only person in roughly 100 square miles of deserted terrain.

I could also see the top of Clisham, the highest peak of Harris, set against the darkening eastern sky. And as darkness fell, Vega, the diamond of the late spring sky, started glowing high overhead. Then, one by one, more stars twinkled on.

The May night was short. At 7am I peeked out the tent to see the sun had already risen. A fire had not been needed in the night, so the sticks my wife gave me were gently set in the fireplace of the cottage; ready to warm the next traveller who might need them—perhaps it would be me.

With my gear packed up I said goodbye to Crolà. At Kinresort I turned north to climb to the high pillar-stone. The way was familiar now, and following stone after stone I headed north. As on the way out, the hardest part was that section of four-foot-high islands of turf floating on black bog. They had to be carefully navigated by picking a seemingly drunken, zigzag course.

Dozens of stones were followed in reverse order from the previous day. The last stone was placed just where the lodge on Loch Morsgail came into view. From there on navigation would be easy. Or so I thought. I was closer to the loch than on my way out and, being lazy, decided to take a direct route to its shore.

To get there I had to traverse a flat stretch of what looked like grassland. It was not grassland. With my pack I weighed about 220 pounds, and on my second step all that weight sent one leg plunging deep into black muck.

Using the knee of my other leg, I was able to keep from sinking any further. That knee was then used to push up and, pulling on heather with both hands, I slowly hauled my sunken leg out; hoping the muck would not suck the boot off. It didn't, and I pulled my leg free. After cursing myself for being careless, I wiped the dark peat-mud off on a clump of green heather, and carried on.

I followed an undulating fisherman's path around the loch to the ruin of a dam that once blocked the loch's outflow. Atop it lay the partial sections of a crumbled walkway. There would be no crossing there, so I continued a quarter mile to the foot bridge that led to the road.

Once back on hard pavement it took a while for tired bog-legs to adapt to a ground that did not quake every time I stepped on it. A leisurely stroll took me to the public road, and then west to the main highway. I followed the highway down to the bridge over the Morsgail River, took off my pack, and then snoozed in the bright afternoon sun.

Crolà – as it was. Photo: AA MacGregor
© National Museums Scotland. Licensor www.scran.ac.uk

Crolà – as it is

Thirty minutes later my wife arrived, bringing a warm kiss and a cold beer. What a way to end what had been an extra-ordinary twenty-four hours.

Postscript

Six hours later night fell on Crolà. High on the moors above, the Postman's Stones stood in the moonlight, patiently waiting to guide the next wayfarer through the bogs. A few months later winter storms blew in off the Atlantic, and Crolà was once again covered with the jetsam of the uncaring. But, hopefully, the Postman's Stones, in time, will lead another traveller to the far shores of Loch Reasort where, perhaps, they will be inspired to pause, toss the junk away, and bring Crolà back to life for a while. If they do, that traveller will have a day to remember. That traveller should be you. And if it is, remember there's some firewood waiting there to warm you up.

23: THE SCHOLAR'S ROAD TO DIREASCAL: HARRIS

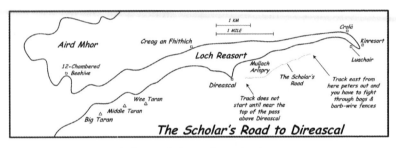

The Scholar's Road to Direascal

Map Reference: Ordnance Survey Landranger 13

WHILE exploring the Hebrides, I occasionally see things that puzzle me, strange things that I research when I return home. Then, if I rediscover some fact or bit of history I had once known, but forgotten while in the islands, I feel a great sense of 'shame-on-you.' For knowing the history of something when you see it, makes the seeing more meaningful. This is the story of one of those experiences.

Over the years I've been fortunate to have spent time in some of the abandoned settlements that dot the shores of Loch Reasort: Kinlochresort, Luachair, Crolà, and the beehives of Aird Mhòr. But there was one that I had not seen, as it is the most remote of them all: Direascal.

Getting there would involve a three day camping trip; hiking into Kinresort on the first day, making a sortie out to Direascal and back on the second day, a hard five mile round trip from Kinresort, and hiking back to 'civilization' on the third day. I say a 'hard' five miles because, although the 1:25000 OS map shows a path from Luachair to Direascal, oddly, it spans only the middle half of the route. I knew from experience that the pathless stretch could be a morass of soggy bog. Given time, I would have eventually dedicated a long visit to Harris to make that three-day hike. But, amazingly, an opportunity to see Direascal fell into my lap; and I did not have to lug a heavy pack over squishy bogs.

I first learned of Direascal while reading Angus Duncan's *Hebridean Island: Memories of Scarp*. In it, he tells of growing up on Scarp and spending childhood holidays in Luachair, at the head of Loch Reasort, seven sea-miles from Scarp. The author recalls one of those stays as follows:

> *I distinctly remember seeing the children (of Direascal) come to the small village (Luachair) at the head of the loch, where my aunt lived, to attend the Ladies' School there. As it was less than three miles away, with a tolerable path for schoolchildren, I visited the hamlet of Dirascal more than once and still remember the position of the three houses, near the water, in a quiet bay of the loch. But it was claimed on behalf of the proprietor that the presence of the houses frightened the deer away, and prevented them seeking winter shelter on the lower levels by the shore.*

Direascal had been cleared of people in the early 1800s to make room for sheep. It was resettled in 1885 by people from Scarp, but the three crofts that were established had a short life. In April of 1900, in order to keep them from 'frightening' the deer, the families were moved to Husinish, on the Harris mainland opposite Scarp.

The 'tolerable path' Angus Duncan referred to was an ambitious undertaking, and had not been completed by the time they abandoned

Direascal in 1900. When they started building the path, workers from Luachair and Direascal met at the halfway point, and each group started building a path back to their respective villages. By the time they left in 1900, the Direascal men had made good progress; the path ended on the hillside, 200 yards east of the village. But work stopped on the other section a half mile from Luachair.

Now here's where that 'shame on you' comes in. I had read Angus Duncan's book in 2005. But six years later, when that surprise chance to see Direascal came during a cruise around the Western Isles, I had forgotten all about his recollection of the school children walking the path from Direscal to Luachair and back. I had also forgotten a passage I'd read in Bill Lawson's 2002 book, *Harris in History and Legend*, which tells why the path had not been completed.

So during that cruise I primarily wanted to see Direascal because it, and the partial path to Luachair, may possibly be the most remote examples of nineteenth-century life in the Hebrides. Walking that path would be a memorable experience, and so I was overjoyed when a strong southerly wind left us no option but anchoring in the bay of Direascal, or as Angus Duncan called it, 'a quiet bay of the loch'.

Once ashore we explored the ruined houses. One was huge, as if it had been used to house a large group of people; possibly a shelter for deer stalkers. A thin dotted line on the map showed the path that led almost to Luachair, and we started searching, but found no sign of it near the village. We worked our way up to the 300-foot-high hill pass below Mullach Airispridh, and just below the summit we found the start of the path. It was an amazing sight, way out there in the middle of nowhere. What lay before us was more track than path, almost a causeway across the bogs, winding its way to the east.

We had only three hours ashore. The round trip to Luachair was over five miles, so I'd have to hurry. This meant abandoning my fellow passengers, as they wanted to amble along and enjoy the wildlife, rather

The Scholar's Road leads across the bogs

than make a forced death-march to Luachair. But that march had to be done; that path had to be walked.

The undulating path started descending, and I flowed down it like water rushing to a cascade. Here and there short sections had sunk into the bog. But these were easily stepped over. At the half-way point I passed the shore of Loch nan Uidhean, where the path crossed the Allt nan Uidhean on a small bridge of stone. My pace was swift, and I became optimistic I had enough time to make the round trip.

Then I noticed something that brought a smile to my face. Whenever the path crested a rise, stone markers had been planted to guide the walker; just like the Postman's Stones I'd followed the year before on the other side of Loch Reasort. Near tiny Loch an Truim I came to a large diamond shaped stone that rose three-feet above the ground. And as I carried on I realised its importance: it marked the end of the path for a traveller headed east, or the beginning for someone headed west.

The diamond marker stone above Luachair

Then my optimism disappeared—before me lay a vast morass of swamp and quaking bog. There was no sign of a path. But with so much time and energy invested in the trek, I could not give up. It was slow going, detouring around soggy ground and black peat hags that would eat me alive if I gave them the chance. My optimism started to creep back, only to be dashed to bits by a barbed wire fence blocking the way. I made a ninety-degree turn and followed it to the south, hoping to find a gate or a stile. I didn't.

There was nothing to do but climb the fence. I found a sturdy post, put one foot up on it as high as possible, and slowly hoisted the other leg over. I almost made it. A barb caught my flimsy waterproof trousers, which I was wearing in place of gaiters, and ripped them to shreds. That was the bad news. The good news—I was over the fence.

I carried on, climbed more fences, and then came to an old keeper's house, evidently still in use, as several bright orange propane tanks sat near the front door. Below the house lay the heart of Luachair: the schoolhouse ruin and the string of blackhouses near the shore. Across the loch stood the cottage at Crolà, the pile of colourful jetsam I'd cleared from it the year before clearly visible on the shore to the west.

A look at my watch showed I'd only an hour left. So I allowed myself a hurried ten minutes to look through the blackhouses where the Scarpachs had lived, and where Angus MacDonald stayed as a child. It was one of these houses that the postman, Malcolm Macaskill, had lived in. It was he who set up the Postman's Stones to Morsgail. Although thirteen years had passed since I'd last been here, on a long walk from Bogha Glas (chapter 17), everything looked the same.

Schoolhouse ruin at Luachair – blackhouse village at centre left

Roofless blackhouses at Luachair

After savouring those ten minutes I started back. In the heat of a fine summer day, tatters of my waterproof trousers fluttering in the breeze, I climbed the hillside to the prominent diamond marker-stone. A few minutes later I was zooming westwards along that marvellous path built 125 years ago.

I reached Dìreascal with five minutes to spare. So I took off the shredded waterproofs, sat on a wall of one of the old houses, and relished a few solitary minutes amongst 'the three houses, near the water, in a quiet bay of the loch'.

Postscript

Two weeks later, back home, I found my copy of Angus Duncan's *Memories of Scarp*, and re-read his experiences in Luachair. I also

224

Direascal

re-read Bill Lawson's *North Harris in History and Legend*, in which he relates how the path had been started at the centre, but never completed. I could have kicked myself for not remembering all this at the time. But still, I *had* walked the round trip to Luachair on the Scholar's Road, just as the children of Direascal had over a hundred years ago.

PART VI:

EXPEDITION AROUND THE LONG ISLE

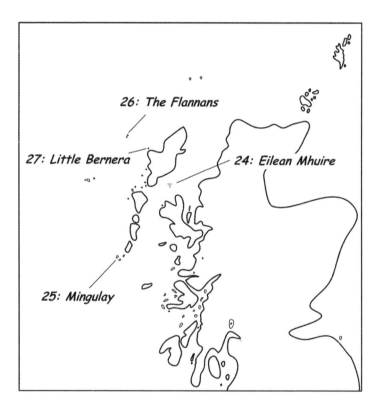

26: The Flannans

27: Little Bernera

24: Eilean Mhuire

25: Mingulay

24: THE ROPE CLIMB OF EILEAN MHUIRE: THE SHIANTS

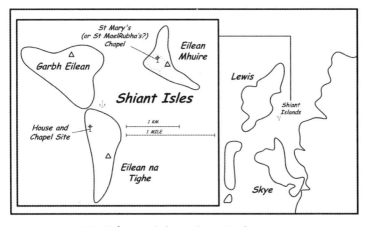

Map Reference: Ordnance Survey Landranger 14

FROM the sea the dusky sky appeared to be swarming with locusts, thick clouds of them swirling through the air. But they were not insects, they were puffins, and tens of thousands were flying back and forth between the sea and their island burrows. Every now and then they suddenly disappeared from the sky, as if there had been an explosion, its force blowing the puffins away. Some crashed to the sea, while others had made a beeline for the safety of their burrows. A bringer of death had made an appearance. An evil looking great skua soared through a now empty sky. A sky that, seconds before, had been filled with life.

When the skua finds a victim, others of its kind join in the feast, and as they munch away bits of bloodied puffin feathers float from the carnage. Once the skuas leave the sky fills again, and the puffins carry on with their performance as if nothing happened.

Sometimes the puffins would land near the boat, see us, and panic. Trying to run away on the water they belly-flop from swell to swell— their little orange legs pumping, their stubby wing-fins frantically flapping. More fish than bird it takes a tremendous amount of effort for them to get airborne. They keep trying and trying, but in a panic they just can't seem to do it. Neither can they make a decision to dive. Wanting to help, you urge them on.

"Come on! Dive! Dive! You can do it! Dive!"

All the while you're wondering what panicked thoughts must be spinning through those little puffin brains.

Run, swim, dive, or fly?
Run, swim, dive, or fly?
Oh me, Oh my,
Run, swim, dive, or fly?

Decisions, decisions. After flopping across the water for about fifty feet they usually heed your advice and dive. This incredible aerial display lasted over an hour, and at the end of it my neck was stiff from looking up.

Poplar Diver lay at anchor in the calm lagoon between the three Shiant ('shant') Islands: Garbh Eilean, Eilean an Tighe, and Eilean Mhuire, which lie in the Minch, seventeen miles north of Skye. We had anchored there a year before, and had seen only a handful of puffins. This time we'd arrived two weeks later in the year. And what a difference those two weeks made. Over a hundred thousand puffins filled the sky.

The following morning I asked Rob Barlow, our skipper, about getting ashore on Eilean Mhuire, the easternmost of the Shiants, as I wanted to see what was left of the old turf dwellings on what was the most fertile of the three islands. I also wanted to see St Mary's Chapel. As its name implies, Eilean Mhuire may be dedicated to Mary, and the tradition of a chapel on the island has persisted for centuries. Rob said we could go have a look-see and, if possible, make a try at a landing. But things did not look promising. Conditions had changed, and a stiff southerly was blowing the sea against the landing place.

Eilean Mhuire is a cliff-girt isle, and as far as I knew there was just one landing spot. We loaded into the inflatable and motored over to it. White capped swells lashed the small beach, so there would be no way to get safely ashore. Another bit of pebbly shore looked accessible, but to get from it to the top of the 160-foot-high cliffs looked like a difficult climb. With the wind increasing, and the water getting choppier by the minute, Rob turned the Zodiac into a narrow inlet to have a last look around. Sheer rock surrounded two sides of the inlet, but the north side was a steep, grassy slope. Narrow terraces laced the hillside there, worn by grazing sheep, which would ease the climb somewhat. I was a bit leery about going up. But then, to our surprise, and my relief, we noticed a thick rope snaking its way down the hill.

One by one we stepped out of the inflatable onto a wet, rocky shelf, and then clambered up to the tail end of the rope. We tugged on it. It felt firmly anchored, but we would not use it to pull ourselves up. It acted more as a bit of insurance to hold on to as we slowly climbed the hill. Reaching the top we found the rope to be tied to a post *almost* securely embedded in the turf. Next to it laid a large stone, obviously put there to pound in the post. Ever concerned for our safety, Rob used the stone to give the post a few whacks in advance of the descent to come.

The top of the island was a luxuriant, green rolling plateau, with a small hill at its eastern end. Eilean Mhuire was known as the garden isle of the Shiants. The total area of the three islands is 500 acres, but

Eilean an Tighe and Garbh Eilean seen from Eilean Mhuire

only thirty of that were arable, and half of those were on Eilean Mhuire. The criss-cross outlines of lazy-bed ridges covered much of the ground; a few ducks floated on a small pond, and here and there stood the overgrown mounds of the old turf dwellings.

Only one stone-built structure was evident. Marked on the map as St Mary's Chapel, it was a rectangular structure, fifteen by ten feet in size. It lay embedded in the side of an earthen mound, perhaps an old burial ground, such that three of its walls were embraced by the earth. The fourth wall, which had been built on the lowest part of the mound, was completely missing, which made me think the chapel now served as a makeshift sheep pen.

Martin Martin started all the confusion about a chapel on Eilean Mhuire when he reported, 300 years ago, that 'Island-Mor hath a chapel in it dedicated to the Virgin Mary'. One of the names for the Shiant Islands is Eileanan Mòra. So the question is; was Martin saying there had been a chapel on Eilean Mhuire specifically; or that there had been one on Eileanan Mòra, meaning the Shiant Isles in general? Adam Nicolson's *Sea Room* (the best book on the Shiants, written by their owner) explains how *Eilean an Tighe* (House Island) was once called *Eilean na Cille* (Church Island), meaning that Eilean an Tighe may have been the original island of the chapel.

That old name for the Shiants, Eileanan Mòra, is mysterious. Mòra usually means 'great', but geographically speaking, the Shiants are not 'big' or 'great' islands. So the name begs the possibility of another meaning. In the seventh and early eighth centuries St Maelrubha worked along the west coast of Scotland and the isles. The church of St Moluag at Eoropie, forty miles away on the north end of Lewis, may have originally been the chapel of St Maelrubha, as he was the patron saint of the Morrisons of Ness. And some guidebooks refer to the chapel at Eoropie as Teampull Mhòr.

St Mary's (or Maelrubha's?) Chapel

There are some twenty places dedicated to Maelrubha, and two are of interest here: Loch Maree, forty miles to the east; and Maaruig, a settlement on the shore of Loch Seaforth, fourteen miles to the west. If you draw a line between these two you'll see it crosses the Shiants. So there's some food for thought that the Shiants' old name, Eileanan Mòra, may mean the Isles of St Maelrubha.

So was the little building on Eilean Mhuire a chapel or not? I don't know. But does it matter? For even if Eilean Mhuire did not have a church, this fertile oasis in the sea must have been visited, if not inhabited and tilled, by the early monks who worked among the people of the isles.

As I reached the top of the island an icy rain-squall blew through. So I took cover in a nook in the turf, where greasy tufts of sheep fleece meant I had not been the first to do so. After donning waterproofs I popped my head up to take in the view. To the south, the cliffs of Trotternish rose from the northern wing of Skye. And a dozen miles to the west, across the Sound of Shiant stood the red-banded tower of Eilean Glas lighthouse on Scalpay.

Leaving my hilltop burrow I circled around to the edge of the western cliffs and looked over to Garbh Eilean. On the previous evening this vast bowl of sky between the islands had been filled with puffins. What a sight it would have been to see that performance from this perch on the cliffs. Below me the steep green slope lay cratered with burrows, and I could see the colourful bills of several puffins curiously peeking out, wondering what I was up to. A few hours later they would be soaring in the dusk along with thousands of their brothers and sisters.

When time came to leave we gathered together at the top of the rope. The rain had dampened the slope, so going down would be more challenging than the ascent. Instead of using the rope, a few decided to zigzag down the narrow terraces; but I wanted it in hand, 'a rope in case.' I descended one terrace at a time, sliding on my behind when the drop was more than a few feet.

Eilean Mhuire seen from atop Garbh Eilean

We all made it safely to the head of the inlet. The wind and rain started again in earnest as we waited for Rob to ferry us back to the boat. The rock walls of the inlet did strange things to the wind, funneling it in circles so that it came at us from every direction. Rob soon motored in and, as the boat was lightly loaded, one of those whirlwinds pushed the boat off course, briefly sending him airborne. He spun around to make another run, this time full speed towards our perch on the rocks. His aim was true and five of us quickly slid down to fill the boat.

It would take a second trip to get the remaining three, including myself, off the island. Ten minutes later Rob was back. Now an old hand at Eilean Mhuire uplifts, he zoomed into the inlet at full throttle. The nose of the Zodiac found its target, a vertical crack in the rocky shelf. Jamie, Rob's son, grabbed the rope and held firm while the rest of us slid onto the hard, wet deck of the inflatable. Jamie jumped in and we were off. Five minutes later *Poplar Diver's* engine rumbled to life, and we had to bid the isle of puffins goodbye.

25: Atop MacPhee's Hill: Mingulay

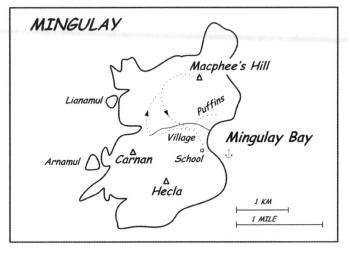

Map Reference: Ordnance Survey Landranger 31

THERE were five of us in the dark wheelhouse of *Poplar Diver* watching Rob pilot the ship through the black, midnight sea. As we neared Barra, our destination for the night, he followed a string of marker-lights that led to the shelter of Castlebay. The car ferry from Oban wasn't due until the following day, so we tied up to its pier. The large black rubber fenders that lined the pilings loomed high over us. Built to deflect the weight of ships like the 280-foot ferry *Lord of the Isles*, they easily cushioned the occasional bump of the seventy-foot *Poplar Diver*. Nearby, and sitting like a phantom on its small rock island, MacNeil's castle of Kisimul could barely be seen in the darkness. Within an hour the slight swell lulled us to sleep.

All six passengers, and three crew, were up early the next morning. The mooring lines were pulled in and we motored out of Castlebay. To starboard, on the eastern tip of Vatersay, lay a low mound, the ruin of Cille Bhrianan, the chapel of St Brendan. Buried there is *Mòr nan Ceann*, Mary of the Heads, the wife of a MacNeil chief. Her name is said to have come from her preference for fresh ox tongue, a once-a-day habit that cost the lives of several hundred cattle a year. Can you imagine what went through the mind of the cook in Kisimul Castle back then, wondering every day how to prepare ox tongue in a new and flavourful way? "Now let me see; would she like it boiled, broiled, baked, or fried; toasted, roasted, on a stick or a brick?"

We swung around to the east side of Muldoanich, a 500-foot-high lump of an island that must have once had a monastery, for its name means the isle of the tonsured ones. The ship then turned to the southwest, and over the next half hour we watched as the isles of Sandray and Pabbay passed by. With binoculars in hand, I scanned in vain for a glimpse of Pabbay's burial mound. On it is one of the few Pictish symbol stones found in the Western Isles, which we visited back in Chapter 9. The stone dates to the seventh or eight century, and had been discovered in 1889 by Father Allan MacDonald, a priest we'll be hearing more of later.

A half hour after passing Pabbay, Mingulay Bay came into view. Mingulay (Miughalaigh) is two miles long, a mile and a half wide, and in outline resembles the shape of Ireland. Together, Mingulay, and the nearby island of Berneray, are Land's End of the Outer Hebrides. If you were to travel due south from these 'islands at the edge of the world,' your first landfall would be Malin Head, 100 miles away on the northern tip of Ireland.

As we approached the bay we spotted a dozen dark specks on the beach. Looking through binoculars, I could see that they were seals lounging on the brown sand, and once they saw us they made a hurried exodus to the safety of the sea. The anchor was dropped, and then Rob and his son Jamie launched the Zodiac. We made an easy landing on the rocks on the south side of the bay, from where we climbed to a track above the shore. The now washed away eastern end of this track once led to a derrick platform. The derrick had been built by the government in 1901 to aid in the launching, and landing, of boats and supplies. But it had been so poorly placed, and constructed, that it turned out to be of little use to the islanders—islanders who left for good in 1912.

Gareth Robinson, another poor soul afflicted with Island Madness, was with me on this week long cruise. I hadn't seen Gareth since we'd met four years before on a sailing trip to St Kilda, and once ashore the two of us set out to climb the island's high points. We decided to start with MacPhee's Hill, at 735 feet, the second highest spot on the island.

Mingulay Bay

Following the track west we came to the schoolhouse. Built in 1881, it saw its last pupil in 1910. Unlike the rest of Mingulay's buildings, its roof is still intact, and it is used as accommodation for National Trust workers. We walked on through the village; its black house ruins engulfed in bracken and sand, and then started up the slopes of Mingulay's central valley. On the way up we passed the ruin of a nineteenth century mill, the stream still trickling through its stones. At the head of the valley we turned north up the shoulder of MacPhee's Hill. A stiff, cold wind blew, but we climbed on anyway. Gareth wanted to hit all the tops, but I had my own reasons for continuing. I'd wanted for many years to stand atop the hill where the marooned MacPhee stood looking for rescue. I also wanted to visit the hill's haunted hollow, where Mingulay's *each-uisge*, its water-horse, is said to dwell in a bottomless well.

A small ravine lay to the south of the summit, a sheltered spot invisible from below. It had to be the infamous hollow, but there was no well. Neither could we see any sign of the dreaded water-horse. In its normal form the monster was hoofed and hairy. But in order to woo the local lasses it could appear as 'a handsome youth with golden hair and laughing eyes.' Once the unfortunate victim fell into its grasp it would drag her back to its underwater lair. No lasses have lived on Mingulay for over a century, so the water-horse must be a bit lonely. But, we hoped, not lonely enough to take a fancy to any hikers who'd happen by.

We sheltered near the summit cairn. It had been here—the high ground nearest to Barra—that the hill's namesake, Big Kenneth MacPhee, regularly came to see if rescue was on the way. He wouldn't have been happy with our view that day, for clouds obscured the islands to the north. The following is one of the many versions of his story:

The Mingulay rent was late, a shipment of feathers and birds. The MacNeil chief wouldn't stand for that—all those ox tongues had to be paid for somehow. So MacNeil sent one of his men, Big Kenneth MacPhee, to inquire why—and probably demand a late fee. MacPhee went ashore alone and found everyone dead. Then he made his big mistake. He shouted to his cohorts on the boat he'd found a village of corpses. Fearing he'd bring plague aboard they deserted him and returned to Barra. MacPhee spent two months alone—some versions of the story say a year and a day—living off whatever fish (or sheep) he could catch. During this time MacPhee, leery of sleeping in the infected cottages, spent his nights in a nook on the hill; a spot that would come to be known as Leabaidh Mhic a' Phee, MacPhee's Bed. From there he looked north to Barra every day, hoping for help to arrive. He was finally rescued. And because the island had to be repopulated, MacNeil gave it to the MacPhees.

Clouds started to move in as we descended the hill. Even though the island's highest point, the 900-foot summit of Carnan, was intermittently obscured, Gareth continued to the top. But I decided to save that for next time, and returned to the village.

Over the past ninety years drifting sands have half-buried the black houses near the beach. It is an odd sight, lintel stones in place a foot or two above the ground. It is as if the homes have sunk in quicksand. The village burial ground lies above the beach, an oval mound surrounded by a stone embankment. An early chapel dedicated to St Columba once stood on the site, and there are some fifty grave stones, most unmarked and covered by sand. This type of raised burial ground is similar to many in the isles, including the one on nearby Pabbay.

The most substantial building was the Priest's House. Built of granite blocks, its ground floor had four rooms and a kitchen, which were used as quarters for visiting priests. The chapel on the upper floor, accessed by an external staircase, had been one large room, forty-five by twenty five feet. It was in June of 1898 that Mass was first held here, celebrated by Father Allan MacDonald, mentioned earlier as the discoverer of the

Pabbay stone. There is a wonderful book about Fr Macdonald, Amy Murray's *Father Allan's Island*, written in 1920. The island referred to in the title is Eriskay, sixteen miles north of Mingulay. Fr MacDonald worked throughout all the Barra Isles until 1905, when he died from influenza at the age of forty-six. Murray's book is a moving portrait of a man who gave his life to a people struggling to survive in these unforgiving isles in the sea.

All the photos I'd seen of the Priest's House showed it to be fairly intact. So I was surprised to see it was almost a complete ruin. I would later learn the roof had blown off during a storm in the winter of 1996–1997. I climbed to the top of the external stairway and looked in on the collapsed chapel, where Fr MacDonald said Mass a century ago. It was a sad mess, littered with fallen roof timbers and shards of the slate roof.

I'd had enough of melancholy ruins, the time had come to join in some fun. The rest of the shore party had gathered on the grassy hillside

The Priest's House

Mingulay puffins on parade

above the northern side of Mingulay Bay. And after taking a look over to where they were, I knew why. The air above swarmed with puffins, and I slowly approached so as to not scare them off. Eddie, one of my fellow passengers, had eased himself nose-to-nose to a group of puffins strutting about on the turf. I crept forward towards him, an inch or two at a time, until I found my own perch near the noisy burrows.

More puffins emerged from the ground, and within a minute a squadron of two dozen birds were squawking and growling in front of me. We sat there for an hour watching, in a trance-like state, the social interactions of these hypnotic birds. They are called Tammie-Norries in Shetland; papageitaucher in Germany (the diving parrots); and frilathios in Spain (the little friars, or, if you're *really* hungry, maybe the little fryers). But I always think of them as the smiling birds. Not that *they* smile with their bright orange, red, and yellow bills. But if you watch people watching puffins, you'll notice a lot of smiles.

When it was time to go we took our smiles to the landing place. Just down the track lay the remnants of the derrick platform. That effort to help the islanders had been too little, too late. On this windswept island they could be cut off for months at a time, and with an ever dwindling population the launching of boats soon became impossible. In 1906 they began to raid land on Vatersay and set up crofts. Several were brought to trial for this in 1908. After serving most of a two-month sentence, an agreement to create crofts on Vatersay was reached, and they were released. Three years later the last residents of Mingulay left the island, and the drifting sands started to fill their homes.

Our next stop would be the Flannan Isles, the scene of Scotland's greatest island mystery. But there was no mystery about what happened to the people of Mingulay. On our arrival we scared the seals away. As soon as we left they took back their beach.

26: On the Seven Hunters:
The Flannan Isles

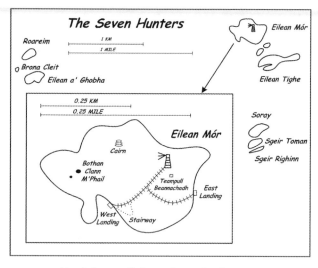

The Seven Hunters

Roareim

1 KM

1 MILE

Brona Cleit

Eilean a' Ghobha

Eilean Mór

Eilean Tighe

0.25 KM

0.25 MILE

Soray

Eilean Mór

Sgeir Toman

Cairn

Sgeir Righinn

Bothan
Clann
M'Phail

Teampull
Beannachadh

East
Landing

West
Landing

Stairway

Map Reference: Ordnance Survey Landranger 13

AFTER leaving Mingulay we made our way up the east coast of the
Uists to dock for the night at Lochmaddy pier. The following morning
we motored north through the Sound of Harris and then set a course
to the Flannans, an archipelago of rocks twenty miles west of Lewis.
The Flannans are also called the Seven Hunters, and when seen from
the east they look like a string of ships on the prowl. Aboard *Poplar*

244

Diver were eight island lovers: Eddie, Liam, John, Andy, Gavin, Steve, Gareth and me. Some came for the wildlife, some for the hiking. As for me, I'd come to see the remnants of human history imprinted on these amazing small bits of land far out in the sea.

In addition to their remoteness, the big draw of the Flannans is the mystery of the light-keepers. The Flannan light, built by the Stevensons, became active in December of 1899. They built two landing stages, one on the east shore of the lighthouse island, one on the west. This allowed supplies and men to be landed regardless of which way the wind and sea were running. Three keepers were stationed on the island, and in December of 1900 they all vanished. When the relief crew arrived at the east landing no-one was there to meet them. They went up to the lighthouse and found the outside doors closed, but an interior kitchen door ajar. In some accounts, an over-turned chair lay by the table. When they searched the island they found signs of severe storm damage at the west landing, but no sign of the keepers. The final lines of Wilfrid Wilson Gibson's poem *The Flannan Isles* describe the moment when the relief keeper, and two boatmen, finally gave up the search for the missing men.

> *Three men alive on Flannan Isle,*
> *Who thought on three men dead.*

Other deaths have occurred on the Flannans. One man fell or jumped from the tower, and several drowned at one of the landings—sinister events for such a small island.

We approached the Seven Hunters from the south-east. Gradually, the tip of the lighthouse on Eilean Mòr, at thirty-nine acres the largest of the Flannans, became visible. Under a cloudless sky we stayed out on deck to watch as the islands rose out of the sea. We rounded Eilean Tighe, the most easterly of the Hunters, and then motored into a fairly sheltered area, a little bay of sorts, that faced to the north-east. The wind came from the south-west, so conditions boded well for getting ashore, and we dropped anchor just off the east landing. In front of us, ten feet above the sea, sat a platform of concrete blocks cemented to the cliffs. Embedded in a recessed slot in the face of the platform was an iron ladder caked with a thick coating of rust, which we would try to use to get ashore.

We loaded on to the Zodiac and motored over to the landing. Rob nosed the small craft into the ladder slot. Then, one by one, we climbed on to the landing. From there, several flights of steep steps led up the cliff to the base of the tramway.

To carry supplies to the lighthouse the keepers had their own little rail system. There were two rail lines, one from each landing stage, and each landing had a crane to lift items off the supply vessel. Using these cranes, all the essentials—water, fuel, and food—were loaded on to a small trolley. Once the trolley was full, words to that effect would be shouted into a speaking tube that ran to the winch-room at the lighthouse. A steam-powered winch would then be engaged, and the trolley pulled slowly to the top. Once emptied, it would coast freely back down to the landing stage, the operator knowing when to slow it down by the amount of cable left on the winch. The trolley was used until the 1960s, when the rail lines were torn out to allow the cement track to be used by a three-wheeled vehicle called the Gnat. The Gnat, powered by a ten horsepower Briggs and Stratton engine, hauled supplies up the track until the 1970s.

The cement track was still intact, but there was no sign of the Gnat, so we'd get no free ride up the cliffs. We started our climb up the lower portion of the overgrown track. Once we'd gained a hundred feet the guano-fed turf that covered it cleared away, and we continued on up the narrow ribbon of bare cement. We soon came to the junction where the tracks from the two landings converge. In much of the literature on the Flannans this point is referred to as Charing Cross, and on the hillside next to it lays the giant gear wheels that once turned the trolley winch.

We continued up the track to *Teampull Beannachadh*, the Church of Blessing. This stone structure is also called St Flannan's Chapel. St Flannan, whom these islands may have been named for, was a seventh century prince of Thomond, in the west of Ireland. He became an abbot and went on a pilgrimage to Rome, possibly visiting the Hebrides during his travels. But there is another, and more likely, source for the Flannan name. Although people sometimes jokingly refer to these islands as 'The Flannel Isles,' that is how the name is pronounced in Lewis, and it may come from the Welsh 'gwlanen' (flannel or wool), as these islands were good grazing ground for sheep.

I entered the chapel by a low opening in its west gable. The sturdy outside walls were two feet thick, and the cramped interior measured five by eight feet. This amazing dry-stone structure started out as a

Lighthouse and Teampull Beannachadh

massive beehive cell that, at some point, was altered into the shape of a chapel. The chapel had been an important site in its day, the scene of many rituals by those who came here to capture birds and gather eggs. One tradition was for the men to remove their shirts on nearing the chapel, and then to pray three times before going to work. They said the first prayer on their knees in front of the chapel, the second while circling it, and the third inside.

It was getting hot, so I performed my own version of the ritual. Standing in front of the chapel I shed a few layers of clothing, and then traversed a section of lumpy ground as I made my way towards two stone structures that stood on the west side of the island. The lumps on the ground were hundreds of eroded rabbit warrens and puffin burrows, where the light-keepers once had a five-hole golf course. With all the holes about, I wondered how they kept track of the balls. I also wondered if some poor puffin ever tried to hatch a golf ball.

On the far hillside lay the golden lichen-stained remains of two beehive cells; one was a three-room apartment, the other a single. These structures are called *Bothan Clann M'Phail*, the bothies of the Clan MacPhail. The MacPhails were watchmen of the Lewis coast. Acting on behalf of MacLeod of Lewis, their main duty was to guard the Morrisons of northern Lewis from the depredations of the Macaulays of Uig. Perhaps the MacPhails used these shelters as a base to keep an eye on the Uig area, due east of here. Or they could have been built by those who came to the Flannans to harvest the birds or gather sheep.

More puffin burrows pitted the top of the hill above the old dwellings. Unlike the colony on Mingulay, these puffins were not inclined to be sociable. They would exit their burrows, see me sitting there, and then hurriedly take flight. I hoped that if I sat still for a while they would return, but they endlessly circled the hilltop waiting for me to leave.

The view beyond the circling birds was stunning. I was sitting atop the tip of a sea mount that protruded just a few hundred feet above

Bothan Clann M'Phail

the ocean. Two miles due west, three other tips of that same mountain broke through the surface of the sea. These were the most remote of the Seven Hunters, the isles of Roareim, Brona Cleit, and Eilean a Ghobha. The air above those rocky islets swarmed with thousands of sea-birds, and beyond them lay nothing but open sea. As it looked unlikely I would have any close encounters with the puffins, I made my way to the lighthouse, all the while thinking on the vanished keepers.

On that December day in 1900 three men disappeared: James Ducat, Thomas Marshall, and Donald McArthur. McArthur's coat and boots were found in the lighthouse, but Ducat's and Marshall's were gone. Could those two men have been out working when something happened? Did McArthur dash off to assist, knocking over his chair in the process? How did he know there was a problem? They had no portable radios in those days. But there had been that speaking tube between the landings and the lighthouse. Could someone have screamed for help into the tube? Or did McArthur, seeing a giant wave approaching the island, hurry down to warn the others, only to be washed away too? The most commonly accepted theory is that building air pressure in a wave-pounded sea cave near the west landing caused a blow-back of surf that swept the men from the platform.

I stood at the door of the seventy-five-foot-high lighthouse, 300 feet above the sea. It was here that Donald McArthur, presumed to be the last of the lost keepers, would have left the building. While standing there I got the notion to put myself in his place, and to find out what it would be like to make a hurried dash down to the west landing.

Somehow, you hear a call for help and rush out of the lighthouse. You follow the trolley track as it curves downhill around the chapel. At Charing Cross you continue straight ahead to follow the track down to the west landing. The track now starts to slope at a serious gradient as

The crane platform above the West Landing – crumbling trolley line at right

it turns to the right in its quick drop down the cliffs. As the going gets steeper you can follow the track along some adjacent cement steps. But now this present-day re-enactment has to slow down. You've reached a section where the steps, and part of the track, have crumbled away over the past hundred years.

If it was a stormy day, this is as far as you'd go. Today, however, is sunny and dry, so you slide down the crumbled track to the base of the trolley line. Behind it, two sets of hidden steps lead down to the crane platform. All that's left of the crane today is a rusty plate that once held it firm to the cement. As you stand on the open platform, the rusted fossils of old iron railings stand precariously between you and an eighty-foot drop to the sea, and in places the railing has entirely disappeared. Were Ducat and Marshall trying to secure the crane here when a wave washed one, or both, of them away? Today is a fine spring day, yet the surf is fierce, and the wind blows the spray up fifty feet. You wonder what this spot must be like in a winter storm.

But you're not done yet, for an even more exposed place waits below. A pathway once made its way from the crane down to the lower landing stage, but sections of it have crumbled away. So you backtrack halfway up the cliff to where another stairway branches off that leads down to the sea. Perhaps McArthur went this way, for it would be the most direct route from the lighthouse to the sea-washed platform of the west landing.

The white cement steps of the narrow stairway lead almost straight down. Its handrails are gone, and the iron posts that once held them are rusting away and bent at odd angles towards the sea. You round a blind drop with nothing but the churning surf visible below. Continuing on, you descend to within twenty feet of the sea. Then the white cement steps disappear, replaced by bare black bedrock. The sea has torn out the final stretch of steps. A hundred years ago those long-gone steps led all the way to the landing platform. But this is as far as you can

Jamie Barlow at the end of the steps above the West Landing

The West Landing

go today. The platform still lies forty feet away and, at the moment, is being scoured by the sea. Anyone attempting to continue on along this path to the surf battered landing will slide into the sea on the slick, black rock.

Standing at the ragged end of these steps above the sea we have to stop our little 'in the footsteps of' experiment, and think seriously about that day a century ago. There have been many strange theories tossed about: giant squids, pirates, and even murder or suicide. But now that you've seen in person how precarious a place the landing is on a relatively calm spring day, there's no doubt in your mind that on that December day in 1900, waves, possibly over a hundred feet high, could have easily swept away all three men.

Jamie, the ship's First Mate, had joined me at the dead-end of the steps above the West Landing, and we kept looking back at the crashing surf as we made our way up to the top of the island. At Charing Cross we turned right to follow the track back to the cliffs above the east landing, from where we descended the narrow cement stairs that zigzag down to the platform. We then watched as Rob motored up in the Zodiac. He nosed the inflatable into the ladder slot, and one-by-one we climbed down the rusty bars and slid into the boat.

We stood on deck for a while as *Poplar Diver* motored east towards Loch Roag, leaving the mystery of the missing light-keepers behind us.

We seemed to stand for an endless while, though still no word was said,
Three men alive on Flannan Isle, who thought on three men dead.

The Flannan Isles – WW Gibson

27: In Search of a Princess: Little Bernera

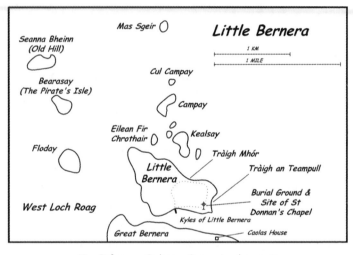

Map Reference: Ordnance Survey Landranger 13

In 1990 I stood on the shore of Great Bernera. The island of Little Bernera (Beàrnararaigh Bheag) lay a quarter mile away, but no one was at home in nearby Caolas House. I could not find anyone to ask, "Can you take me to Little Bernera?"

Ten years later I was on Uigen pier in west Lewis. Little Bernera sat five miles away on the other side of Loch Roag. I asked Murray MacLeod, who operated a speedboat service on the loch, if we could go there.

"No, it's too windy, but I can drop you on Pabay Mòr."

A year later I was again on Uigen pier.

"Murray, can we go to Little Bernera?"

"No, the sea's too rough. But I can drop you on Vacsay."

Another year passed. I was in the Minch enroute for North Rona on the ship *Poplar Diver*. Sea conditions were bad and Rona might be inaccessible. Instead of spending several hours in heavy seas, with little hope of landing, I suggested going around to Loch Roag and paying a visit to Little Bernera. But we decided to try for Rona. Little Bernera still patiently waited.

Another long twelve months passed by. I was on *Poplar Diver* again. After a visit to the Flannans we were motoring east to Loch Roag. As we neared the Pirate's Isle of Bearasay, Rob, the skipper, asked if I had a suggestion for a destination. Did I! Over a dozen years of waiting were about to end.

Little Bernera is 341 acres in total. It is separated from the island of Great Bernera by a narrow channel known as the Kyles of Little Bernera. Great Bernera itself is linked to the mainland of Lewis by a bridge built in the 1950s. So you can easily drive to Great Bernera and get within a quarter mile of the shores of Little Bernera. But as I'd found out so many times, that last quarter mile can be quite an obstacle.

Why did I want to visit Little Bernera so much? There were two reasons. The first was a book that put into words the intense attraction that I had come to have for the Hebrides. As with the characters in the book, my obsession with the isles started with a summer visit—long, lovely days that drew me back year after year. Then experiences in other less seasonable times of the year brought me to a more realistic and meaningful appreciation of a place 'so beautiful and so desolate at the same time.' The book is *A Princess of Thule*, written by William Black in 1873.

Black was born in Glasgow in 1841. He wrote over two dozen books, and in the 1870s his novels were immensely popular. In *A Princess of*

Thule the island princess, Sheila Mackenzie, is partly based on Isabella MacDonald of Great Bernera, which is referred to as the island of Borva in the novel. Black based the character of Old Mackenzie (Sheila's father—the King of Borva) on Isabella's father, John MacDonald. MacDonald was in the employ of Donald Munro, the chamberlain of Lewis, who was infamous for his failure to keep promises to the Bernera people as to their grazing rights on Lewis, which lead to the Bernera riots of 1874. The MacDonalds lived in Caolas House on the shores of the Kyles of Little Bernera. And their graves are above *Tràigh an Teampull*, temple strand, a small beach of white shell sand on (to quote Black again) 'the island where the burial ground is.' That island is Little Bernera.

In the novel, William Black also made use of the legend of Gealachos. During the early days of the Norse raids on the Hebrides, there lived on Little Bernera Gealachos, the daughter of the island priest. Her name meant Fairfoot, and her favourite place on the island was a knoll near St Donnan's Chapel above Temple Strand. She was kidnapped from there by Sweyn, king of the Norseman, and taken to Norway. Ensconced in Sweyn's great hall for seven years, she led a sad existence, resisting the king's persistent wooing. The king finally relented, returning her to Little Berneray to live out the rest of her life, which she devoted to helping the people of the island. To quote from the end of the story of Gealachos, as told in Donald Macdonald's *The Lews*:

> *She made merry with those that made merry, and visited the bereaved and mourned with those that mourned; and where there was illness she was there to lend a hand and help with the nursing, for she was a born nurse. She lived to a great age, and when she died she was taken and buried on the edge of the temple strand, where she sleeps so peacefully within sound of the waves which gave her such great pleasure in the happy days of her youth.*

In *A Princess of Thule* Black captures the tourist's love for the Hebrides, which anyone can feel during visits in the summer. On a holiday in Lewis the leading man of the novel, Frank Lavender, falls in love with Sheila Mackenzie, the island princess who *carries with her the mystery of the sea in the depths of her eyes; and the music of the far hills in her voice.* Lavender marries Sheila so as to take this summer idyll home with him, thinking that

> *she would appear in London as some wild plumaged bird, hailing from distant climes, and before she had lived there long enough to grow sad, and have the weight of the city clouding the brightness of her eyes, she would be spirited away again into this strange sea-kingdom, where there seemed to be perpetual sunshine, and the light music of the waves.*

But once she's in the city things go awry. I won't tell you more; you'll just have to read the book. The story was so popular, that, in 1882, L Frank Baum based his first play on it: *The Maid of Arran*. Baum would go on to write *The Wizard of Oz*.

The second reason I wanted to visit Little Bernera was to see what, if anything, remained of St Donnan's chapel. On Easter day in the year 617, St Donnan, along with over fifty followers, suffered the red martyrdom. In other words, they were murdered. These killings took place on Eigg, one-hundred miles south-east of Little Bernera. Donnan started his mission in Scotland around the year 580, and as a result of his work there are settlements called Kildonnan sprinkled all over mainland Scotland and the isles.

Never heard of St Donnan you say? Think again. His name is printed year after year on every Scottish pictorial calendar, and it shows up in most picture books of Scotland. St Donnan founded a church on a small island in Kintail, and on that site today sits the castle of Eilean Donan (St Donnan's isle), the most photographed castle in Scotland.

I live a long way from the Hebrides, yet I'm reminded weekly of St Donnan when a logo featuring the castle is flashed on the television prior to showings of BBC programmes.

After leaving the Flannans *Poplar Diver* anchored for the night in the Kyles of Little Bernera. In the morning we landed on the island at a small cement pier used for off-loading sheep. In a nearby cove stood the crumbling remains of an old stone jetty used when the island was inhabited, and above it sat the empty shells of several stone cottages. From there I made my way to the highest point of the island, which I reached after crossing the boggy floor of a small hidden glen, where fields of old lazy-beds rippled across the wet ground.

From the top of Little Bernera I could see its satellite islands dappling the waters of Loch Roag. There was tiny Harsgeir, flat Floday, the hump of Seanna Bheinn (the Old Hill), Campay, Kealasy, Eilean Fir Chrothair, and Bearasay. These last two are on my list of islands to visit someday, Eilean Fir Chrothair with its beehive cell, and rocky Bearasay, the Pirate's Isle. In the early seventeenth century, Neil MacLeod and forty of his followers had a stronghold on Bearasay. From this small cliff-girt isle they launched their raids against the 'Gentlemen Adventurers' foolishly sent to Lewis by James VI, the wisest fool, to 'civilise' the Outer Hebrides. They eventually caught Neil, and he ended his days swinging from an Edinburgh scaffold.

I crossed to the north-east coast and came to Tràigh Mhòr; Little Bernera's great beach, a long stretch of white sand rolled smooth by the receding tide. With the sand beneath it, and blue sky above, the sea was the colour of turquoise. A few minutes later, several of my fellow travellers from *Poplar Diver* were skinny-dipping there in the cold, languid water. After rounding the eastern tip of the island I came to a field of tombstones set above a small cove. On the far side of the burial ground stood what looked like a chapel, its walls intact, but with no roof. As I approached, it became clear it was not a ruin, but a burial

Tràigh Mhòr, Little Bernera

enclosure built to look like a chapel. In front of the enclosure lay the rectangular foundation of an old structure. Nothing had been built in its space, and no graves intruded on it. Centuries ago this may have been the site of St Donnan's chapel; its stones long since tumbled and carried away for other uses. I walked around the old church site, and when I looked over the four-foot wall of the burial chapel, I found the Princess.

In the novel there is a dream scene of her funeral:

They put the coffin in the stern of the boat; and in absolute silence, except for the wailing of the women, they pulled away down the dreary Loch Roag till they came to the island where the burial ground is. They carried the coffin up to the small enclosure, with its rank grass growing green, and the rain falling on the rude stones and memorials.

No rain fell, but rank grass was still growing green among the old tombstones. And Loch Roag looked anything but dreary as the sun glinted off the sea, the surrounding islands, and the distant headland of Aird Laimisiader.

There were three large memorials in the enclosure. The first, crowned with a six-foot-tall granite cross, marked the grave of Isabella MacDonald. The second marked the grave of her husband, Dr Roderick Ross, and the third her father and mother, John MacDonald and Catherine Stewart. The inscription on Isabella's tombstone read:

> IN LOVING MEMORY OF
> ISABELLA MᶜDONALD
> WIFE OF R. ROSS
> WHO DIED 27TH APRIL 1890
> AGED 43 YEARS
> NOBLE AMIABLE AND TRULY GOOD.
> HER LIFE WAS A SACRIFICE FOR OTHERS.
> DOING JUSTLY, LOVING MERCY AND WALKING
> HUMBLE WITH HER GOD.
> BLESSED ARE THE MEEK, THE MERCIFUL, THE PURE.

So there on this lonely little island, rarely visited, lay the grave of the Princess of Thule; at least that's the title Black's novel has bestowed on her memory. Hardly anyone reads Black's works today, so the occasional tourist who comes to Little Benera for a day on its beaches, its truly wonderful beaches, may notice the graves, but most will not know the story behind them.

Dr Ross, Isabella's husband, has his own place in island history. He was sent to North Rona in May of 1885 to perform a post-mortem on the bodies of Malcolm MacDonald and Murdo MacKay. These were the two men who, after a dispute with the Free Church minister in

The grave of Isabella MacDonald

Ness, had gone to Rona in a self-imposed exile. Less than a year after they arrived on Rona both men were found dead.

It was an enchanting spot—the little burial chapel set atop its knoll near where Donnan's church once stood, and where Gealachos 'sleeps so peacefully within sound of the waves.' Below it lay the walled burial ground, with a sprinkling of modern stones set amongst a hundred ancient ones. Some stood straight, many lay halfway tipped or completely fallen.

On the shore below the cemetery the gentle surf rolled into Temple Strand. It must be a very different place in the winter, for a reinforced stone wall had been built into the hill above the beach to prevent the sea from undermining the graveyard. I spent a tranquil hour in the enclosure trying to copy down the hard to read inscriptions on the MacDonald tombstones. The memorials have been worn by a century of Hebridean winters, and here and there splotches of gold and white lichen obliterated some of the deeply carved letters.

It was hard to turn my back on this spot I'd looked forward to seeing for so many years, but my time was up and I had to leave. Thirty minutes later we were all back aboard *Poplar Diver*. With the anchor raised the boat motored its way south through Loch Roag. At Callanish we went ashore to have a look at the stone circles; the crowd of visitors a stark contrast to the quiet morning on Little Bernera. We passed by the island again on our way out of Loch Roag, and I could see the granite cross rising above the Princess's grave. Once past the cliffs of the Pirate's Isle I watched as Little Bernera disappeared astern.

But there was still one more remote spot to visit, on yet another island, before I would complete this pilgrimage to a princess...

Three days later I was 130 miles away on the island of Mull driving the single-track road to Duart Castle. It was seven o'clock in the morning, so the castle would not be open. But I had not come to see the castle. Thousands of tourists visit Duart each year, but few, if any, pay a visit to what I was looking for.

I arrived at the castle's large car park. There were spaces for dozens of cars and buses, but as it was early mine was the only car there. I followed a path that led away from the castle towards the shore. The meagre track cut through fields of head-high bracken. The morning dew made for soggy going, so I had to stop and put on waterproofs to keep from getting soaked. Once through the rampant bracken I reached the short cliffs above the Sound of Mull. As I walked along the rocky headland two rusting barbed wire fences blocked the way, and I

The William Black Memorial Light

had to step out over the cliff edge to crawl around the end of each one in turn. After a half-hour of slow hiking I came to a stone tower set on a grassy shelf above the sea.

Duart means the black height, and here on this black height stands the William Black memorial light. This eighteen-foot-high circular light-tower was built in 1900, two years after Black died. With its parapets of grey stone it looks like a miniature castle. The adjoining stair tower is crowned with a conical cap that rises six feet above the parapets. There is an entrance door set in the base of the tower, and a black metal plaque lies embedded above it. The plaque has an engraving of a feather pen set amongst intertwined foliage, and the words:

263

TO THE DEAR MEMORY OF
WILLIAM BLACK
NOVELIST
ERECTED BY HIS FRIENDS
AND ADMIRERS IN MANY
LANDS ON A SPOT WHICH
HE KNEW AND LOVED

William Black brought romantic visions of the Western Isles to a generation in the nineteenth century. But he is now forgotten. It is unfortunate Black's memorial is in such an out-of-the-way spot. But, that said, it sits next to one of the most heavily-travelled tourist routes in Scotland. Just offshore a large, black MacBrayne's ferry, *The Isle of Mull*, sailed by. The boat bustled with hundreds of tourists on their way from Mull to Oban. I could see passengers on deck looking over to where I stood, and wondered what they were thinking about, seeing a

The burial ground at Tràigh an Teampull – MacDonald enclosure to the right

figure standing alone on this remote headland so early in the morning. I know what I was thinking about; Little Bernera, that day on its beaches, that day in search of a princess.

Postscript

Four years after my visit to Little Bernera I came across this description (TS Muir) of the chapels on Little Bernera:

> ...there is an open burying-ground, containing a few slabs, plain, but of ancient form; and elevated on a rocky mount, close by, are some remains of the ground-work and part of the east wall, of the chapel of St Michael. Part of another chapel—that probably mentioned by Martin as having been dedicated to St Donnan—was till not many years since standing on a lower part of the shore; of it no trace remains.

Portrait of Isabella MacDonald and her parents, c. 1860
Courtesy of Roderick MacLeod, grandson of Isabella

265

So, what I thought at the time was St Donnan's, had been a chapel dedicated to St Michael. That meant one thing, and it was a good thing. I needed to go back to Little Bernera to see for myself if no trace remained of the Chapel of St Donnan.

PART VII:

EXPEDITIONS TO NORTH RONA

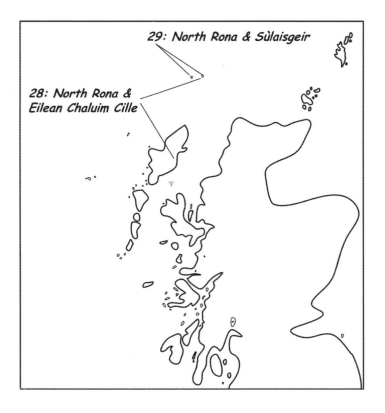

29: *North Rona & Sùlaisgeir*

28: *North Rona &*
Eilean Chaluim Cille

28: Inside Ronan's Cell

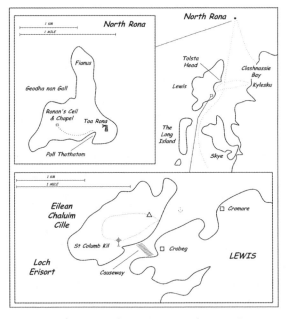

Map References: Ordnance Survey Landranger 8 & 14

Part 1: An Eilean Chaluim Cille Sabbath

SOMEONE was peeking out at me from behind a slightly skewed curtain. They obviously didn't approve of what I was doing, but I continued on to the graveyard anyway. I had a little island all to myself. But the nearby mainland village of Cromore lay just to the west, across a narrow arm of Loch Erisort. On that Sunday afternoon most of its residents were indoors, faithfully observing the Sabbath. Some were also observing me.

Sabbath aside, Cromore was once a bit busier than it is nowadays. A passenger ferry used to run across the mouth of Loch Erisort, passing the Barkin (birch) Islands as it made its way from Cromore to Crossbost, some two miles to the north. But these days, unless you have a boat, it's a twenty-five mile drive along curvy single-track roads to travel between the two villages.

I was on *Eilean Chaluim Cille*, the isle of St Columba, in the Lochs district of eastern Lewis. I didn't get there along those single-tracks, but by boat. I was halfway through a week long cruise aboard the ship *Poplar Diver*. She is a converted rescue boat, seventy feet long by eighteen wide. Her bread and butter trips involved taking National Trust work parties to St Kilda. But she occasionally made an island-hopping cruise like this one, and our main destination for the week was North Rona. We had just made our second crossing of the Minch, waiting for the weather to improve for a dash up to Rona, and I was in a bad mood. The sea snarled. Rona looked to be a lost cause.

We'd set out from Oban a few days earlier, with stops at Canna and the Shiants. On a sunny Canna day I'd followed a precarious sheep track down the cliffs to Sgòrr nam Bàn-naomha which, along with St Ronan's cell on North Rona, are the oldest Christian ruins in Scotland. That had severely whetted my appetite to get to Rona. But after leaving Canna the weather had deteriorated. Taking a respite from the rough seas we anchored in the sheltered waters near the mouth of Loch Erisort. It was an unforeseen bonus, finding myself so near the historic island of Eilean Chaluim Cille. So I asked to be set ashore to pay a visit to the ruins of St Columb Kil (NB 385 210).

Eilean Chaluim Cille was renowned for its fertility in the middle ages. Monks from Iona grew fruit on the island and, in 1549, it's said

MacLeod of Lewis had an orchard and market garden there. These days the island is used for grazing sheep, and from the boat I could see them munching away on the turf-clad remains of the old cultivation ridges that covered much of the island.

Once ashore I made my way down the east side of the island to St Columb Kil. The church looked to have been the centre of a good sized settlement in its day. Two large enclosures, several hundred feet in length, lay parallel to the shore, and between them an old track led down to the ruin of a jetty on the rocky beach. The eastern enclosure looked like it had been bombed, and in it were the slight remains of a building with only two walls standing. The western enclosure was more intact, and at its centre stood the ruin of St Columb Kil.

There is not much written about Eilean Chaluim Cille, though Donald MacDonald's *The Lews* does devote a short chapter to it. In it he mentions St Columb Kil was one of only two pre-reformation churches in this part of Lewis. It had never been a parish church, but was highly venerated, and a sought after place of sepulchre for the people who lived around Loch Erisort. The only description of the church I've come across is this from TS Muir's *Ecclesiological Notes*, where he describes the site as it was in the summer of 1855:

> *In a shockingly-conditioned burial-ground … is a not greatly ruinated chapel, dedicated to St Columba … with features much resembling those of the other Long Island chapels. The east elevation, which is nearly entire, contains a flat-headed window, 4 feet by six inches, and in the west gable there is a smaller one of the same shape. The south side contains a narrow lanciform window, and a broken doorway on its left; the north side is down to the ground nearly, except a bit at its west end.*

The north-east end of the enclosure wall was tumbled, and I stepped over it to enter the still shockingly-conditioned burial ground. The

The Church of St Columb Kill

east gable of the church had partially fallen, and in the south wall the lanciform window was still there, though probably more ruinated than in 1855.

Rising from a thicket of nettles, several stubby tombstones poked through the ground, both inside and outside of the church. One large tombstone, relatively modern, stood centre-stage; a dour, grey-stone monument, its top clad with a thick growth of moss. Most of its lettering was worn and lichen-stained, so that, sadly, I could not read the name. Even sadder was that St Colum's Church is just one more example of island history rotting away, falling apart, stone by stone.

I left the church enclosure and wandered through the island's interior. Reaching the highest point I waved over to *Poplar Diver* to let them know I was ready to be picked up. The high ground was heathery scrub, but the low ground was a fertile greensward, where monks once tended fruit trees. Those monks would not appreciate it here today, for

272

the island is criss-crossed with a matrix of taut barb-wire fences, not a single stile in sight.

Once I was back aboard *Poplar Diver* the ship's engines were fired up, breaking the Sunday quiet, and we motored away from sleepy Loch Erisort. Hopefully we would find a good anchorage for the night and, if the next day dawned well, make one last attempt to reach North Rona. If it dawned not so well, we'd have to retreat to Oban in defeat.

Note: If you want to visit Eilean Chaluim Cille you won't need a boat. A gravel causeway now connects it to the mainland. So put on some sturdy boots, make your way to road's end at Crobeg, then wander across the stony track to see what's left of St Columb Kil.

Part 2: Into Ronan's Cell

We anchored that night south of Tolsta Head. The forecast the next morning was grim, more of the same stiff wind we'd put up with all week. Should we try for Rona, or go somewhere else? That was the question on everyone's minds. After breakfast we started motoring towards Rona, leaving the decision until we got a feel for the sea to the north.

The Minch was heaving off Tolsta Head when we took a vote. The results were evenly divided. Half were for steaming fifty miles through rough seas to attempt an improbable landing. The other half, including myself, thought it would be best to look for a more certain landfall, possibly in the sheltered waters of Loch Roag on the other side of Lewis. I was surprised I felt this way, for Rona has been such a desire for so long. But I could always try again to see her. And a day ashore on somewhere like Little Bernera sounded much better than enduring several hours of heavy seas, only to glimpse Rona and not land.

The vote being so close, the decision was made to try for Rona. We passed Cellar Head, where I spotted the roofless remains of Dune Tower and its deserted chapel sitting high on the headland. A few minutes later the Dougal monument atop the cliffs of Meall Geal stood out against the skyline, and then the sight of the Butt of Lewis lighthouse announced we were in the open sea. Surprisingly, conditions actually improved. And, after several hours of ploughing north through rolling swells, the 350-foot-high hump of Toa Rona appeared low on the horizon.

Three miles out from the island a dark spot on the west side of Rona started to appear: the village ruins. We closed in on the cliffs at *Geodha nan Gall*, the Cove of the Strangers, just below the village, where the heavy swell boded ill for landing. From there we went around the northern tip of the island to check out another landing place on the Fianuis peninsula. But the surf there would swamp anyone attempting to get ashore. Heading south we rounded Toa Rona, the modern lighthouse on its summit looking as out of place as the generator tower and assorted blights on St Kilda. By now we'd nearly circumnavigated the island, and had yet to find a safe landing place.

Our last chance came as we pulled into Poll Thothatom on the south-east side of the island. The narrow gut of the inlet looked promising, and so we loaded into the inflatable and motored towards the shore. A landing looked possible—the swell was minimal, and the only obstacles a few seals calmly eyeing us near the rocks. But it wasn't going to work. Perpendicular cliffs completely surrounded the little inlet and, even though we could get onto the rocks, we'd be trapped there.

Back aboard *Poplar Diver* I was in a funk, all hope of getting ashore had vanished. Then Rob Barlow, the Skipper, decided to have one more look see. So, once again, we piled into the inflatable and headed back to the shore. A rock shelf at sea level was spotted. Between swells Rob nosed the inflatable in, and one at a time we jumped on to the barnacled rocks. (Thank you, Rob!)

We were ashore, but time was short. The weather was ominous, and having spent the better part of the day getting this far we had just an hour before we needed to be steaming towards a sheltered anchorage for the night. There was no way to see everything I'd been planning on seeing for so many years.

My God, how I wanted to climb to the top of Toa Rona, how I wanted to cross over the ridge and see Tunnel cave, how I wanted to walk out to the tip of Fianuis and do some seal watching. But I'd have to save all those for next time, because most of all I wanted to crawl into St Ronan's Cell.

Passing the sites of several stone covered wells I made my way along the southern cliffs towards the village. The first sign I was near it were immense fields of lazy-beds. Then the stones of the chapel and cell appeared, and I was there. In the burial ground to the west of the chapel, crusted with lichen and precariously leaning at a forty-degree

St Ronan's Cell

Entrance to St Ronan's Cell

Inside St Ronan's Cell

angle, was the only modern marker. Now sadly illegible, this is the memorial stone to Malcolm MacDonald and Murdo MacKay who died here in strange circumstances in 1885.

Time check: thirty minutes left. The first order of business was to recreate an 1887 photo, possibly the first one of the site. The photo shows the naturalist JA Harvie-Brown reclining on the turf of the burial ground next to the chapel. In the foreground of this old photo you can see the three-holed Rona cross, which has since been removed from the island and is now in the Ness Historical Society Museum. The cross has the figure of a man carved on one side, and the holes pierce his throat and armpits. No one knows why the cross was holed, but the stone may have connections to the sheela-na-gigs, for on its shaft is carved an exaggerated phallus.

In the 1887 photo the chapel is in fairly good condition. But though extensive re-building had been done in the 1930s it is now in sad shape, as most of the western wall has collapsed. I was in too much of a hurry to take the time to find a position where I could place the camera to take in both the chapel and myself reclining on the ground like Harvie-Brown. So I settled for a self-portrait standing on the same spot.

Time check: twenty minutes left. Low down in the east wall of the chapel was the entrance to St Ronan's Cell. Several inches of sheep-muck covered the ground, and as the portal is only three feet high you have to squat down and either waddle in on your feet like a penguin, or crawl in on all fours through the slime. By now Andy Parrot had joined me, one of my fellow passengers, and we both choose the waddling method.

Everything I'd read said fulmars would be nesting inside, just waiting to spew. But we found the cell deserted. The interior was spacious, most of it lying below ground level. A small aperture above the entrance lit the stone roof eight feet above, and the meagre remnants of an altar lay at ground level against the east wall. How old was this thing? I'd read the chapel building is something like 800 years old, but the original cell…? How old would *it* be? Maybe 1200 years?

We waddled back out of the cell. Our time had run out. We'd spent only thirty minutes in the village. We could have used a week. We hurried back over the lazy-beds, along the cliffs to Poll Thothatom, and then scrambled down the rocks to the shore. At the landing we came upon a sad seal, still able to move about, but entwined in a tight loop of fishing line cutting into its skin, a permanent torture. We tried to get close, thinking to grab it and cut the line. But it was not to be. The seal slid into the sea when we approached.

One at a time we reversed the landing procedure, and in quick order we were all soon back aboard. The weather was indeed getting worse as we started our way south to find safe harbour in Clashnessie Bay. I'd had only an hour ashore, but what an hour it was.

29: Return to Rona and Afloat off Sùlaisgeir

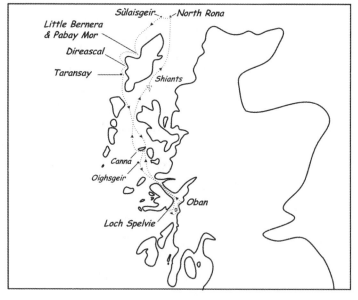

Map References: Ordnance Survey Landranger 8, 13, 14

IN THE last chapter I wrote about a rushed, hour long visit to North Rona, and all that I'd do on a future visit when I had more time. Nine years later, on the first day of the summer of 2011, I set off for Rona again aboard the ship *Hjalmar Bjørge*.

We left Oban with nine passengers, and one dog aboard. Seven (the ship's dog) has been on more islands than many an island-bagger. And as we set out, other than what was for dinner, Seven and I had one thing on our minds. Would we be able to land on Rona? The odds were against us, for the wind and sea must be calm to get ashore on that island, forty miles north of the Butt of Lewis. To help even those odds the cruise was ten days long, which would allow us to wait for a break in the weather, if needed.

Our first night was a calm anchorage in Canna's Tarbert Bay. The following morning, as we cleared the north of Skye, a strong westerly started to blow, and it continued to blow as we approached the Shiants. The usual anchorage between the islands would be untenable. So we anchored off the west side of Garbh Eilean and spent a few hours on the island; exploring the Bronze Age roundhouse ruin at Annat, and climbing *Glaic na Crotha* (cattle hollow) to the summit, where we were rewarded with a view over the Minch. Verdant Eilean Mhuire, with its large puffin colony, lay a half mile to the east; due south was Rubha Hunis, the northern tip of Skye, and just beyond it lay South Rona. But there was no sign of that other Rona, the one we were headed for, ninety miles to the north.

The next morning, as we motored past the Butt of Lewis the sea-state worsened and the ship had to plough her way through large swells that occasionally broke over the bow. On nearing Rona we saw that the only possible landing place would be Poll Thothatom, on the south-east side of the island.

Then, unbelievably, the sea calmed, the sun came out, and we were blessed with a true summer day. The inflatable was lowered, and our skipper, Mark Henrys, guided it into that same cleft in the rock where I'd landed nine years before. Once ashore, we climbed a steep hill to the lush blanket of grass that covers the south half of the island.

St Ronan's Cell and Chapel

My first destination was the village, as I wanted to see if it had changed since my last visit. As I walked towards it I was attacked. A sudden whoosh overhead, and then a sharp *kark-kark*, as a pair of bonxies started a series of strafing runs, trying their best to get a piece of my scalp. Their attacks ceased as I neared the village.

Rona village has some of the most amazing ruins in the Hebrides. At times, upwards of 30 people lived here, surviving off the birds, seals, and the island's seventeen arable acres. The entire population starved to death at least once. In the 1800s only six acres were under cultivation, and the last permanent residents left in 1839.

Getting down on all fours I crawled into the 1200 year-old St Ronan's cell, which Fraser Darling rightly called the Heart of the Island. A fulmar was nesting inside, and I carefully stood as far from it as possible. Then I noticed something wonderful I'd missed on my

Crosses inside St Ronan's Cell

Fulmar nesting next to the altar in St Ronan's Cell

rushed visit all those years ago. Propped against the wall were three beautiful stone crosses, each a foot high.

One of the crosses did not look like a tombstone, and may have once been mounted near the altar. The fulmar was nesting snuggly against the altar, and if it hadn't been there I'd have stayed longer in this, the inner sanctum of the Hebrides. But the fulmar was getting nervous, turning in circles and occasionally jabbing its beak at me. Not wanting to get spat on, I crawled back out.

West of the burial ground I came to the house where Murdo MacKay and Malcolm MacDonald died in 1885; less than a year after they had come to live on Rona. I stood at the doorway where they discovered Malcolm lying dead on his side, then walked inside the roofless ruin to where Murdo had been found dead, covered with a tartan plaid. The authorities suspected foul play, and three months later an autopsy was performed here on Rona. The following is an abridged extract from the autopsy report Michael Robson includes in *A Sad Tale of the Sea*:

> *During a snow storm McKay is taken ill of an attack of inflammation. McDonald attends his companion, and likely enough wants his regular sleep and meals. But other responsibilities force him to face the storm, perhaps seeing to the sheep. On his return he finds his companion dead. He removes the body from the bed, for it must be laid out and washed. He takes a jug to fetch water … Once beyond the door he sits down to collect his thoughts. Sadness and the want of sleep induce him to lie down … Sleep creeps on, he becomes benumbed and expires.*

What a sad tale indeed. Except for a tilted tombstone there is no sign of the men's presence. I tried to read the stone's inscription. But over a hundred years of winter storms had taken their toll, and only a few letters were legible.

MacKay & MacDonald tombstone, Sùlaisgeir in the distance

After paying my respects to those men, and the generations that lived and sometimes starved on Rona, I climbed to the central ridge of the island. How I wish I could have seen what Fraser Darling saw up there in the winter, seals lounging 200 feet above the sea. I then descended to Fianuis, the narrow peninsula at the north of the island and walked to a sheep fank near the tunnel cave that penetrates halfway through the peninsula.

Fraser Darling and his family lived near here to study seals in the late 1930s. Darling estimated there were 5000 seals, but now, in summer, not a single one was hauled out on the low, rocky ground. I walked over that ground to sit for a while at the northern Land's End of the Western Isles. Next stop, the Faeroes, 160 miles over the horizon.

With an hour left I started back up the ridge. No Bonxies attacked, and neither did I have the distraction that tempted St Ronan. While

Tunnel Cave

climbing this ridge with Saint Brianuil, Ronan said to her "What beautiful legs you have." Brianuil decided isolation was taking its toll, so she packed up and moved to Sùlaisgeir.

I sat on an odd knoll that rises from the ridge. Its name is *Sìthean a Croer*, which may mean the hillock of the cattle fold. And as I basked in the sun, I cracked open a beer to celebrate the privilege of having so much time on Rona. (As you may have guessed by now, one of my loftier goals is to have a beer on every Scottish island.)

Only ten minutes of that time was left, and I had not yet climbed Toa Rona, the top of the island. If I rushed I could make it, but I did not want to rush. I wanted to savour what might be my last minutes on the island. Toa Rona could wait for another visit. After finishing the beer I held a fist in the air to ward off the bonxies and then started down to the landing.

Toa Rona seen from Fianuis – the hump of Sìthean a Croer at right

The next visit came much sooner than expected—the very next day. After spending the night anchored off Rona, we awoke to calm seas and went ashore again. I climbed Toa Rona, bonxies chasing me up its grassy slopes to the top. Standing at the summit cairn I tried to blot out the sight of the lighthouse built in 1984, and revelled in the isolation. We were completely surrounded by sea, the only visible land the low double hump of Sùlaisgeir, 10 miles west.

A lazy hour was then spent on the west end at Caolas Lòba Sgeir, where the antiquarian T S Muir camped in 1860. I felt a connection to Mr. Muir, for his first visit to Rona had also been an hour long, and it took him several years to return. Through binoculars a snowstorm of gannets could be seen soaring over Sùlaisgeir, where I hoped we'd be shortly. I then took a seat atop Sìthean a Croer to savour my last few minutes watching bonxies, and the island.

286

Postscript: Sùlaisgeir and Return to Little Bernera

After leaving Rona we floated for over an hour off Sùlaisgeir, staring up in awe as gannets avalanched off the cliffs and soared overhead. We also saw the cairns built by the men of Ness, who come here to catch the guga, the young gannets. One large cairn stood out from the rest, said to mark where St Brianuil (of the shapely legs) died. The day was getting on, so we reluctantly throttled up and headed south. We had seven days left to explore the Hebrides. During those days we did some memorable things: going ashore on Pabay Mòr, Taransay, Canna, and the south shore of Loch Reasort to walk the most remote path in the Hebrides, the Scholar's Road from Direscal to Luachair.

We also spent an afternoon on Little Bernera, which gave me a chance to make good on that promise I'd made eight years before to

Cairns of the men of Ness on Sùlaisgeir

return (see chapter 27). I wanted to find out if, as TS Muir reported in 1859, that no trace remained of St Donnan's Chapel.

He was wrong. Lying on a narrow neck of land, just below the MacDonald burial enclosure, I found the rectangular outline of a structure pushing up at the turf. It had to be the remnants of St Donnan's. Someone had gone to great effort to preserve the site, for the base of the little promontory had been reinforced with cement to protect it from the battering surf.

I had the burial ground all to myself. No birdsong, no voices, only the gentle surf breaking the silence of the sea. Little Bernera is a thin place, so I was not truly alone. I had the company of Gealachos and the Princess of Thule, who both sleep there peacefully within sound of the waves.

Sron na Lice, the south-west tip of Sùlaisgeir

PART VIII:

TIME TRAVELLING THROUGH THE ISLES

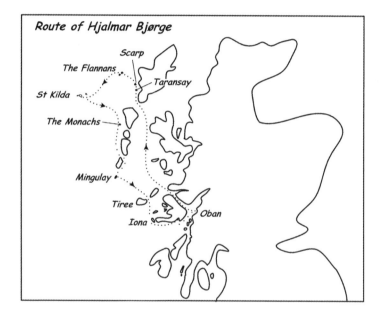

Route of Hjalmar Bjørge

Scarp

The Flannans

Taransay

St Kilda

The Monachs

Mingulay

Tiree

Oban

Iona

Map References: Ordnance Survey Landranger 13, 18, 22, 31, 48

30: Once Round the Hebrides

When continually feasting on goodies, what do you save for last? That was the dilemma I faced while putting together these island stories. Which island should I end with? The more I thought about it, the harder the choice became. So I decided to be lazy. I decided to make another pass by the entire dessert table. And as for that last island, I wouldn't pick it, I'd let *it* pick *me*.

For several years in a row I'd gone on one of the small-boat cruises offered by Northern Light Charters. One of their regular offerings was exactly what I wanted. Departing from Oban, it went to Kilda via Scarp and the Flannans, and then returned via the Shiant Isles. This itinerary would take me past two dozen old island friends, and with Scarp I'd make a new acquaintance. So on a dark, January morning, I booked the trip, getting the last available berth. Then came the hard part: seven months of waiting.

Day 1: To Tobermory

Oban, on the first Saturday in August, was hot, muggy, and packed with tourists. Railway Quay was in chaos, Caledonian MacBrayne in the process of expanding their ferry terminal. I'd left my hire car parked next to a garage, dropping the keys through a letterbox with hopes the car would be there when I returned in a week. With a heavy pack slung over my shoulders, and dragging a suitcase behind, I marched through Oban's busy streets to the waterfront. I was lucky to have the suitcase, for the trip had gotten off to a bad start: British Airways had lost my luggage in the bowels of Heathrow Airport. For three days I'd lived in borrowed clothing. Fortunately, my bags finally showed up—six hours before the boat departed.

I found *Hjalmar Bjørge* tied up at Railway Quay. Built in 1963, she served for thirty-three years as a rescue ship for the Norwegian fishing fleet. Seventy-five feet long, and twenty wide, this ninety-ton powerhouse was the belle of the quay. With her navy blue hull, and her name proudly emblazoned in bold chrome letters on her large wheelhouse, she drew an appreciative eye from every passerby. With a capacity of over 5000 gallons of fuel she can travel 3000 sea miles, crossing an ocean if needed. Northern Light acquired her in 2002, making several alterations so she could carry twelve passengers in comfort. The correct pronunciation of her name is something like *Yal-muh Be-yor-gay*, which is a bit cumbersome, so she's often called *Hal-muh George*.

Hjalmar Bjørge is owned by Hannah Thompson and Mark Henrys, who together operate Northern Light Charters. Mark would be skipper for our week long outing, and the other crew members were Rachel and Heather. Heather had been cook on my trip to North Rona aboard *Poplar Diver*, so I knew we'd be in for some good food. It took an hour to load the dozen passengers and their gear. I met my cabin-mate for the trip, Roy; and then one by one, the other passengers: Joe and Diane, Susan and Hugh, Pippa, Rosemary, Felicity, Isabel, Bill, and John. Most had been drawn to this trip for the opportunity to see wildlife and visit St Kilda. None had as bad a case of Island Madness as I did, though Bill Coull and John McCallum came close. They had tried to get to the Flannan Isles the year before, hoping to see the location of Scotland's most intriguing island mystery. But rough seas had bounced the passengers around so much they'd had to turn back. They were trying again to see an island that had eluded them, a situation I was all too familiar with.

At 5pm Rachel untied the mooring lines from the quay, and we set out for the thirty mile cruise to Tobermory. We tied up to a mooring buoy in the yacht-filled harbour, and during dinner we thought the setting sun was playing tricks, when we saw a pink-winged gull flying around the bay. But the bird was indeed pink, someone having coloured its wings with a permanent marker. Cruel, but it didn't bother the gull. In fact, it seemed to exude an air of superiority as it soared above its lesser coloured companions.

From there on the week's itinerary would be free form. Weather would be the driving force. We'd have to go with the flow, landing when we could, observing from afar when we couldn't. I was counting on the cruise offering up a few surprises. Little did I know I'd set foot on three totally unexpected islands.

Day 2: Return to Taransay

We set off early Sunday, having breakfast while motoring past Bloody Bay. As the lighthouse tower on the Point of Ardnamurchan passed to starboard, the small isles of Rum, Eigg, and Muck came into view. We could see Eigg's south coast and, as we continued north, Muck slowly eclipsed the site of Massacre Cave.

Next came Canna, its southern cliffs outlined in the hazy horizon; cliffs where a narrow sheep track will lead you down to the nunnery cashel and its bathhouse sunk in the cliffs. Following the Skye coast to the north we crossed the Little Minch and entered the Sound of Harris. To port lay Berneray of the beaches. It hid from view the island of Vallay, and I wondered if Erskine Beveridge's old mansion still lay there rotting away. Ensay passed by; Ensay House and its sea-gate standing above their small sandy bay. My day there had been one of discovery. I'd been given the key to the chapel of Christ Church, and found dune covered Manish Chapel on the island's northern shore.

Then the first surprise of the trip occurred. We'd had a long day at sea, so a bit of shore leave was due. Mark anchored *Hjalmar Bjørge* in a lagoon well known to me, and in short order we were afoot on Taransay. I had one thing on my mind, and that was to get a decent photo of St Taran's cross. Not one of the dozen I'd taken in the past measured up to Seton Gordon's picture of it in *Afoot In Wild Places*, a photo that had sparked much of my interest in these far off isles.

We landed a stones-throw east of the cross and I made my way to the lone croft house-cum-bothy above the shore. From there I could see St Taran's cross perched on the hillside. Reaching the stone, I walked around to the side with the cross and stopped, astounded. On my previous visits the cross had faded into stone still recovering from a wet winter. Now, in mid-summer, the cross shouted out of the sun-bleached rock. It looked as if it had been carved yesterday, not centuries ago. When I saw the developed photos two weeks later I would be stunned again. The cross had been captured in all its glory, and almost as well as Seton Gordon had done seventy years before.

From the cross I climbed to the interior of the island to pay a return visit to Loch an Dùin. The clank of the rattle stone sounded underfoot as I crossed the causeway to the fort. It was still an overgrown, ankle twisting, hodge-podge of stones, and I lingered for a while to enjoy the solitude. In the hot, still air, no midges were about. But something impressive was; for a forest of antlers stippled the skyline to the north. A dozen deer stood frozen in their tracks high on the ridge, spying down on this intruder in their midst. I held my breath and returned their gaze. As soon as I exhaled they scattered, and I watched as a string of antlers sank below the ridge.

With ten minutes of shore leave left I headed back to the beach, reaching it just as Rachel approached in the inflatable. With all of us back aboard *Hjalmar Bjørge* we crossed the sound to anchor for the night off the strand of Tràigh Rosamol on the Harris coast.

St Taran's Cross

As dusk approached, the dark hills to the north took on an impenetrable look, jealously guarding their secret. For eight miles away, set in a loch in the deserted Harris interior, lies The Island that Likes to be Visited: The Isle of Mary Rose. It is a place I'll remember forever. A place where you can sit on a fairy knoll, the portal to Tìr nan Òg, and listen to the silence of the hills.

Day 3: Scarp and the Flannans

Early Monday we landed on Scarp. As I ventured into its derelict church a sudden racket disturbed the quiet morning. The musty pews were occupied, not by worshippers, but by several scraggly sheep. They had been asleep, and my intrusion sent them into a panic. I was blocking the only way out, and the frightened animals ran pew-to-pew, seeking escape. Backing out the door I let then make a dash for freedom.

In 1881 over 200 people called Scarp home. By 1971 the population had dwindled to seven. The island's moment of fame came in 1934, when Gerhard Zucker experimented with rocket powered mail delivery. After the fuse was lit, instead of shooting 1000 feet across the channel to Harris, the rocket exploded. The mail got a little charred.

I walked through the church. Its floorboards, those still in place, were half rotted. An open bible lay perched atop the raised pulpit. Unfortunately my fleecy congregation had fled so there was no one to read to. (The church was restored as a residence several years after my visit.)

I explored the abandoned schoolhouse next—but only after repeating the sheep clearing process. Before leaving the village I wandered around the cemetery, a grassy mound with a mix of modern stones and old slabs with no inscriptions. One of the newer stones marked the grave of Angus MacDonald, a minister born on Scarp in 1877. He died in 1959, a dozen years before the last permanent inhabitant left. His memorial is one we should all hope for:

Chòmhraig mi an deaghchòmhrag,
Chrìochnaich mi mo thurus,
Ghléidh mi an creidimh

I have fought the good fight,
I have finished my journey,
I have kept the faith

Walking west I came across the strangest sight in the village. Next to what had been the shop stood a faded, red phone-box. It had been a while since anyone made a call, as the door lay off its hinges, the phone was gone, and a nesting bird flew out as I poked my head in to take a look.

To get a view of the entire village I climbed to the summit of 587-foot-high Beinn fo Thuath, and as I reached the top several sea-lochs came into view. Loch Reasort could be seen three miles away on Harris. At its mouth, on the Aird Mhòr peninsula, sat the ruin of the twelve-chambered beehive dwelling. A wonderful place to camp— provided you're up to a twenty-mile hike through the Lewis hinterland. To the north of Resort opened the mouth of Loch Tamnavay. If you want to experience a nearness to a long departed way of life, spend a night there in the deserted clachan of Aird Bheag. Where, while sleeping next to roofless black houses and a forgotten walled garden, you'll be serenaded by barking deer, and awakened by cuckoo birds.

After all the hurried climbing I needed 'a wink on mother knee.' So I walked down to the shore to take a snooze on the grassy hillside.

Looking north from above Scarp village

Five seconds after closing my eyes my scalp started tingling. My face and arms did likewise. I breathed in, tasting something unpleasant. I opened my eyes to see the air filled with thousands of midges battling over every bit of exposed skin. On went the repellent, on went the assault. Swatting like a mad-man I finally found relief atop a bit of high ground, where a slight breeze kept the beasts at bay.

An ambitious day of travel lay ahead. After our morning on Scarp we were going to visit the Flannan Isles en-route to St Kilda. The Flannans lay thirty miles to the north-west and, after two hours of sea travel, the flotilla of small islands came into view. I had hoped to get ashore on *Eilean Tighe* (House Island), to see the ruins of its two stone dwellings. But it was not to be.

It is not until you get past Eilean Tighe that the east landing on the lighthouse island of Eilean Mòr comes into view. What we saw there was not good. A heavy swell pounded both the landing, and the rocky shore of Eilean Tighe. Landing on either would be impossible. We circled round to the infamous west landing, where the light-keepers may have been swept away in 1900. The swell was higher there, and we could see the ragged end of the washed away steps, a dead-end that had stopped my intended descent to the landing stage the year before. As we bounced around on the swell I took a photo of Bill and John, thumbs up and smiling, their dream of seeing the Flannans close-up fulfilled.

After leaving Eilean Mòr we passed the farthest of The Seven Hunters, the islands of Eilean a Ghobha and Roareim, and then motored west into open sea.

Day 4: A Second Voyage to St Kilda

It seemed as if it had been yesterday, and not five years, since I'd last stood in the village on Kilda. Everything looked the same; the only difference was that Warden Andy had been replaced by Warden Natalie.

No, Kilda is not a prison—the only thing locked up is the pub. After being welcomed by the National Trust Warden, who warned us not to wear waterproofs on the steep grassy hillsides—standard advice to all visitors—we were free to wander. On my first visit I'd camped in a field above the Puff Inn (the island pub) and had spent most my time hiking the hills. This time I would do something different, a house-by-house tour of the village.

I started near the cannon that had been installed in 1918, after a German submarine shelled the island's radio transmitter. The sharp-eyed Kildans had been excellent sub-spotters, and the Germans knew it. From there I followed the old main street west to the village, a collection of old black houses set between 'modern' white houses built in the 1860s. I wandered into each dwelling, one by one, reading in David Quine's guide book about who had lived there, trying to imagine what each house would have looked like back then.

After an hour I reached house 5, where I lingered for a while. This had been the heart of the village. The last residents were Annie and Neil Ferguson. Neil was the island's last Postmaster, and the Post Office had been a tin shack adjacent to his home. There were two old photos taken here I wanted to recreate as best I could. The first was Alasdair Alpin MacGregor's picture of Neil Ferguson, mailbag slung over his shoulders, entering the post office for the last time on August 27, 1930.

The post office is gone; the space where it had sat is now a small grassy area, a foot or two above the level of the street. But the stone steps that once led up to it were still there, steps that Ferguson is standing on in the photo. I stood on the spot where he'd posed seventy-four years ago just as my camera, perched twenty feet away, flashed.

Nearby lay the site of another famous picture, AM Cockburn's image of the St Kilda Parliament in session. The Kildans would meet to plan the day's activities, and the photo shows fourteen men, a boy, and several dogs gathered along Main Street. Some of the dogs in that picture were probably among those intentionally drowned when they evacuated the island a few years later. I tried to recreate that picture, too. Other than the fact that the National Trust had re-roofed the houses, the buildings have not changed in eighty years. The hills in the background were the same. But there was one big difference. My picture had no sign of life.

At the end of the village I hiked up to the site of the medieval settlement, which had been occupied until the black houses were built in the 1830s. I penguin-waddled into the low dark entrance of *Taigh an t-Sìthiche*, the house of the faeries, one of the oldest structures on the island, and then continued uphill. Dozens of stone cleits and beehive cells dotted the area, Soay sheep lounging atop the ones topped with turf. Above the head dyke I passed several small springs. I paused to taste the water from one of them, Tobar Kilda, its mouth protected by stones embedded in the surrounding turf.

Where Parliament sat

From Tobar Kilda I started the climb to the Gap, the cliff-saddle between the hills of Oiseval and Connachair. Bonxies attacked as I passed the large elegant stone enclosures in An Lag, the big birds swooping down from behind. I raised one fist in the air (I might have also raised a finger) and walked on. Six hundred feet above the sea I reached the cliffs that face out to Boreray, where fulmars surfed on the air currents sweeping over the Gap.

I had hoped to climb Oiseval. But that goal was thwarted when a thick mist blew in to hide its top. So it was time for plan B: to stand atop the Lover's Stone. The stone protrudes from the south cliffs of the island and, as I neared it, the swirling mist struck again. With visibility reduced to three feet, and since it's an 850-foot sheer drop from the stone to the sea, I decided to leave climbing it for another time. Still in the mood to climb, I headed over to Ruaival, a lower hill at the south tip of the island.

It started to rain as I boulder hopped up Ruaival. Its summit is a large sloping table top rock that was slick with water, so I didn't stay long. Living in the past, I then repeated something I'd done before, and made my way over to the weirdly propped Mistress Stone. It, too, was a slippery seat. So instead of dancing on it to impress any nearby maidens, I slid down the slick stone gully underneath it and started back to the village.

The walk there took me across some of Kilda's steep grassy slopes, where I'd been warned, two times now, not to wear waterproofs. But with the rain coming down in buckets, I kept them on. That was a mistake. I slipped and started to slide on the grass. A level bit of sheep track halted my unintended descent after a few feet. So off came the overtrousers and I continued on, getting wetter with every step.

I met up with the others in the village. We were all soaked, but because the Puff Inn didn't open until half-four, there was no place to dry off. Finally, someone took pity, unlocked the door of the pub, and turned on the electric fire. We were shown to a large drying room, where coats, gloves, and hats were left hanging on a large complex of hot pipes. Back in the silent pub, the well stocked bar securely locked behind a metal curtain, we gathered around the heater to warm up. Then, a half hour later, the strangest moment of the trip occurred. The same fellow who'd let us in earlier came back. He rolled up the steel curtain—the bar was now open for happy hour—and turned on a large television.

Sitting in a pub on one of the farthest Hebrides, double whiskies in hand, bare toes warming in front of the heater, we watched football for an hour. You have to buy a double at happy hour, as they don't sell singles. But the large drink cost just ninety-four pence. For tax reasons the Puff Inn could not make a profit, so it offered the cheapest booze in the UK. At half-five the steel cage clattered back down, happy hour was over, and we made our way back to the ship. (Note: The Puff Inn is no longer open to the public.)

Then the passengers mutinied. Our tentative itinerary was to return east through the Sound of Harris and pay a visit to the Shiant Isles. But there were not so quiet mutterings of "Monachs, Mingulay—Monachs, Mingulay" coming from several quarters, mainly John. Now a visit to the Monach isle of Ceann Ear was something I'd wanted for many years. Mingulay, too, would be a bonus. On my one previous visit I'd not had time to climb to its summit. As the weather boded well for landing on both, I added my voice to the mutinous chorus: "Monachs, Mingulay—Monachs, Mingulay." No dissenting voices sung out. So, in the words of the Mingulay Boat Song: 'Hill you ho boys, let her go boys, we're heading to Mingulay'.

Day 5: To the Monach Isles, where the Monks of old
Dug a tunnel to the nunnery (or so I was told)

The following morning we left Village Bay and started a clockwise circumnavigation of St Kilda. As we passed below the southern cliffs we could see the Lover's Stone protruding high above. Then Mark took the ship through the narrow channel between Hirta and Soay, almost touching the arch of Soay Stac.

We then nosed into Glen Bay, on the north side of the island, and steamed towards the mouth of tunnel cave. From my vantage point atop the flying bridge I could see the sloping ledge that leads down the cliff face. Once we were in position to look through the cave, memories came flooding back; memories of sliding down the slippery end of that ledge while hanging on to a rope; memories of stepping past tide pools to the tunnel's far end to find a view of Boreray and its attendant stacks.

Tunnel Cave seen from the sea

Mark turned the ship about and we then crossed four miles of sea to the stacks. Ten feet from the vertical side of 564-foot-high Stack Lee the engines were throttled back, and Rachel and Roy dropped their fishing lines into the water—a steady rain of guano made it a perfect fishing hole. Roy's unbaited triple-hooked line had been in for only a minute when he pulled out two pollacks and a mackerel. Roy dropped his line in again just as Rachel hooked a pollack, and in the blink of an eye pulled out another full haul. After fifteen minutes of fishing they called it quits—having caught enough for the nights' fish pie. (But oh how I hate fish pie!) Mark throttled the engines up and we motored past Boreray, its small patch of stone shelters clinging to a precipice 750 feet above the sea.

From there it was forty miles to the Monachs. Four hours later we rounded the western-most Monach, the island of Shillay, with its

Afloat off Stac Lee

133-foot-tall red-brick lighthouse. Shillay once had a monastery, where the monks had maintained a fire beacon. We anchored off the small sandy isle of Shevinish, to the east of which lies the main island of *Ceann Ear* (East Head). Contemporary with Shillay's monastery, East Head was said to have had a nunnery. These two establishments are the subject of an old bit of island humour. As the tale goes, the Monach monks, looking for a bit of extracurricular activity, dug a tunnel under the sands from the monastery to the nunnery.

Once ashore on Ceann Ear I walked around *Loch nam Buadh* (the Loch of the Virtues) to a cluster of roofless ruins arranged around several enclosed pens, and what must have once been a garden. The nunnery had been near here, close to the fresh water loch. But the loch-water may not have tasted all that good to the nuns. In his book *The Peat Fire Flame*, Alasdair Alpin MacGregor relates a tale of the Monach *each-uisge*, the water-horse which dwelled in the loch. The islanders wanted to kill the monster, so their bull was led there and left to do battle. The water-horse arose from the depths and the two went at it tooth and hoof. The next day they found a pair of bloody lungs floating on the loch, but no one could tell if they were those of the bull or the water-horse.

On the east side of Ceann Ear I came to the shallow bay of Port Ruadh. Above the shore sat the ruins of several stone dwellings. Lobster fishermen sheltered here in the early years of the twentieth century, and there's a photo of them standing next to their turf-roofed huts in MacGregor's *The Farthest Hebrides*. Though littered with jetsam, the stone foundations were still there, and in the corner of each a fuzzy-grey gull chick squawked on a nest.

I meandered around the wind- and rain-swept island for an hour; circling back to the Loch of the Virtues to take another look at the abandoned homes. Back on the west side of the island I stood on Faodhail a Chinn Ear, the sandbar that connects Ceann Ear to Shivinish.

The tide was high, so unless I could find that mythical monks' tunnel I couldn't cross over. But I'd have to look for it another time, as the others had gathered about the landing place, and I could see Mark approaching in the inflatable. We boarded the Zodiac and, as it sped us back to *Hjalmar Bjørge*, we were surrounded by seal heads bobbing on the swell, a dozen curious pairs of intelligent eyes watching us pass by.

Anchor raised we headed south, turned the corner around South Uist, and crossed the Sound of Barra. After motoring past the airfield on Tràigh Mhòr we wove our way between the isles off the east of Barra. A splash landing on that beach aboard a Twin-Otter aircraft had been the highlight of a winter visit to the island. There had been talk at the time about the demise of the air-service. But I'm happy to report you can still fly to Barra and land on the beach.

An hour later we neared the dark hulk of Kisimul Castle, perched on its rock in the calm waters of Castlebay. After dropping anchor (and a dram or two) we were rocked to sleep like babies on the gentle swell.

Day 6: Return to Mingulay

The next morning I was on the hills of Mingulay, making a long awaited walk up Carnan. On my first visit to the island Gareth Robinson and I had climbed MacPhee's Hill, the island's second highest hill, and where the marooned MacPhee had come looking for rescue. Gareth had continued to the summit of Mingulay, making a windy climb up Carnan. But I'd wanted more time in the village. So I'd spent my last hour ashore wandering through the sand engulfed black houses, and enjoying the antics at the puffin colony on the north side of Mingulay Bay.

As it was August, and there were no distracting puffins around, I set my sights on climbing Carnan. A stiff breeze blew, and Mark wasn't too happy with the anchorage. So as he put us ashore we were warned to keep an ear out for the ship's horn. A toot or two meant we were to return as soon as possible.

I walked across the soft sands to the village and, with the sun burning down through a cloudless sky, walked up Mingulay's central valley. I passed the sad ruin of the priest's house, and at the top of the valley came to the vertical cliff of Biulacraig, a 700-foot drop to the sea. From there, a steep climb of 200 feet led to the broad flat top of the island.

At the southern edge of the summit plateau I had a clear view over to the lighthouse on Barra Head. Even though I stood at an elevation of 900 feet, I was only 200 feet higher than the lighthouse, which at 700 feet is the highest elevation light in the UK. At the centre of the table-top summit I hopped onto the trig-pillar. Far to the north-east rose the mountain of Heaval on Barra, where the white marble statue of Mary and Jesus holds aloft the Star of the Sea. And I thought of a long ago winter morning when I'd sheltered near that star-beacon during a storm of frozen rain.

Then I performed the ritual I've mentioned in some of our earlier island visits. It is something I always do when reaching the top of an island. If there is a trig-pillar I hop atop, otherwise I stand on the highest ground. Then, facing each point of the compass in turn, I recite Kenneth MacLeod's *Road to the Isles*. Its third verse is:

> *It's the blue Islands that are pullin' me away,*
> *Their laughter puts the leap upon the lame.*
> *It's the blue Islands from the Skerries to the Lews,*
> *Wi' heather honey taste upon each name.*

What a piece of magic Kenneth MacLeod left the world. It is indeed the blue Islands that are pulling me away. Each and every one of them, their terrain once tinged blue by peat smoke, and still embraced by blue sea and sky, has made me forget my worries for a while; putting a leap in a spirit that tends to get lame after a year of work.

So if you feel the same way, the next time you pass through Taynuilt, on your way to the isles of the west, be sure to visit Muckairn Church on the hillside above the highway. Stand below the ancient stone sheela-na-gig mounted high on the wall of the church, and then start walking south. Where the burial ground starts to slope down you will find the grave of Kenneth MacLeod. Stop and pay your respects to this man who has kept alive some of the poetry and lore of the Hebrides.

It was hard, but I pulled myself away from the sights, sounds, and smells of the summit of Mingulay. Halfway to Hecla, the next hill to the south-east, a pair of bonxies attacked. As they did, I continued to pick my way across the soft grassy slopes, alternately holding one fist or the other in the air. Then I heard a faint roar, followed by ever-decreasing echoes from the surrounding hills. It was as if someone far-off had puffed on a tuba. I didn't want to understand what the eerie sound meant. But I did. It had been the ship's horn. The ever-increasing wind was making the anchorage untenable, and Mark needed to get *Hjalmar Bjørge* out of the bay as soon as possible.

Oh how I wanted to pretend I hadn't heard the horn and continue that amazing walk; cross to the summit of Hecla, and then descend to the old settlement site at Skipisdale. But the horn had to be respected—I did not want to end up stranded like MacPhee. So an abrupt ninety-degree course change to port was called for.

It was hard to leave that vista of heather hills, the sea, and the myriad distant isles. When someone asks what it is that draws me here year after year I sometimes struggle for words. Try to quote *The Road to the Isles* to someone that hasn't a clue as to what the isles are, and their eyes will glaze over. If you were to ask me that question, short of asking you to read this book, I think I could best answer it by showing you the last minute of the film *Waking Ned Divine*. In it we see the main characters standing atop a deserted coastal headland that looks very Hebridean, toasting the memory of the departed Ned. Then the camera

Barra Head seen from the summit of Mingulay

flies over hills that rise high above the sea; the audience soaring along with it, over a landscape so 'beautiful and so desolate at the same time.' Then, all too soon, those hills disappear in the sea-mist to the haunting strains of *The Parting Glass*. The "Oh God, how I wish I was there now" thoughts this scene imparts, along with the realization of the intense physical need to be part of such a wonderful land and seascape, exactly describes the emotional pull of these isles.

I was halfway down the hill when I saw Mark, in the inflatable, pick the others up from the rocks on the far side of the beach and speed them back to the boat. In the summer heat I hurried past the sandy burial mound and ran onto the beach, hopping over the shallow stream that cuts through the thick brown sand. I scrabbled up the rocky outcrop on the beach's northern shore, and on its far side found Mark waiting alone in the inflatable, the outboard idling. Sweat-drenched I slid aboard, leaving behind the last island of the year.

We then set a course to the south-east, aiming for narrow Gunna Sound between Coll and Tiree. After forty-five miles the low shore of Tiree's coast came near, and along with it another barrage of island memories.

Amongst the rocks on Tiree's shore lay the Ringing Stone, where while napping one autumn morning I'd been pelted by hail. Once we'd passed through Gunna Sound the hills of Rum could be seen to the north; hills that rise high over Papadil, the green vale of St Beccan. I'd tempted fate there, too—wearing waterproofs while climbing its grassy slopes in the rain. The Dutchman's Cap and Lunga then passed by, and behind them could be seen Staffa and Inchkenneth. The hidden entrance to Lunga's tunnel cave, and the chapel on St Kenneth's Isle, had been two hard earned island prizes. And as for Staffa of the Green Ray, it definitely needed another visit. I'd yet to make it to the *Gunna Mòr* (the canon), a natural cavity bored into its cliffs.

We were soon off the west coast of Iona where Carn Cùl ri Èirinn, Columba's cairn with its back to Ireland, could be seen standing atop the south-west corner of the island. It had been only a year since I'd stood there trying to see if Ireland was visible or not. Èirinn was not seen that day. But it had not been a true test of the Columban tale, for it had been a foggy day, and nothing was visible.

We next passed the Kidnap Isle of Erraid, and then followed the coast of the Ross of Mull east past the Torran Rocks, Gorrie's Leap, and Carsaig Arches. Our destination for the last night was Mull's Loch Buie, which we reached in the twilight. Above the head of the loch rose the dark tower of Moy Castle. I'd wanted to see the castle's water filled pit-prison ever since reading about it in Boswell's Journal. It is kept locked, as I'd found to great disappointment on my first visit to Mull. But I'd returned a dozen years later, after having made arrangements to see the castle with the owners of nearby Loch Buie House. They told me the tower is kept locked for fear that someone will fall into the pit, a gruesome fate, and something that actually happened to one of their dogs—though it had been rescued. I was led into the ground floor of the keep, then up a narrow stairway to a small side chamber. A dusty plywood panel, four feet across, was lifted off the floor to expose the prison. Halfway down the dark hole lurked a flat surface of pitch-black water. It had been a terrible place to put someone. Though they wouldn't drown, for there's a rock at the bottom where a prisoner could stand to keep his (or her) head above water.

Day 7: The Last Day

In the morning we motored out of Loch Buie and turned to the east. Several old friends then passed to starboard. First was Scarba. On its far side spun the whirlpool of Corryvreckan. A whirl round those waters had capped a day of wandering the rough terrain of Scarba. In the foreground lay the jewelled chain of the Garvellachs. The head of the chain is Dunconnel, where an ancient zigzag stairway of stone will lead you to the top of the island where the 'Great Castle of Dunquhonle' once stood.

Next in line was a diamond in the rough, Garbh Eileach. As it was late summer, the bracken jungle of the rough isle would be sprouting in full strength, creating an unruly jungle for anyone who'd attempt a landing. Behind Garbh Eileach lay the crown jewel of the chain, Eileach a Naoimh, the monastery island of Brendan and Columba. In my binoculars I could see the trig-pillar atop its spine, a magic place to sit and be surrounded by nothing but islands.

Two other acquaintances then made a close pass. Lumpy Belnahua, with what's left of her terrain moulded, like stone-waves, above the flooded quarries, and her ghost-town buildings rising from the tall grass. And behind her tiny Fladda, its lighthouse and walled garden taking up the entire island; a garden that is a sad sight nowadays, red blossomed fuchsias the only remnants of a past glory.

An hour later we motored into Oban Bay, where Rachel and Heather jumped ashore to secure the mooring lines. We all said our goodbyes, then I walked through Oban's still crowded streets to retrieve my car, seeing more people in five minutes than I'd seen for the past week— and yes, the car was still there. A few days later I flew home; west over sea, seven miles above Mingulay. My quandary over picking a final isle had been resolved. And, as hoped, I hadn't picked it, Mingulay had picked me.

Summit pillar, Mingulay

312

AN ISLAND TO END: RETURN TO RAASAY

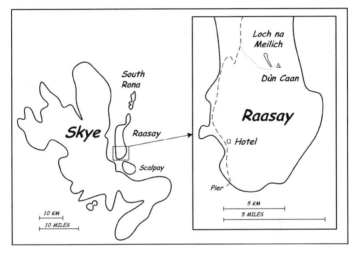

Map Reference: Ordnance Survey Landranger 24

THE island visits you've just read were, for the most part, ordered sequentially from south to north. But this last visit is out of sequence, deserving a place of honour at the end, as it was an experience that turned out to be the genesis for these books.

Back at the beginning of Chapter 5 we were on Raasay, where a surprise-knock on a hotel room door thwarted my plan to climb Dùn Caan. So let's return to that very room, several years later. I had come back to Raasay to try that trek again, for there was a ritual I needed to perform atop the island.

Three years had passed since my walk to Raasay's Dùn Caan had been waylaid by a knock on our hotel room door. And as I loaded my pack I half expected another knock, but there was none. My wife drove me three miles north along the island's only road to drop me at the start of a trail. To reach my Shangri-la I had 1000 feet to climb. Powered by anticipation, I effortlessly followed the trail as it steadily rose to the south-east.

There were two stages to the ascent. The first was a mile and a half tramp that took me to the green highlands near *Loch na Meilich*, the loch of the bleating sheep. It has been a while since any sheep have bleated here, for the loch is Raasay's water supply. My destination was then in sight. A three hundred-foot-tall altar stood before me, the top of Dùn Caan. Climbing it would be the final stage of the ascent.

The last bit of climbing was almost too easy, and I was soon standing on a humpy, slightly tilted plateau, an altar table a few hundred feet in diameter. At one end rose a four-foot-tall trig-pillar; the altar's altar. To

Dùn Caan seen from Loch na Meilich

prepare myself for what would follow, I took a bag of crisps and a can of beer from my pack, and then hopped onto the pillar.

As I sat on the pillar I savoured every drop of beer. Though, as you'll learn, I should have brought brandy. The historic figure in whose footsteps I was following feasted here on cold mutton, but I'd chosen smoky bacon crisps for my pre-ceremonial repast. Ten miles to the north I could see Meal Acairseid, the high ground of South Rona, where another pillar seat offers just as incredible a view.

The Isle of Skye filled the western and southern horizons. If you look at a map of Skye, you'll see why its name means winged-isle, for it resembles the spread wing of a sea eagle. Raasay and Rona are detached feathers of that wing that have chosen to go their own way. But they've not gone far, for they still lay cradled in the lee of Skye. The distracting view took my mind off the task at hand, but only briefly.

So, you ask, what exactly had been calling me to come to this spot for so many years? The answer is I wanted to repeat something that happened here in the eighteenth century.

In 1773, James Boswell (sans Dr. Johnson) picnicked atop Dùn Caan with Lady Raasay and her daughters. The following is from Boswell's Journal:

> … *then we mounted up to the top of Duncaan, where we sat down, ate cold mutton and bread and cheese and drank brandy and punch. Then we had a Highland song … then we danced a reel …*

So why was such a seemingly trivial event, one that spanned only a few minutes centuries ago, so important to me? Because Boswell's journal of his Hebridean tour with Samuel Johnson was one of the first island journeys written with a personal touch. His story has inspired countless others, including me, to follow in his footsteps, and fall in love with these islands. And dancing a reel atop Dùn Caan epitomised the whole freedom of their two month island wander.

There was another reason it was important, an even more personal one. But one that I would only realise several years after the ritual had been performed.

When I had savoured the last drop of beer, I was braced to do the deed. I slid off the pillar and set the camera to timer mode. (I had to record what I was about to do, but I didn't know if I could ever share the picture.) Suddenly I realised I had no idea how to dance a reel—could it even be done solo? So I started to do a jig, going round and round in circles. At first I felt quite silly and had visions of Boswell jigging in his grave. And as I spun I thought I was merely mimicking the act of an admired figure, recreating a long gone moment in time. But doing the jig planted a seed, one that would eventually sprout to reveal the true reason I had been driven to dance.

At last, dizzy from the jig (and the beer) I collapsed on the turf to catch my breath before heading back down the mountain.

A few years later I recalled that mountain dance, trying to understand what had driven me to do something so odd. And as I did, I daydreamed myself back to the top of Dùn Caan. I was jigging around the summit once again. The horizon rotated. The Cuillin Hills of Skye spun away, replaced by the hills above Applecross. The revolving panorama repeated and repeated. The view of the outside world became a blur... then my daydream came to a stop. That seed planted years before sprouted. It bore some amazing fruit.

I realised I'd been driven to dance because someone two centuries ago had taken the time to share a memory. I needed to do the same. It had taken that bizarre jig on an island mountain for me to realize it. To make me aware I had a need to share, as Boswell did, island experiences that would otherwise fade from memory. If I didn't ... well, the thought was too horrible to contemplate. At an estate sale, fifty years in the future, someone would pay three dollars for scrapbooks filled with island photos: mute photos, their stories untold. I could not let that happen. It has taken ten years, but those stories have now been told.

The islands we've visited in these stories are unique places; places I've come to love, both the deserted isles, and the inhabited isles. I will never forget solitary wanderings on uninhabited islands like Barra Head and Pabbay. Never forget exploring old houses and burial grounds while thinking about the history, the legends, and the long gone people who once lived there, whose descendants are now scattered throughout the Hebrides and the world. On those lonely isles I like to stand inside the holy ground of their tumbled dwellings, where you can sense the lingering human presence—some centuries old, some millenniums old—and wonder what life was like when people called these now empty islands their home.

Best of all are visits to the inhabited isles, many flourishing with their own flavour of Gaelic, a language that requires perceiving and describing the world in new ways. Speak a few words of Gaelic to a stranger and you'll make a friend. So visit the islands. Learn their history, and some Gaelic. For only then you will know the true meaning of *Dh' fhairich mi roc nan eilean*; I have smelled the tangle of the isles.

I would like to leave you now, seated back on the trig-pillar atop Dùn Caan, enjoying the amazing vista over Skye and Rona. Sit there and view, in your mind's eye, all the places we've visited in these pages: the ruins of South Rona's Dry Harbour, the cliffs of St Kilda and Mingulay, St Ronan's Cell, the Well of the Cross, and solitary nights in Aird Bheag and Crolà, to name a special few.

And as you think back on all those places, seated high atop Raasay, look west towards the setting sun. In the words of Robert Louis Stevenson, your eyes will kindle with the brightness of the sea, and, as I've come to learn, your heart will kindle with the joy of being.

THE END

THE ISLANDS BOOK TRUST –
high quality books on island themes in English and Gaelic

Based in Lewis, the Islands Book Trust are a charity committed to furthering understanding and appreciation of the history of Scottish islands in their wider Celtic and Nordic context. We do this through publishing books, organising talks and conferences, visits, radio broadcasts, research and education on island themes. For details of membership of the Book Trust, which will keep you in touch with all our publications and other activities, see www.theislandsbooktrust.com or phone 01851 880737.

The Islands Book Trust, Ravenspoint, Kershader, South Lochs, Isle of Lewis, HS2 9QA (01851 880737)